Millways
of Kent

SOUTHERN CLASSICS SERIES
Mark M. Smith and Peggy G. Hargis, Series Editors

Millways
of Kent

NEW INTRODUCTION BY
Dan Huntley

NEW PREFACE BY
John Shelton Reed

JOHN KENNETH MORLAND

THE UNIVERSITY OF SOUTH CAROLINA PRESS

Published in Cooperation with the Institute for
Southern Studies of the University of South Carolina

© 1958 University of North Carolina Press
New material © 2008 University of South Carolina

Cloth edition published by the University of North Carolina Press
First paperback edition published by the College and University
    Press, 1964
This paperback edition published by the University of South
    Carolina Press, Columbia, South Carolina 29208

www.sc.edu/uscpress

Manufactured in the United States of America

17 16 15 14 13 12 11 10 09 08   10 9 8 7 6 5 4 3 2 1

Library of Congress Cataloging-in-Publication Data

Morland, J. Kenneth (John Kenneth)
    Millways of Kent / John Kenneth Morland ; new introduction by Dan
Huntley ; new preface by John Shelton Reed.
        p. cm. — (Southern classics series)
    "Published in cooperation with the Institute for Southern Studies of the
University of South Carolina."
    Originally published: Chapel Hill : University of North Carolina Press,
1958.
    Includes bibliographical references and index.
    ISBN 978-1-57003-726-9 (pbk : alk. paper)
    1. Cities and towns—Piedmont (Region)—Case studies. 2. Piedmont
(U.S. : Region)—Social conditions—Case studies. I. University of South
Carolina. Institute for Southern Studies. II. Title.
    HN79.A13M6 2008
    307.76'70975743—dc22
                                                                        2007043529

This book was printed on Glatfelter Natures, a recycled paper with 50
percent postconsumer waste content.

Publication of the Southern Classics series is made possible in part by the
generous support of the Watson-Brown Foundation.

Contents

Illustrations

Photographs

Series Editors' Preface

Part of the "Kent trilogy," John Kenneth Morland's *Millways of Kent* focuses on the blue-collar workers of York, South Carolina, particularly those engaged in factory labor. In his compelling new introduction, Dan Huntley explains how Morland's affable nature as much as his investigative skills gave him unprecedented access to every level of mill culture and enabled him to pepper his narrative with poignant descriptions of workers' joys and sorrows, their hopes and fears, their triumphs and failures. Replete with fascinating observations about the culture of racial and class segregation, the importance of the larger national context, the power of cultural isolation, the lasting effects of industrialization, and the legacies of ethnic consciousness, *Millways of Kent* stands as a profoundly insightful book about an important southern constituency rarely lent such a skillful an ear or given such an articulate voice.

Southern Classics returns to general circulation books of importance dealing with the history and culture of the American South. Sponsored by the Institute for Southern Studies, the series is advised by a board of distinguished scholars who suggest titles and editors of individual volumes to the series editors and help establish priorities in publication.

Chronological age alone does not determine a title's designation as a Southern Classic. The criteria also include significance in contributing to a broad understanding of the region, timeliness in relation to events and moments of peculiar interest to the American South, usefulness in the classroom, and suitability for inclusion in personal and institutional collections on the region.

MARK M. SMITH
PEGGY G. HARGIS
Series Editors

New Preface

> There are three major versions or styles of living in Kent: that of the "town" whites, that of the "poor white" mill villagers, and that of the Negroes. These three groups form the larger society of Kent. Each exhibits a distinctive organization of customs, attitudes, and values. Each is a subculture—a variation of American culture, Southern Piedmont style.
>
> Hylan Lewis, *Blackways of Kent*

In 1946 the Rosenwald Fund awarded a grant to the University of North Carolina's Institute for Research in Social Science to support an ambitious program of southern community studies under the direction of the anthropologist John Gillin. The plan called for studies in five different locations. Gillin himself was supposed to produce a monograph about a coastal fishing village on North Carolina's Core Sound, and graduate students were to write dissertations—ideally to become books—in four other, very different southern settings: a plantation community in Alabama's black belt, an Alabama "piney woods" community, a mountain town in western North Carolina, and a textile mill town in the South Carolina piedmont. At the end Gillin was to draw on all of the studies to write a summary volume on the culture of the modern South.

Six graduate students were sent into the field for periods of a few months to a year. Charles Peavy, who had just completed a University of Chicago master's thesis on Melanesia, was assigned to Brewton in the piney woods. Morton Rubin, fresh from his

UNC master's thesis on a Basque community in Spain, went to Alabama's Dallas and Wilcox counties. Vladimir Hartman, another UNC doctoral candidate, studied Newland, North Carolina, in the Appalachian mountains. And in 1948 and 1949 three students—one black, two white—went to the South Carolina town they agreed to call "Kent."

Ralph C. Patrick Jr., a Chapel Hill graduate and a doctoral student at Harvard, was originally signed up to study the entire town himself, but when he concluded that he could not do justice to Kent's mill people and black population, Gillin recruited J. Kenneth Morland, a graduate student at UNC, and Hylan Lewis, a University of Chicago doctoral candidate who had just joined the faculty at Atlanta University, to study those communities while Patrick studied "Town" (i.e., white, nonmill) Kent.[1]

All six graduate students gathered copious field notes, but the project was never fully realized.[2] Gillin had a great many other irons in the fire, notably in the area of Latin American studies, and when he left Chapel Hill for the University of Pittsburgh in 1959, he took his field notes on the Core Sound community with him and never wrote his monograph.[3] Nor did he write his overview volume, although a 1951 article (with Emmett Murphy), "Notes on Southern Culture Patterns," suggests what the book might have looked like.[4] It presents a table showing the presence or absence of some two hundred characteristics in each of the seven "subcultures" studied. "Illegal moonshining and bootlegging of alcohol" were found in all seven, for example, as were "family reunions for the extended family," while an "ideal pattern that women should never hear swear or curse words" was not found in the coastal subculture and "beer parties" were observed only in the plantation, piedmont town, and pinebelt subcultures.

Some of the graduate student researchers were more productive. Peavy apparently never finished his dissertation on the piney woods community (although approximately 1,500 four-by-six-inch sheets of his field notes are in the project files), but Hartman's dissertation on the North Carolina mountain town was eventually completed in 1957, and Rubin's 1951 book, *Plantation County*, was based on his UNC dissertation of the previous year.[5]

Two of the three students who went to Kent also published their dissertations, Lewis's *Blackways of Kent* in 1955 and Morland's *Millways of Kent* in 1958.[6] Both books are now recognized as minor classics of southern ethnography, and it is appropriate that the University of South Carolina Press should reissue them in a series devoted to classic works on the American South.

A book based on Patrick's study of Kent's "Town" whites was all that was needed to complete the picture, but Patrick never published *Townways of Kent*. Nearly twenty years ago I approached Patrick's widow about editing her husband's dissertation and finding a publisher for it. I never met Patrick (although he and I both taught at the University of North Carolina), but I had known about his dissertation for some time. I do not recall where I first learned about it: possibly from Robert Wilson, my colleague in the sociology department at North Carolina and Patrick's Harvard classmate, who tried unsuccessfully in the early 1980s to interest Harvard University Press in publishing *Townways*. Both as a student of the South and, after 1988, as director of the Institute for Research in Social Science, which had supported the research in the first place, I was eager to see Patrick's book in print. Mrs. Patrick was delighted—so much so that she graciously gave me her personal copy of the dissertation. Several southern university presses (unlike Harvard) saw the point of publishing this missing piece of the larger Kent puzzle but, perhaps understandably, were unwilling simply to trust that Patrick's manuscript could be revised to make an acceptable book. I was reluctant to undertake the required revisions without a firm commitment from a publisher, so I put the project aside for more than a decade.

I regret that Mrs. Patrick did not live to see her husband's book in print (she died in 1997), but it is fitting that *Townways of Kent* should finally appear in conjunction with *Millways* and *Blackways*. Each book portrays life within one of Kent's communities and describes how members of that community saw their town.

Together they give us three radically different yet complementary angles of view on the same small southern town at midcentury. Half a century later, readers must be struck immediately by how much, and how rapidly, the South has changed.

The three books also tell us something about how American social science has changed. Beginning in the 1920s, Robert Park, his students and colleagues at the University of Chicago, and other researchers associated (at least in retrospect) with the "Chicago school" produced a string of studies examining urban neighborhoods and subcultures as well as small cities and towns such as Robert and Helen Lynd's "Middletown" (Muncie, Indiana) and W. Lloyd Warner's "Yankee City" (Newburyport, Massachusetts).[7] The Kent studies were anchored in this tradition.

At the time the boundaries between sociology and anthropology were indistinct and permeable. Although Warner taught in a department of sociology, for instance, he was trained as an anthropologist and directed the work of the anthropology students who wrote *Deep South*, a study of caste and class in Natchez, Mississippi.[8] Just so, although John Gillin, director of the Field Studies in the Modern Culture of the South project, was an anthropologist, both Lewis and Morland were writing dissertations for departments of sociology, and Patrick's dissertation was in an interdisciplinary "social relations" department. In their subsequent careers the three Kent researchers remained hard to classify. Patrick was identified primarily as an anthropologist, though teaching in a school of public health. Morland maintained a dual identity as sociologist and anthropologist, serving as professor and chairman in the sort of joint department that survived mostly in small colleges such as his. Lewis was clearly a sociologist, but his best-known student was to be Elliot Liebow, whose dissertation, published in 1967 (with a foreword by Lewis) as *Tally's Corner*, was in anthropology.[9]

As the Kent studies were being completed, however, the distinction between anthropology and sociology was about to become clearer. The main current of sociological research, even at

the University of Chicago, soon turned away from the ethno-
graphic Chicago school toward the sort of quantitative analysis,
often of sample survey data, championed by the competing
Columbia school. Even under the capacious tent of American
sociology, the sort of community study done by Morland, Lewis,
and Patrick would barely survive; it quickly became primarily the
province of anthropologists willing, or obliged, to turn their attention from the Third World to communities closer to home.

For sociology as a discipline, this marginalization of ethno-
graphic work has had many consequences. No doubt there are
both good and bad, but certainly one of the unfortunate ones has
been that little of what sociologists do these days appeals to general readers as the best ethnography can. No work of sociology is
likely to match the more than 700,000 copies that *Tally's Corner*
has sold. (Community studies may now be making a bit of a come-
back within sociology, but if so, it is in a new, postmodern guise
that does nothing to invite the attention of readers more interested in description than theory.) However much today's sociology
dissertations may contribute to the sociological enterprise, it is
safe to say that almost none will be worth reading in fifty years.[10]
And how few of those will be worth reprinting—as these three dissertations from half a century ago unquestionably are?

NOTES

1. J. Kenneth Morland, interview with editor, February 11, 1992.
Another student, Barbara Chartier, spent two weeks in York's mill villages; she interviewed mothers and administered psychological tests to
schoolchildren for her master's thesis, "Weaverton: A Study of Culture
and Personality in a Southern Mill Town" (University of North Carolina,
1949), much of which Morland later incorporated in his *Millways of Kent*
(Chapel Hill: University of North Carolina Press, 1958). Morland also
recalls that a Duke University student, Dorothy Reynolds, visited York to
administer Rorschach tests to mill people, but the Duke University
library has no indication that she wrote anything about her research.

2. The students' field notes, except for those of Hylan Lewis, are now
archived among the Field Studies in the Modern Culture of the South

records, no. 4214, Southern Historical Collection, University of North Carolina at Chapel Hill. Lewis's notes and correspondence about the project are with his papers, boxes 188–89, Amistad Research Center, Tulane University, New Orleans.

3. When Gillin was dying from lung cancer (he died in 1973), he showed Morland an "enormous box of notes" and asked if he would be interested in writing them up, an offer that Morland had to decline (Morland interview). It is not clear what became of the notes; they are not in the John P. Gillin Collection at the University of Pittsburgh (RG 90/F-75, Archives Service Center).

4. John Gillin and Emmett J. Murphy, "Notes on Southern Culture Patterns," *Social Forces* 29 (May 1951): 422–32.

5. Vladimir Hartman, "A Cultural Study of a Mountain Community in Western North Carolina" (Ph.D. diss., University of North Carolina, 1957); Morton Rubin, *Plantation County* (Chapel Hill: University of North Carolina Press, 1951).

6. Both were published by the University of North Carolina Press after UNC sociology professor George Simpson decided not to write a single-volume study of "Kent" based on the three students' fieldwork (Morland interview).

7. Martin Bulmer, *The Chicago School of Sociology: Institutionalization, Diversity, and the Rise of Sociological Research* (Chicago: University of Chicago Press, 1984); Gary Alan Fine, *A Second Chicago School: The Development of a Postwar American Sociology* (Chicago: University of Chicago Press, 1995). On "Middletown," see, for example, Robert S. Lynd and Helen Merrell Lynd, *Middletown: A Study in Contemporary American Culture* (New York: Harcourt, Brace, 1929). On "Yankee City," see, for example, W. Lloyd Warner and Paul S. Lunt, *The Social Life of a Modern Community* (New Haven, Conn.: Yale University Press, 1941).

8. Allison Davis, Burleigh B. Gardner, and Mary R. Gardner, *Deep South: A Social Anthropological Study of Caste and Class* (Chicago: University of Chicago Press, 1941).

9. Elliot Liebow, *Tally's Corner: A Study of Negro Streetcorner Men* (Boston: Little, Brown, 1967).

10. John Shelton Reed, "On Narrative and Sociology," *Social Forces* 68 (September 1989): 1–14.

New Introduction

In the fall of 1948 three graduate students—one black and two white—visited York, South Carolina. They would spend the coming year living in this community of four thousand people, taking notes on life among the three groups who made up the place they called "Kent": the prosperous white merchants, the poor white mill workers, and the blacks.

These researchers' legacy is a unique snapshot of a southern hamlet at midcentury, a community in transition, its family farms disappearing in the face of a growing semiurban and industrial landscape. Their work is akin to that of a John Audubon sketching a soon-to-be-extinct species such as the passenger pigeon or Carolina parakeet.

Hylan Lewis, a doctoral student at the University of Chicago, wrote about the black community. His work was published as *Blackways of Kent* by the University of North Carolina Press in 1955. Ralph Patrick Jr. lived among the white merchants and wrote his dissertation for Harvard University. His intended book, "Townways of Kent," was never published, partly because of his concern for the privacy of the people he portrayed. John Kenneth Morland, a former Chinese scholar at Yale University who became a UNC sociologist, studied the mill workers. The University of North Carolina Press published his dissertation in 1958 as *Millways of Kent*.

The graduate students were under the direction of the renowned anthropologist John Gillin of the University of North

Carolina at Chapel Hill. Funding for the landmark studies came from the Rosenwald Fund, which had provided critical funding for the creation and support of black schools throughout the South, and from UNC's Institute for Research in Social Science.

The Kent trilogy was part of a larger sociological experiment to study the similarities and differences during the first half of the twentieth century in five communities representing the major subregions of the South: the plantation region (or what remained of it in the post–Civil War era), the western mountains, the piney forest belt, the coastal fringe, and the piedmont.

Gillin defines the piedmont as the region between the Appalachians and Atlantic Ocean, stretching from southern Virginia through the Carolinas and into the northern portions of Georgia and Alabama. This was an area particularly devastated by the Civil War, with much of its infrastructure—railroad lines, ports, foundries, and manufacturing facilities—still in shambles in the 1870s and 1880s. It was at that time that progressive politicians and influential newspaper editors began to speak of the New South, which could be lifted off the economic ash heap by textile mills and the financial boom they would spur. Of course, what was really fueling this Babbitt-like civic boosterism were northern industrialists seeking a cheap labor force—uneducated workers from bankrupt farms who could be intimidated into not joining the unions that were beginning to dominate the industrialized Northeast. Wages in the Carolinas were less than half those in New England.

By the 1890s the textile industry had begun to burrow into small towns across the piedmont. Mills of red brick—kilned from the red clay that defined the region—were sprouting in communities where both long- and short-staple cotton had once reigned as king. Politicians from nearby Gaston County, North Carolina, boasted that their towns had more shuttle looms than any place outside of industrial England.

Morland brought to the sociological study a bedrock respect for these blue-collar workers, similar to the admiration expressed by James Agee and Walker Evans in their seminal work *Let Us Now*

Praise Famous Men. His work also echoes classic texts written about the South and mill workers, works such as W. J. Cash's *Mind of the South* and Liston Pope's *Millhands and Preachers.* Reading Morland's book half a century after it was written, the reader is struck by the image it presents of a relatively young nation, not far removed from its victory in a global war, but still seeking its identity in the new world order. Gillin writes in his foreword to *Millways of Kent* about the specter of world communism: "On this side of the Iron Curtain we tell ourselves that we have evolved a system that gives the common man a chance— a chance to be a fully participating member of national society, even of the world community of free men. Every man, woman, and child of the Free World is supposed to be a functioning member of the free world of human beings" (xxxii). Morland agreed. "These people need no defense and no praise," he wrote in his introduction to *Millways of Kent.* "Theirs is a way of life essentially meaningful and satisfying to them" (xxxviii).

In less-experienced hands this book could have become a densely written, academic treatise with cardboard characters interspersed with impenetrable pages of graphs and pie charts. But Morland's skills as an oral historian enabled him to breathe life into these anonymous workers as flesh-and-blood humans reflecting on the daily challenges, joys, and disappointments of trying to make a living in a small American town at midcentury. Morland immersed himself in mill culture with the zeal of an anthropologist parachuting into a tribe of Stone Age foragers in the Amazonian rain forest.

Although mill workers had a reputation for being notoriously clannish and suspicious of outsiders, Morland's easygoing nature allowed him unusual access to their daily lives. To better acquaint himself with their world, he worked and lived on a family farm for two weeks, lived with a retired mill couple for six months, and ate his meals at a mill boardinghouse. He was later joined by his new bride, Margaret, who assisted him in his studies by joining church circles and neighborhood quilting bees.

Except for a brief mention in York's weekly newspaper and a meeting with a mill owner (who approved of the study but suggested Morland lie to mill workers about his intention to study mill culture), Morland did not bring attention to himself. And he was able to ingratiate himself into the day-to-day workings of the mill village. He attended mill church services, sang in choirs, and attended prayer meetings and revivals. He even taught Sunday school. He also attended weddings, funerals, baptisms, family reunions, and ball games and went on hunting and fishing trips. He spent time in the pool halls, cafés, dance halls, and beer parlors.

Morland discovered that the shadow of the mills loomed over everyone, whether at the top of society or struggling at the margins. He writes of the daily discrimination mill workers faced whenever they left the narrow boundaries of their mill village. In one instance a Kent physician, plainly disgusted at the idea of treating mill workers, speaks candidly of dealing with their lack of personal hygiene and flings open a clinic window to rid his examining room of their "mill-worker stink."

What Morland discovered was remarkable in the post–World War II economic boom times in the United States: a white subculture in the South that in some ways was more segregated than the black community. Although he was able to move freely between the homes of mill workers and the homes of lawyers and doctors, he found that a white mill worker was no more likely than a black person to be invited to sit down for a Sunday dinner with a respectable white town family. Mill worker families lived in isolation from the rest of York's citizens—worshiping at their own churches, shopping at their own corner groceries, playing baseball in their own mill-based athletic organizations. Even at the public schools, mill children were subject to a more subtle form of segregation: they may have been in the same schools as town children, but they were much more likely to be routed to noncollege curriculums. The mill workers were so isolated, in fact, that they resembled recently arrived Irish, Italian, or Chinese immigrants in the early nineteenth century, who were pushed into ghettos in large metropolitan areas such as New York City. The racial and conservative political climate Morland encountered was such that he and his colleagues felt the need to cloak the town in a pseudonym, a tactic common among researchers intent upon gaining trust in smaller towns, where locals were often more distrustful of outsiders. (More than twenty years before the Kent project began, Robert and Helen Lynd studied the power relationships and life in a small midwestern town, later identified as Muncie, Indiana. Their fieldwork was published in 1929 as *Middletown*.) The town the researchers chose—York, South Carolina —was across the Catawba River and just south of Charlotte.

York and its sister city of Lancaster, South Carolina, were named for the English textile cities of York and Lancaster. The region was settled in the mid-1700s by the Scots-Irish, a feisty, independent group who mostly had come south along the Philadelphia Wagon Road, which cleaved the piedmont along a northeast-by-southwest axis. York County was a hotbed of backcountry guerrilla fighting during the American Revolution, and many Rebels fought nearby at Kings Mountain, one of the war's turning points. Less than a century later, York County had the dubious distinction of hosting the last full cabinet meeting of the Confederacy after the fall of Richmond. The town had once been considered the "Charleston of the Upcountry" with its Victorian homes, mild climate, and fertile cotton fields. It even had its own female academy and a military academy. But like much of the region, York was devastated by the South's shattered economy during the last decades of the nineteenth century. During the volatile Reconstruction period, York was so wracked by civil unrest and Ku Klux Klan activity that it was occupied by two companies of Federal troops well into the 1870s. President Grant declared martial law in the county in 1871, and nearly two hundred whites were jailed for Klan-related crimes.

Some of the scions of the town's waning aristocracy initially fought the establishment of textile mills in the 1880s and 1890s, fearing that the mills would become a magnet for lower classes of people from an even poorer region of the South—the western Carolina mountains. But the town's merchants were hungry for industry and gladly issued bonds when mill owners sought capital. By the early twentieth century, four textile mills were humming in York. Surrounding the factories were several hundred plain wooden houses laid out Monopoly-style. Despite the modern trappings of the industrial age—iron machinery and electricity—the mills were more analogous to the feudal serfdoms of the Middle Ages in Europe. The larger mills often came with a castlelike mansion occupied by the mill owner. The mills, operating twenty-four hours a day, were highly structured organizations, and the mill villages were built to resemble those in New England, in which the workers walked to their jobs to spin cotton and weave fabric.

The mills, which initially employed children as young as six until the federal government forbade the practice, were governed by supervisors with near total control over practically every aspect of workers' lives, from the workplace to the rents on their homes. Some mills even operated grocery and clothing stores, where workers would be issued credit. A large portion of a worker's weekly paycheck was often spent on company housing, food, utilities, and clothing, leaving scant cash by payday, an arrangement later lamented by Tennessee Ernie Ford in his song "Sixteen Tons." It was a corporate paternalism not far removed from the tenant farmer system, which was just a step above slavery, trapping impoverished families in an almost inescapable cycle of poverty.

The level of control was so completely instilled in mill village culture that it was hard to imagine a life beyond the shrill shriek of the mill whistle. Until the 1970s a Gaston County, North Carolina, textile mill operated a chapel within its plant (with a mill-paid minister) so that workers could be baptized, married, and buried without ever leaving the factory floor. Imagine that type of work arrangement today at Microsoft or IBM—or imagine a local company paying part of the salary of the school superintendent and principals.

Most all of the mill workers in York were without union representation and without many of the workers' rights enjoyed by their counterparts in the North. Older teenage children of mill workers often dropped out of school and were forced to leave home if they did not go to work in the mill. It was an overtly paternalistic system in which mill owners had undue influence over the lives of their workers. Ironically, many of the mill workers' ancestors had escaped a similar life in Europe in order to come to the New World.

Morland writes of how the mills were highly structured organizations in which there was little outlet for worker creativity or even for suggestions about how to improve mill efficiency. For the most part, mill owners considered the workers little more than interchangeable cogs in a machine driven by profit and production quotas.

As an example of the level of control over the private lives of workers, most mills, including those in York, operated three shifts six days a week, with shift changes at 3:00 P.M., 11:00 P.M., and 7:00 A.M. Shift changes were preceded by blasts of a huge steam whistle. The day's clocklike regimen was so complete that few workers had a wristwatch or alarm clock in their home: the only clock that mattered was the mill clock.

I was three years old when Morland's book was published in 1957. I'd heard tales in the 1970s about the researchers who came to York, but I never knew anyone who had read their books, which were hard to locate outside of a librarian's reference desk. In the 1980s I wrote a story in the *Charlotte Observer* about *Blackways of Kent* and interviewed Hylan Lewis and some of the people in his book. Several are still living and can recall humorous anecdotes from the time when the researchers came to town. At first, they said, the researchers were tailed by the York Police and variously suspected of being communists, labor organizers, FBI agents, or simply northern troublemakers who were openly talking to blacks. A few fondly remember taking the "city boy" to a muddy fish seining complete with Mason jars of moonshine.

Morland said he enjoyed his time in York and was intrigued to learn of the ambiguities of mill life. For example, he observed that although most all mill workers considered themselves Christians and many belonged to a church, he began to notice distinct differences in mill churches and town churches. Mill worker weddings in churches were a rarity, and many mill workers considered church weddings ostentatious. Most mill workers were married by a justice of the peace, followed by a small ceremony in their homes. Often no rings were given, nor were wedding presents. Some of these customs were driven by economic circumstances, but some also by a Puritan-like culture that shunned "uppity airs." Members of the town's Wesleyan Methodist church did not believe in wearing rings of any sort. In one wedding Morland attended, the groom gave the minister a five-dollar bill, which the minister returned. The couple, he said, needed the money more than he did.

Morland also writes of families who became detritus of the mills—broken by violence, abuse, and alcoholism. He profiles the dregs of the mill community, the floaters and drifters, the "lint heads"—unattached men who "work a few weeks in order to save enough money for a week of loafing and drinking and a bus ticket to the next mill town" (38).

Although Morland certainly observed racism, violence, alcoholism, and even thievery in the mill villages, he maintains that such behavior was relatively rare. He pronounces that the bulk of the mill people he met and studied were "good people," "three-dimensional, warm, generous, and vibrant" (xxxvii).

And despite all the negatives, many workers who were born and raised on the mill hill will argue today that they were not exploited. They will tell you how the mills were the best things that ever happened to them. They will tell you how in the early days the mills would drive old school buses into the hills of Appalachia to recruit new workers, promising a "new life with good wages." And the mills would literally move entire families with their belongings to a textile mill village. These same workers will tell you that the first time they had "inside plumbing" and a flush toilet was in mill housing. The mills, they said, provided their first light bulb, refrigerator, and radio. Their children, for the first time, got to ride a bus to school and had cash to buy shoes instead of bartering with crops. And there are tens of thousands families who bettered themselves through textile work, the parents sacrificing so their children could go to college and escape the cycle of poverty that had claimed families for generations.

I know this because I'm the son of two Carolina textile mill workers and I've conducted oral histories with dozens of textile workers who were born on the mill hill. Carolina textiles enabled my parents to send their four children to college, the first of seven generations in the Carolinas to go to college. They worked in textile mills so their children would never have to.

It has been more than twenty years since I first read *Millways of Kent*, and I'm struck by what a rare gem this little-known work is. It's a moving, intimate chronicle of a world that no longer exists. The American textile industry began declining in the 1960s, hit hard by low-wage imported fabrics. Although York's four mills are still standing, their huge windows are bricked up. They serve mostly as cheap warehouses, decades removed from being the economic beehives they once were. The mill houses also still exist in York; all were converted to private ownership by the early 1970s. Low-income whites, some blacks, and an increasing number of Latinos now occupy the plain, almost identical, white-siding houses with their distinctive "built-in" porches and sharp-angled roofs.

The mill era has come and gone, but through studies such as this, we learn about our past and see how it intersects with the future. As I write this, a California billionaire is launching plans for another unique economic subculture for the piedmont. From the dust of a former mill in Kannapolis, North Carolina, a bio-technology research center is taking shape. One of its more inno-vative features is nearby housing—so that its employees, like those who worked in a different industry a century ago, will never be far from work.

Foreword to the First Edition

W hatever it may be in politics, the "Solid South" is not "uniformity" in mode of life, or in what anthropologists call "culture." It is a collection—more or less integrated—of subcultures, differing in important details among themselves, even in the same type of community. In the series of investigations we called "Field Studies in the Modem Culture of the South," we set out at the University of North Carolina to elucidate the differences—and the similarities—of living patterns in five important "subareas" of the southern region of the United States: the Plantation area, the Mountains, the Piney Forest Belt, the Coastal Fringe, and the Piedmont.

The Piedmont Crescent is of particular significance. It stretches from Virginia, through North Carolina, South Carolina, and northern Georgia, into northern Alabama. It was there that the "New South" was envisioned in the 1880's. Its foundations were to be the southern textile industry. Through this beginning, it was thought at the time, the South would enter the modern world with a balanced economy and a progressive mode of life. The pattern in the Piedmont, however, was not to be that of the great industrial cities of the North, but one of village and small city industry, recruiting its workers from the surrounding rural areas, attempting to integrate the factory with the older agrarian pattern of life. For over seventy years now the Piedmont has been industrialized in this sense, and as large-scale industry moves into the region, the Piedmont is receiving first consideration for location. It is the one subarea of the South, generally speaking, that has something of an industrial background and tradition. Yet the work force of the textile mills is in many ways different from the factory labor class of other parts of the country. It is practically one hundred percent "Old American," it has received no appreciable admixture of European immigration for nearly two hundred years, it has had practically no experience with the metropolitan type of organization and culture, and it is closely allied traditionally with the southern Piedmont small-farm type of life and that of the mountain coves, which, in fact, many of its members still follow on a part-time basis.

The community we here call Kent was chosen with considerable care to represent the different phases of culture to be found in the Piedmont mill towns at mid-century. It had about 4,000 people and therefore was not too large to be studied by three field teams. It had four textile mills each with its surrounding village where the workers lived. Some Piedmont mill towns have only this. But Kent also had a considerable Negro population, whose culture Hylan Lewis has ingeniously explored in *Blackways of Kent* (Chapel Hill: The University of North Carolina Press, 1955), one in the present series of studies. It also had an old aristocracy, a small though ambitious middle class, and an emerging "new rich" element that considered itself progressive in business and community welfare projects and wished to "tune in" Kent to the booster type of patterns common in many other parts of the country. The old aristocracy, middle class, and "new rich boosters" collectively exhibit *The Townways of Kent* analyzed by Ralph Patrick, Jr., scheduled for publication in 1958.

The life ways and social organization of the mill workers and their families are the subject of the present volume by John Kenneth Morland. In keeping with the general plan of The Field Studies in the Modern Culture of the South, Morland did not do a problem-oriented investigation. In the course of a year in the field he and his associates thoroughly acquainted themselves with many mill workers and their families, and they familiarized themselves with the pattern of action, expression, thought, and feeling. Morland lets the facts speak for themselves. But in this introductory word to the reader I may allow myself to express a few reflections, a few questions these facts raise.

The mill people are physically and functionally an important part of the total Kent system. Without the mills and these people to operate them, Kent would probably be nothing but a country political and trading center, which it was before the mills came. Yet at the time of this study in the late forties the mill workers were in many respects actually more segregated than the Negro elements of Kent society. It is also difficult to see how they were less despised and discriminated against by the dominant white elements. If one were a member of a mill village, he had no more chance of being invited to dinner by "respectable" white families than had a Negro, nor could he entertain much greater expectations of marrying into a "respectable" white family, going to the same college where their children go, belonging to their clubs. And there were few if any open pathways whereby the mill workers' children might work up into a status of social acceptance by the other whites in Kent. The mill people lived very much in a world of their own. Although they spent their lives within walking distance of the town people, the culture of their villages was, in many ways, something apart. Their aspirations were restricted, their frustrations were somewhat ingrown, their world view was definitely limited. The mill village culture was almost as encapsulated as if it were that of a recently arrived immigrant group. Among the Negroes, on the other hand, there was an intimate awareness of many patterns of middle- and upper-class white life, conveyed by domestic servants, and a certain "intellectual" leadership kept closely in touch with national trends, particularly those affecting the Negro race.

A world-wide social revolution is in progress, and it is particularly noticeable among the so-called underdeveloped peoples. All experts agree that this is not merely a power struggle between two static systems, Democracy and International Communism. The struggle is for the good things of life, for self-expression, for faith (even though secular) in ideals that make life worth living. On this side of the Iron Curtain we tell ourselves that we have evolved a system that gives the common man a chance—a chance to be a fully participating member of the national society, even of the world community of free men. Every man, woman, and child of the Free World is supposed to be a functioning member of the free world of human beings, guaranteed an opportunity to develop the best that is in him.

Are these mill village people, reported so vividly by Dr. Morland, members of the modern world of free peoples? Dr. Morland carried out his study with no such question in mind, and he points to no morals in his exposition. But can anyone read his report without wondering?

Morland did this study of Kent in the last years of the forties decade, while much of the older pattern of the southern mill life still persisted there. In other words, the mill people of Kent as here described still represented the old ways of life and organization in the early stage of transition. Already in Kent, and more so in many another southern mill community, things have begun to change. Management has adopted a concerted policy of selling off the company-owned houses to private buyers. Many of these purchasers are mill workers, but some are townspeople, such as small shopkeepers and service workers, who thus infiltrate the mill villages and tend to break their isolation from other parts of the community. The fact that most textile mills now have some contracts with the government which prohibit the employment of children under 18 years of age except in restricted hours (and not at all at night) has lengthened the period of education for the youngsters and brought them in closer touch with the currents of the greater world outside. The pattern of voluntaristic organizations with a community welfare orientation is beginning to be taken into the mill communities. These and other innovations are not changing the pattern of the mill communities overnight, but they are slowly transforming the textile workers and their families into something closer to the general image of the self-respecting, intelligent labor force of modern industry.

Dr. Morland's account abundantly demonstrates that the mill workers are "good people," with innate organizational abilities, realism, and adaptability. As modern industrialism moves into the area and as the workers widen the horizon of their world view, they may well be able to evolve a new pattern. The image of "village industry" has long occupied the minds of critics of the older slum-and-factory system. Here in the Piedmont is a large labor force which still has ties to the land and the rural tradition, but is accustomed to the discipline of machine industry. Given a pattern of life of wider range, in which their own leadership and interests might develop, there might well emerge a new form of labor "partnership" with management, whereby industry would be integrated to the people and the land of the South.

The manuscript of this book has been prepared for the printer under the efficient direction of Dr. Katharine Jocher, editor of the publications of the Institute for Research in Social Science of the University of North Carolina. The Field Studies in the Modern Culture of the South, under the direction of the writer of this Foreword, were supported by grants from the Rosenwald Foundation and the aforementioned Institute.

JOHN GILLIN
Chapel Hill
August, 1957

Preface to the First Edition

The anthropological fieldworker studying his own culture by the participant-observer method is faced with several problems. One springs from the fact that he is studying a pattern of life of which he is a part. This can mean, on the one hand, that because of his very familiarity with the culture, he might inadvertently overlook important aspects. On the other hand, he might hesitate to describe what is highly familiar as being so well known to possible readers, as well as to himself, as to appear trite. Another problem arises from the nature of social science, and of all science for that matter. This is the difficulty of attempting to generalize about whatever phenomenon is being reported. No two things are alike, nor are any two human beings and their behavior identical. Thus, any generalization is an abstraction from the specific realities which have been observed, and, in a sense, any generalization oversimplifies the particulars which form its basis.

These problems challenged me throughout my study of the Kent mill people. How I wrestled with them and attempted to solve them are implicit in the chapters which follow. But I wish to say explicitly at this point how they were resolved generally, at least to my own partial satisfaction.

As I understand it, the task of the participant observer is to record as accurately as he can the things that he sees and to interpret them in the total context of the way of life of the people being studied. And he must try to observe and participate in as much of the life as he can, checking and rechecking particular observations to find out whether trends toward regularity appear. As long as this is done, persistently and carefully, he allows the chips to fall where they may; that is, he does not worry about triteness or sensationalism. He reports and generalizes about a way of life as he finds it, nothing more and nothing less. He does not report it because it is different or unusual or anything else. He reports it because, so far as he can determine, it exists.

At the same time, there were important safeguards guiding my study of the subculture. The *Outline of Culture Materials* (G. P. Murdock, *et al.*, New Haven: Yale University Press, 1945) provided a useful, detailed check list of the aspects of culture that should be covered in a complete report. The director of the study, Dr. John Gillin, proved a dynamic source of guidance as he checked my weekly field notes. Even with such helpful guides, this account of the life of Kent mill people does not pretend to be a complete picture, if indeed such a picture could be given under any circumstance. But it is my strong hope that the observations reported are accurate and objective enough so that they can add in some small way to the knowledge of human beings in general and of southerners in particular.

The problem of generalization was dealt with in a similarly pragmatic manner. Granted that each mill person is an individual different from all other individuals (and the better I came to know them the more individualistic I realized they are), it was obvious that they also have a great deal in common. In looking for their similarities, I was aided considerably by using as a basis of comparison the lifeways of surrounding groups: white townspeople, rural people, and Negroes. But when did I know something was "typical"? Again, I could only report what I found repeated numerous times, in different persons, on different occasions. Where statistical checks were possible and appropriate, they were used. But since a study of this type is exploratory among such areas as feelings, attitudes, and general outlook of the mill people themselves, statistical measurement would have been not only most difficult but also not always desirable. Yet it is possible in such exploration to determine whether an attitude expressed by one or two persons is repeated by others, either spontaneously or as the result of probing by the fieldworker. Therefore, my chief concern was not whether something observed was typical of a "majority," but whether it occurred with any degree of regularity among the mill people that I came to know.

Furthermore, all actual behavior accurately reported, whether or not anything is known about how typical it is, is *factual* and can add to the storehouse of knowledge about human beings. A great deal of what is recorded in the following pages gives verbatim quotations and descriptions of particular happenings. In other words, it might be called "straight reporting," done systematically within an anthropological theoretical framework. This can give other students the chance to utilize firsthand data in drawing their own conclusions, perhaps different ones in some cases from those I drew. This is not to minimize, however, the basic function of the scientist in looking for trends and patterns and in abstracting generalizations.

Since the participant observer can be considered an instrument through which aspects of the way of life of a people are delineated, his own personal feelings are kept out of the report as far as possible. There might emerge from such an objective analysis the picture of a group of flat, cardboard figures rather than the three-dimensional, warm, generous, and vibrant people I found the mill villagers to be. From the moment of my first visit to the villages, when I was met by cold, unresponsive stares, to the day a young mill couple presented my wife with their vacuum cleaner to the time of my first return trip when I was greeted by an elderly mill woman—"It's Kennuth come home!"—the experiences I was privileged to share and the friendships I continue to cherish have meant that the "instrument" is an altered one in that my own feelings and attitudes about mill people have been irrevocably affected. And I had vividly demonstrated for myself the truth of the universal report by anthropologists that when a people come to realize that the fieldworker is there to understand and not to criticize or change or sell something, this fieldworker is warmly received.

These people need no defense and no praise. Theirs is a way of life essentially meaningful and satisfying to them, even in the face of the challenges and changes before them. And theirs is a life essentially meaningful and significant to an anthropologist, because they are a human group, adjusting to life as they find it through the millways they have learned as children and which they share with fellow villagers and which they will pass on in modified form to their children.

I am especially grateful to Dr. John Gillin for invaluable guidance and encouragement throughout the study. Both my original interest in and understanding of anthropology were stimulated by him, and I am dependent upon his teaching and writing for many of the theoretical concepts employed in this study. A grant from the Institute for Research in Social Science made possible the twelve months' stay in the field. Discussions with Dr. Ralph Patrick and Dr. Hylan Lewis about the uptown and Negro sections of Kent increased my understanding of the relationship of mill people to the rest of the town. My wife was in every way a co-worker on the project, contributing not only warm encouragement but also keen observations and insights, particularly about mill women. Miss Harriet Herring gave me the benefit of her intimate knowledge of the industrial South in a critical evaluation of the first draft of this manuscript, and Dr. Katharine Jocher helped immeasurably in guiding the manuscript into its printed form. Finally, I am deeply indebted to unnamed persons in the mill village sections of Kent, for without their cooperation and friendship this study could never have been made. Although many persons have helped to make this study possible, I must accept full responsibility for the data and analyses presented and for any shortcomings and mistakes therein.

JOHN KENNETH MORLAND
Lynchburg, Virginia
May, 1957

Millways
of *Kent*

To Martee

Studying the Mill-Village Subculture

CHAPTER 1

THE MILL-VILLAGE sections of Kent make up an integral part of the town of Kent, yet they can be viewed as a separate and distinct part. Just as they cluster in geographical areas that are distinct from other areas of Kent,[1] so do they practice a way of life that is distinct, a way of life that might be termed a subculture.[2] The chief purpose of my study of the mill people was to discover and delineate the basic patterns of their way of life. To do this I entered into the life of the mill people as far as they would permit an outsider, and I observed, listened, questioned, and took part in a number of their activities for a twelve months' period, from August, 1948, through July, 1949.

Techniques of Study

An outsider is not readily accepted in these tightly knit sections, especially one who appears in the strange role of field-

1. Two other separate areas, geographically and culturally, are "town" and Negro. Ralph C. Patrick, Jr., studied the "town," and Hylan Lewis the Negro. Both Patrick and Lewis were in Kent during part of my stay and shared their findings with me. Lewis' study of the Negro community has been published as *Blackways of Kent* (Chapel Hill: The University of North Carolina Press, 1955). Patrick's book on the middle- and upper-class people of Kent is in preparation for publication.

2. John Gillin points out in *The Ways of Men* (New York: Appleton-Century-Crofts, 1948), pp. 186–87, that the development of such subcultures may be based on locality and interests, both of which characterize the mill-village sections. They occupy separate areas and have the cotton mills as a dominant interest.

worker. Various "covers" for getting into the mill-village sections were considered, among them the possibility of posing as an insurance agent or a salesman. Such roles were suggested by the out-of-state owner of the largest mill in Kent, with whom this matter was discussed before the study was begun. He felt that the mill people would not respond if they knew they were being studied. While such an approach might have had an immediate advantage in gaining entry into the villages, it was rejected as being detrimental to the study in the long run. I was sure that sooner or later the mill people would realize that my primary aim was not to make a living as a salesman, and such realization might have increased suspicion to the point of making communication impossible. Therefore, from the start I told the people in as simple language as I could that I was helping with a study of the South and that the town of Kent had been chosen as a part of that study. I added that many people, especially those in the North, did not understand southerners (and the mill people agreed), and that I needed their help and cooperation so that those outside the South could really know how southerners lived. Throughout the study and in retrospect I have never doubted the soundness of this frank, open approach.

My introduction to the leaders in the mill-village sections as well as to those in the "town" sections [3] was greatly helped by Ralph C. Patrick, Jr., who had begun his field research in Kent several months earlier. Together we explained to the mill superintendents and to leading citizens in the town the reason for my being there. A short article appeared in the local weekly newspaper telling of my arrival, my association with Mr. Patrick, and the purpose of my stay. Through the help of the minister of the mill Baptist church, I was able to rent a room

3. "Town" sections include those areas other than the mill-village sections and the segregated Negro districts. "Town" people are whites who do not work in the mills (with the exception of the mill superintendents and over-seers). They include, in Patrick's terminology, the "blue bloods" or aristo-crats, and the "red bloods" or the "good, plain people."

with a retired mill couple at a point focal to three of the four mills. For six months I lived with this couple and took my meals at a mill boardinghouse.

I had hoped to secure a job in the mill, working for perhaps three months to provide a more natural relationship with the mill people. But cotton textiles were in a slump during my entire stay, and the mill superintendents were unwilling to give me a job when regular operatives were out of work. And, of course, I did not want to take a job from a regular worker.

The family with whom I lived and the mill workers with whom I ate at the boardinghouse provided a helpful orientation into the villages and proved to be never ending sources of information. At first mill people were highly suspicious of me. Rumor had it at various times that I was a private detective, a company spy, an F.B.I. agent, a labor organizer, and a communist. Many thought that the explanation of my presence as a student learning about the life of the community was a "cover" for some other work, and there were numerous speculations about my "real" purpose. If a mill person was seen talking to me at length, so I learned toward the end of the study, he was later teased by fellow mill villagers with the taunt "I see you've been feeding the spy." Suspicion was never completely overcome, but it was allayed to the extent that I could take part in many phases of the life of the villages and could come to know a few of the people very well.

There were many ways in which I was able to participate. I attended mill church services, prayer meetings, revivals, and church suppers, and I sang in church choirs and taught Sunday School. I went to weddings, family reunion suppers, birthday parties, and funerals. I watched baseball, football, and basketball games in which mill boys participated. I was invited on fishing and hunting trips and played various sports with older mill boys. I frequented the pool rooms, cafés, dance halls, and beer parlors where some of the mill people spent their leisure time. Ability to use a camera proved helpful in gaining invitations to special happenings in the villages, and pictures taken on such occasions were valuable records of the subculture. Color slides were made of people and events in each of the village sections, and there were frequent requests that I show these slides. They were shown in twenty-two different mill homes and in the mill and town schools.

Informants helped me work out a map locating all mill houses and the names of the families living there. For several months, during the earlier part of the research, I made visits to approximately every third house in the four villages, using a simple schedule to record such information about the members of each family as date and place of birth, occupational history, place of birth and residence of relatives, years of education, church and other organization membership, forms of recreation engaged in, newspapers and magazines received. The information gathered in this way proved valuable statistically, but, more important, the schedule provided something concrete to do during the first part of the visit. After the schedule had been filled out and put away, a lengthy, informal conversation usually followed. This informal conversation might have been more difficult and awkward without the introduction the formal questions provided. Furthermore, the use of the schedule helped relieve the anxiety some people felt regarding what my study involved. The people were accustomed to church, school, and national censuses, and the schedule reminded them of these.

Because most of the mill workers stem from farm backgrounds and because some of them live on farms and commute to and from the mill, I made numerous visits to the surrounding countryside. Through the help of the county agricultural agent and his assistants, I met and visited several prominent farmers. Also, I took the schedule to 15 country homes where textile workers lived. For two weeks I lived and worked on a farm three miles from Kent where an ex-textile worker ran the farm while his wife continued to do mill work.

At the end of six months my wife joined me, and we moved to an apartment in the town section. We made daily visits to the villages and maintained connections with mill life by exchanging meals with mill families, attending church in the villages, and going to movies, dances, and plays with mill friends. My wife was invited to stork showers, house showers, and auxiliary meetings at the churches, all strictly women's affairs.

Other methods of data collection supplemented observations, participation, and the use of a schedule. Interviews were held with doctors, lawyers, grocery-store clerks, ministers, teachers, mill officials, the probate judge, the chief of police, funeral directors, labor organizers, and others who dealt with mill people. Through the help of the principal of the consolidated Kent school, compositions on "The Story of My Life" were assigned to all pupils above the seventh grade.[4] Among the 369 children who wrote compositions, there were 129 who had one or more parents in textile work, including 92 whose parents lived in the Kent mill-village sections, and a content analysis was made of these compositions. Two special studies were made of aspects of the subculture and the results were incorporated into this report. Miss Barbara Chartier of the University of North Carolina dealt with child-rearing customs. The other consisted of 75 Rorschach tests given by Miss Dorothy Reynolds of Duke University. I used a wire recorder on occasion, especially to record church services and informal gatherings. Data were classified according to the *Outline of Cultural Materials* by George Murdock, *et al.* (New Haven: Yale University Press, 1945).

The participant-observer method of study proved advantageous in many ways. Emphasis in the study was on the functional analysis of mill customs, and it was only through observation of and participation in the life of the villages that

---

4. A copy of the outline of this assignment together with two of the compositions is found in Appendix B, pp. 265-71.

the functions of customs and their interrelations could be ascertained. Verbalizations could not be relied upon exclusively, whether from town people or from mill people; neither could statistical information afford everything needed. Both verbalizations and statistical measurement had to be interpreted with the point of view of the mill people in mind. And the only way that point of view could be gained was by living and working with mill people, constantly observing what they did, as well as what they said. The mill people tended to be suspicious and were not highly articulate, but even so, they almost always had time to talk, in an unhurried, leisurely manner. When I visited homes to have schedules filled out, the mill people were always ready to give an hour or more of their time to answering questions and chatting amiably.

There are, at the same time, weaknesses in the method. In such an intimate study of culture, the personality of the investigator is bound to have an important effect on the study. The participant observer is first of all a person interacting with other persons, and the type of person he is will determine, in part, the type of informant attracted to him. Much of the time the situation is entirely undirected, as it must be to maintain normal conditions, and this means that a great deal of what the observer sees, whom he meets, and what activities he engages in must be left to chance. Of course the investigator can do a great deal about making his own opportunities, but he must be careful lest his own attempted manipulation influence unduly the behavior of those being observed. Precautions were taken against impressionism by checking information gained from one person several times with information gained from others. Also, the numerical data from the schedules were guards against the conceptions of the culture gained from a few informants with whom I became especially well acquainted.

It is not possible, obviously, for any one person to participate in all phases of village life. Age and sex groupings forbid that. But in defense of this apparent weakness, although no single study can encompass the whole of a subculture, an objective and systematic study made of human behavior in its natural context can contribute in a special way to a science of human relations.[5] Also, it can delineate at least the principal patterns of the subculture from which can proceed more detailed studies of particular aspects.[6] And it might be added that this kind of sequence in research could provide a meeting place, methodologically, for cultural anthropology and sociology. The anthropologists could make the more general study, followed by more exact measurement in specific areas by the sociologist.

Underlying Assumptions

The following broad principles underlay the approach to the study of the Kent mill-village sections: (1) Social behavior in the mill villages is capable of scientific treatment; that is, it can be observed, classified, and generalized about.[7] (2) Such behavior may be summarized in terms of patterns or consenses of what is proper belief and activity in certain situations.[8] (3) These patterns of behavior are adaptive and functional in the sense that they are meeting felt needs of the mill villagers.[9] (4) The way of life of the people in the mill sections is a functional whole, and no part of this whole can be understood if removed

5. Conrad Arensberg, in "The Community Study Method," *American Journal of Sociology*, LX (1954), 120, claims that the study of a community is not the study of whole cultures or of communities, but is rather "...the study of human behavior *in* communities; that is, in the natural contexts, made up of natural and full human cooperative living...."

6. Miss Chartier's study of child-rearing practices mentioned on page 5 is an example of such possibilities.

7. George Lundberg expounds this in his *Social Research* (New York: Longmans, Green and Co., 1942), especially pp. 1–22.

8. Elaborated by M. J. Herskovits, *Man and His Works* (New York: Knopf and Company, 1949), pp. 201–13.

9. See John Gillin, *op. cit.*, pp. 176–77, 188–90, 238–40.

from its context.[10] These principles are implicit, for the most part, in the description of the subculture, but occasionally they are made explicit where it is believed they aid in interpretation.

References to Other Studies

Although this study is primarily a firsthand account of life as it is lived in the Kent mill-village sections, it makes comparisons from time to time with other findings regarding southern mill workers. It makes no systematic attempt to find out how typical the Kent mill workers are of the cotton-mill operatives in the Piedmont area, but, wherever it appeared helpful, it has referred to other works of a comparable nature.[11] These studies happen to be ones with which I am most familiar, and doubtless others could have been used. Indications from these comparisons and from conversations with persons working closely with mill people in other parts of the Piedmont are that the ways of life developed by all southern mill people are much the same.

10. B. Malinowski, *A Scientific Theory of Culture* (Chapel Hill: The University of North Carolina Press, 1944), p. 150; see also A. R. Radcliffe-Brown, "On the Concept of Function in Social Science," *American Anthropologist*, XXXVII (1935), 397.

11. Those most frequently referred to include: a study of seventy-five married women and their social activities in Greer, South Carolina, in S. W. Hutton, Social Participation of Married Women in a South Carolina Mill Village (unpublished master's thesis, University of Kentucky, 1948); a study of five hundred cotton-mill families in North Carolina by J. J. Rhyne in *Some Southern Cotton Mill Workers and Their Villages* (Chapel Hill: The University of North Carolina Press, 1930); a study of the interaction of churches and cotton mills in Gaston County, North Carolina, by Liston Pope in *Millhands and Preachers* (New Haven: Yale University Press, 1942). Also of special help, both in method and content, was James West, *Plainville, U. S. A.* (New York: Columbia University Press, 1945), a study of rural people who appear to have much in common with the Kent mill-village people.

Order of Presentation

To begin, this study depicts the cultural setting or situation in which the mill-village mode of life is carried out, and then devotes five chapters to the major social institutions, or the "main-trunk activities," as the Lynds term them:[12] although the mill subculture is to be regarded as a functioning whole, for the purpose of analysis that subculture may be broken down along the institutional lines of economic life, marriage and family, enculturation and schooling, religion, and use of leisure time. The political aspect appears as a part of the next chapter on the relationship of the mill sections with the town and the surrounding rural areas. Although prestige differentiation among the mill people themselves is not at all highly crystallized, it is significant enough to be treated in a chapter on social stratification. The relationship existing between the subculture as a whole and the manifest traits of the mill people conditioned in the subculture is explored in another chapter. Finally, the most important factors in the change the subculture is undergoing are discussed, along with their possible influence for the future.

Note of Caution

Throughout the following pages are numerous examples of cases and happenings that illustrate the point being made. Note that these examples are illustrative and by themselves not meant to document what has been said. Generalizations are made only after they have been checked and rechecked several times. Again, this report deals mainly with the delineation of patterns or consenses of behavior, or, as Gillin has stated it, the trends toward uniformity that run through individual

12. Robert S. and Helen Merrill Lynd, *Middletown* (New York: Harcourt, Brace and Co., 1929).

variation in the performance of customs.[13] Before such trends can be abstracted, a number of cases must be observed. It would be a contradiction in terms to delineate the consenses of behavior or trends toward uniformity from a single case. However, to help make particular patterns clearer and more concrete, such illustrations serve a vital purpose.

13. Gillin, *op. cit.*, p. 184.

The Setting of the Mill Subculture

CHAPTER 2   THE SUBCULTURE of the Kent mill-village sections exists and functions in a particular setting or situation, and before describing the subculture itself it is well to have a picture of this situation. A useful set of categories for analyzing a cultural situation has been developed by Gillin,[1] who demonstrates that there are four general components which lay down the conditions under which a culture must operate: (1) the environmental or habitat component which places limitations especially upon the economic aspects;[2] (2) the social or demographic component, including the numerical size and distribution of the group; (3) the human component or the biological characteristics of the group; (4) the foreign or surrounding cultural component. These categories, interpreted rather freely, provide the framework for discussing the setting of the mill-village subculture.

Environmental Component: Geographical Features and Natural Resources

The town of Kent is located in the heart of the rolling hills of the Piedmont crescent which extends roughly from Danville, Virginia, to Birmingham, Alabama. It is the county seat of Kent County and shares with the rest of the southern Pied-

1. John Gillin, *The Ways of Men*, pp. 198–209.
2. Elaborated by M. J. Herskovits, *Man and His Works*, pp. 162–65.

11

mont the resources for agriculture and industry which make
the area one of the most productive in the Southeast. Both the
climate and the soil make possible diversified agriculture. In
Kent County the average annual rainfall is 48.3 inches, and the
mean annual temperature is 61.6 degrees, making possible an
average of 227 growing days in a year.[3] In 1945 there were
4,043 farms, averaging 80.6 acres each and producing as main
crops cotton, peaches, turkeys, hay and grain, dairy products,
and livestock. Cotton remains the most important crop despite
the diversification begun after World War I and strongly
encouraged by the county agricultural agents even now.

Although Kent County was still more than 50 percent rural
according to the 1945 Census, industry employed more persons than agriculture. In 1947 the farms had an estimated seven
thousand workers while industry employed over ten thousand,
mostly in the 21 textile plants in the county. The combined
value of manufactured products was almost $100,000,000 in
1947, while the total value of crops harvested in 1945 was more
than $5,500,000.

Kent is located just two miles from the geographical center
of the county. It is 754 feet above sea level on the fall line between the two rivers which form the main parts of the eastern
and western boundaries of the county (see Figure 1, page 13).
Both of these rivers have power dams which provide electricity for the textile plants as well as for other power needs in
Kent. Also they have made fishing and other water sports possible, particularly on the backwater of the Iroquois River.

*Social Component: Historical Development and Description of
the Mill Sections*

Kent is an aristocratic town that glories in its past. Its lovely
colonial houses with white columns and large trees shading
spacious lawns testify to the grandeur that was. When industry

3. These and other figures are from the U. S. Census.

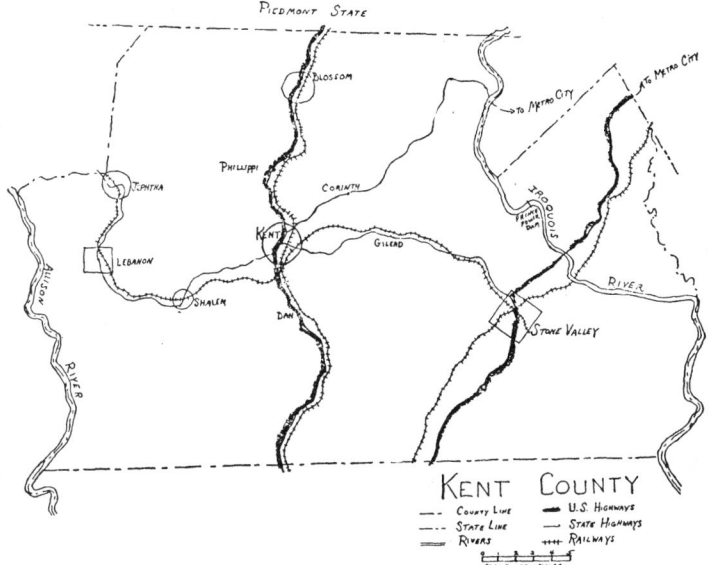

FIGURE I. Map of Kent County

began coming into the Piedmont area, Kent was already a well-established town whose leaders were satisfied with things as they were. According to oral tradition, Kent could have been a center on the main line of the Southern Railway but for a few prominent citizens who objected to the noise and smoke the trains would bring. Now two unimportant branch railway lines cross at Kent, each with two trains a day. The leaders of Kent were indifferent toward establishing cotton mills in the town when mills began "breaking out like the measles" in the Piedmont area. Consequently, Kent has been outstripped in growth and development by progressive Stone Valley, 16 miles to the east.

In 1940 the population of Kent was 3,494, and in 1949 it was estimated to be between 4,000 and 4,500. Stone Valley, on the other hand, had an estimated population of five to six times that of Kent in 1949, and with the addition of new industry, including a forty-million-dollar celanese plant, it will grow even larger and more influential than Kent. Another important county neighbor of Kent is the cotton-mill town of Blossom, nine miles to the north. Blossom has about the same population as Kent and provides staunch rivals of Kent High School and of the Kent baseball team. Just over the state line, 32 miles to the northeast, is Metro City, a city of one hundred thousand people. Many of Kent's citizens, including some of its cotton-mill workers, go to Metro City for special shopping and entertainment attractions. The radio programs and newspapers emanating from Metro City and Stone Valley find their way into almost every Kent household.

Kent is surrounded by a number of rural villages and hamlets of from one to three hundred people. Almost all of these villages have Biblical names, the same as those of the Presbyterian churches around which they have grown. Members of these villages do their trading in Kent, especially on Saturday, and their children go to Kent High School after finishing their local elementary schools. Many of the present mill operatives were born in these rural sections and attempted to farm there before entering mill work.

The story of the rise of textile plants in the South is also the story of their rise in Kent. It is well to review the conditions under which the mills sprang up in the South, for such a review gives many clues to understanding present-day life in Kent's mill villages. The year 1880 is generally accepted as the date for the beginning of the rise of southern textile mills as an important industry.[4] Following the disastrous effects of the War between the States, southern leaders began to realize as never before the need for finding new, diversified economic activities to replace the old cotton culture. They saw that the

4. Herbert J. Lahne, *The Cotton Mill Worker* (New York: Farrar and Rinehart, Incorporated, 1944), p. 50; Broadus Mitchell, *The Rise of the Cotton Mills in the South* (Baltimore: Johns Hopkins University Press, 1921), p. 77.

South had to build an industry of her own if she ever expected to achieve a healthy economic condition. The logical place to start was the cotton mill, for the South had the elements that would make it successful. The cotton-mill campaign began as a deliberate undertaking by economic, political, and even religious leaders. In Salisbury, North Carolina, a mill was started as the result of a religious revival. The evangelist preached against the sin and corruption of the city, but observing that little could be done until the people had a chance to earn a decent living, he concluded that next to religion, Salisbury needed a cotton factory.[5] Newspapers joined in with editorials and stories exhorting the South to gain economic strength and independence by building its own industry. Mills were looked upon as patriotic, philanthropic endeavors to pull the South out of the mire of dependency and give work to the landless and poor. Of course the mills attracted enterprising entrepreneurs who saw a chance for reaping profits in competition with northern mills.[6]

One of the most important factors in the rapid growth of southern mills was the ready supply of cheap labor. Impoverished by the war, many tenants and farmers were barely able to eke out an existence, and it was this unsuccessful farming group that furnished the labor to operate the mills. At first only the poorer tenants were drawn to the factories. But as cotton and other farm products took a sharp drop in price because of the competition of foreign markets and the depression of 1893, even the more able farmers were forced to seek the better economic opportunities offered by the mills. As the need for labor increased with the success and growth of the mills, the circle from which labor was drawn grew wider. It

5. Mitchell, *op. cit.*, p. 136, n. 163.
6. In regard to the rise of the cotton mills in Gaston County, Liston Pope, in *Millhands and Preachers*, p. 20, concludes: "Almost without question, the desire for profits was fundamental, and religion appears to have been partly a mask for economic advantage from the very beginning, whether or not it was consciously so used."

began to tap the hill people who had been fighting a losing battle trying to cultivate corn and tobacco on their rocky hillsides.[7] Labor scouts went far back into the mountains and induced entire families to leave their homes and travel at the expense of the mill to partake of the higher wages offered by the mill. These rural people poured into the mill villages by the thousands, welcoming the chance to work for 12 to 14 hours a day for what seems to us today a mere pittance. Young children worked these long hours for as little as 10 cents a day.[8] These dispossessed farmers were often badly disillusioned by what they found at the mill, but at least it was a living.

Most of the early mills were constructed in more or less isolated spots where water power was readily available. The result was that houses and stores had to be provided by the mill owners for this influx of workers, and this practice persisted even when mills were located in or near existing towns. These houses were usually built in the same style, a few at a time as the mill expanded, until finally a small village surrounded the factory. This set the pattern that has existed down to the present, a pattern in which the mill owners have exerted a high degree of control over the entire life of the village. Such control often extended beyond the economic life to religion and education, since the mills also had to provide churches and schools. In recent years, however, this control has decreased, particularly in education since, in most states, public consolidated schools have superseded small privately operated schools. Mill owners have found, too, that such villages are no longer a profitable investment; consequently many mill-village houses have been sold to the workers and to others.[9]

7. Ben Robertson in *Redhills and Cotton* (New York: Knopf and Company, 1942), gives an impressionistic picture of this.

8. A fifty-nine-year-old woman of Kent reports working in 1901 in Stone Valley at the age of 11 for 10 cents a day. In 1906 she worked 12 hours a day in Kent for 84 cents.

9. *Cf.* Harriet L. Herring, *Passing of the Mill Village* (Chapel Hill: The University of North Carolina Press, 1949); also *infra*, pp. 38-40.

The rise and growth of the mill villages, then, show exceedingly rapid economic and social changes. This movement from farm to mill is a dramatic case study in the rapid shift of an agricultural population to urban and industrial life. According to Mitchell, "The cotton mill operatives came immediately from the soil. The cotton manufacturing South sprang directly from the cotton growing South. It is probable that never before or since in economic history has an agricultural population been so suddenly drawn into industry.... The picture is one with a cotton mill in the foreground and acres of cotton plants in the background." [10]

As we have noted, Kent was comparatively late in organizing its mills. Stone Valley had six mills, one of them established almost twenty years earlier, when Kent's first cotton mill began operation in the spring of 1897. The Kent newspaper from 1880 to 1905 carried letters of enthusiasm from Stone Valley correspondents, telling of the rapid industrial expansion of what they liked to term "our Magic City." Stone Valley offered every inducement to attract the mills, while Kent scorned them for many years. On June 7, 1895, an article appeared in the Kent newspaper protesting the fact that cotton factories were being built in surrounding towns while no effort was being made to build one in Kent, and predicting that unless a factory were erected, Kent would lose its trade and decline in importance. An editorial in the same issue agreed that a cotton mill would speedily bring good dividends on the money invested and that it would contribute materially to the business interests of the town, but the editor foresaw no dire results to trade and business if a factory were not erected; rather he felt that it was a matter of individual enterprise, and that it was entirely dependent upon those who had sufficient money to invest. According to a number of the older Kent mill workers, Kent businessmen wanted to build cotton mills,

10. Mitchell, *op. cit.*, p. 173.

but their wives objected. They did not want any of "those terrible mill people" in Kent.

In 1896 a group of Kent's businessmen formed a board of incorporators and sold stock in the Kent Cotton Mill. The next year they erected a spinning plant and a village just outside the city limits. The local newspaper printed editorials praising the enterprise and carried articles describing the progress in building, the opening of the mill, and the success of the mill in operation. The other three mills in Kent were founded within a few years thereafter—the Townsend in 1899, the Neilson in 1905, and the Locksley in 1907. As in the case of the Kent Cotton Mill, each of these mills was founded with local capital. In 1913, the Kent Cotton Mill ran into financial difficulties and had to be sold. It was bought by the Cromwell Company, which already owned a chain of mills in the Piedmont, and now is known as the Cromwell Mill. The other mills changed hands several times and today are owned by the Reginold brothers, who formerly worked in cotton mills in a neighboring state. Thus the four mills are divided between two corporate managements, one local and the other with headquarters in an adjoining state.

From twelve to fifteen hundred people, about one-third of Kent's population, live and work in the four mill-village sections. The small, one-story, frame mill houses, many of which are so close to the street that there is no space for a lawn, are in sharp contrast to the beautiful homes of Kent's aristocracy. They are monotonously alike in appearance, built close together, and many are on unpaved roads that become nearly impassable in wet weather. Only within the last few years have paved streets been laid down through any of the mill sections. Water is supplied by a single spigot in the house or by a well sometimes shared by several families. Only the houses in which foremen live have sewage outlets, and outhouses are the rule.[11]

11. Since this study was made, inside plumbing has been installed in all houses in Kent in accord with a state law.

The Cromwell, with 124 houses, is the largest mill section, and it is the only section in which all the houses are owned by the mill. About half of the houses lie just outside the Kent city limits on "Old Hill," and the others just inside the town line are on "New Hill." The Old Hill houses are usually of the same L-shape design (see Figure 3, page 21), and the inside walls are ceiled with boards. Houses on New Hill vary in design and have plastered walls and ceilings. New Hill houses are frequently preferred by Cromwell workers to those on Old Hill because of their newer construction and location within the city limits. Workers living inside the city can send their children to the downtown school, rather than having them go to the smaller county school, located near the mill on Old Hill. All of the Cromwell houses rent for 25 cents a room a week. Twelve additional homes on Charlesville Street (see Figure 2, page 20), bordering the Cromwell section, are owned or rented by mill workers employed by the Cromwell mill. They are, in effect, a part of the Cromwell village.

The other three mill sections are in the immediate vicinity of the smaller Reginold mills. The Locksley section has 43 houses, the Neilson 49, and the Townsend 42. When the Reginold brothers purchased the three mills in the mid-thirties, they bought only about one-third of the houses in the village sections. The others were purchased by townspeople, who rent them to mill families, and by a few of the mill workers. These houses vary in appearance, depending on who owns them. Those owned by the mill are usually in good repair, and they rent on a subsidy basis, comparable to that for the Cromwell houses. Most of the houses owned by workers are well kept and have frequently been improved by such things as cement steps, grass lawns and flowers, and porch railings. Those in poorest repair are the ones owned by townspeople who rent them for an average of three dollars a week. The Reginold houses are more cheaply constructed than those in

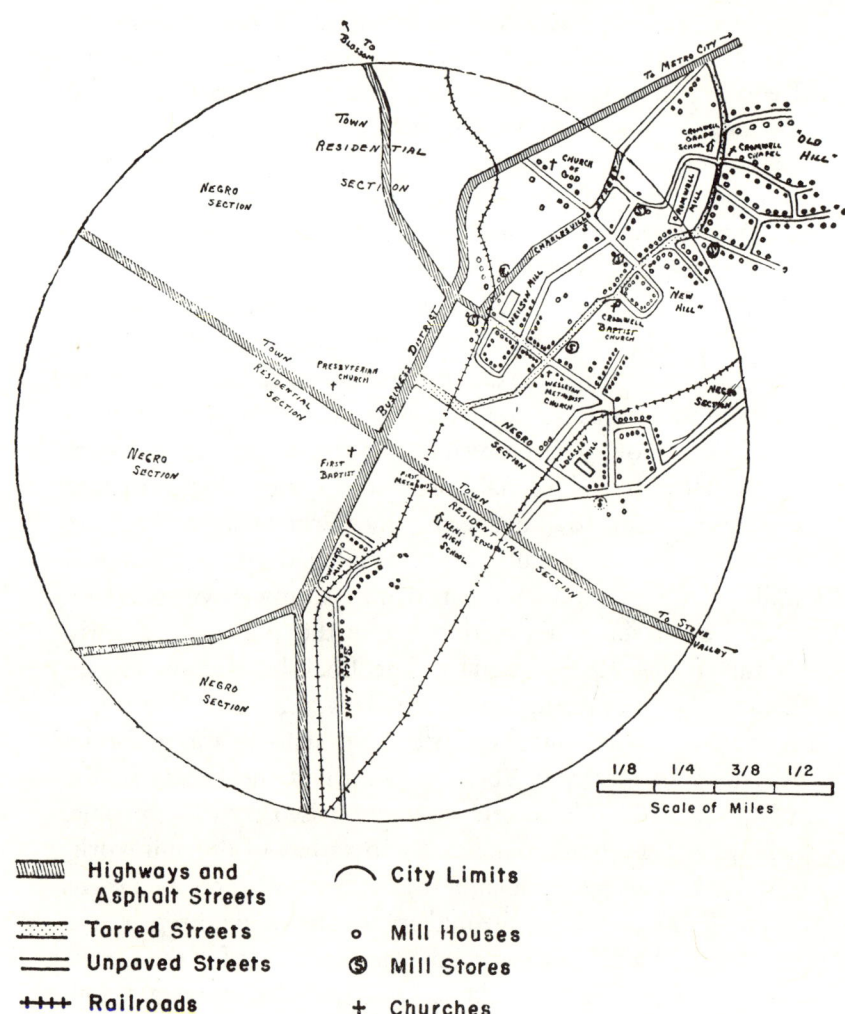

FIGURE 2. Map of Town of Kent

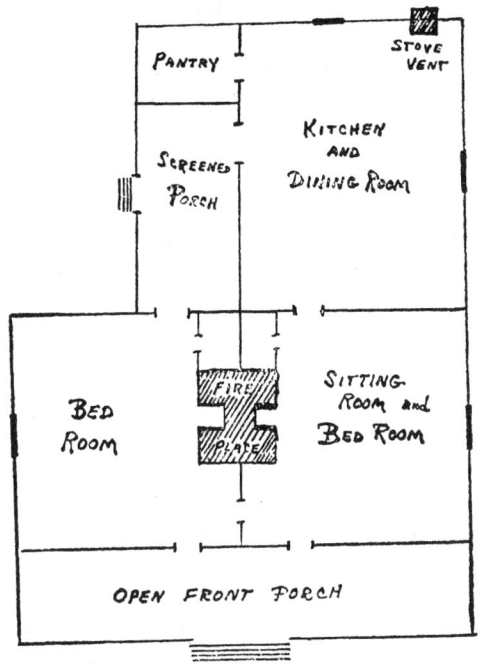

FIGURE 3. Floor Plan of Typical L-Shape Cromwell House

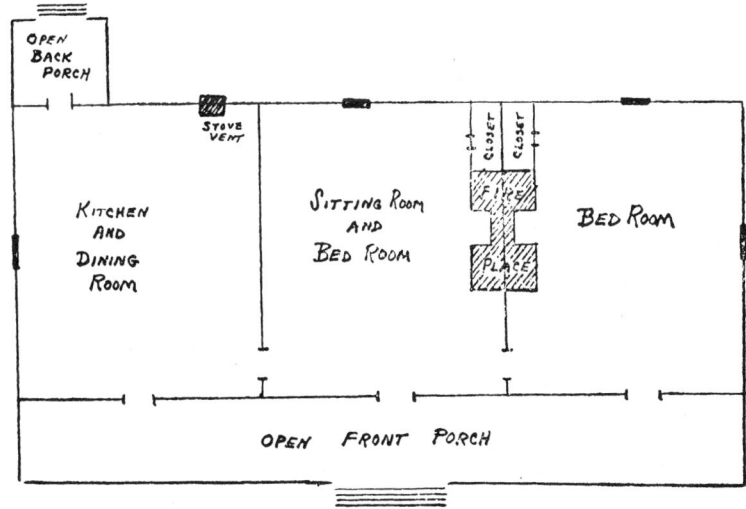

FIGURE 4. Floor Plan of Typical Neilson-Locksley House

the Cromwell, and, although they vary in design, the most usual type is rectangular, with three rooms parallel (see Figure 4, page 21).

About one-tenth of those who work in the Kent mills live in the surrounding rural areas, where they do part-time farming in conjunction with their mill work.[12]

The Human Component

All of those who live in the mill-village sections are racially white, and most of them appear to be descendants of the Scotch-Irish Presbyterians who first settled the area.[13] To discover additional characteristics of the mill people, a survey was made of approximately every third mill home, which constituted 96 of the total of 270. As indicated in Table 1, over

TABLE 1. OCCUPATION OF FATHERS OF 192 KENT MILL FAMILY HEADS *
IN 96 FAMILIES, BY MILL-VILLAGE SECTION

Village	Farm		Farm-Mill †		Mill		Other ‡	
	No.	Percent	No.	Percent	No.	Percent	No.	Percent
Total	100	52.1	35	18.2	44	22.9	13	6.8
Cromwell	59	54.6	17	15.7	27	25.0	5	4.6
Locksley	11	42.3	7	26.9	6	23.1	2	7.7
Neilson	20	62.5	4	12.5	4	12.5	4	12.5
Townsend	10	38.5	7	26.9	7	26.9	2	7.7

* Includes husband and wife in each family.
† "Farm-Mill" means that parents farmed before entering mill work.
‡ "Other" includes carpenters, mechanics, saw-mill workers, store clerks.

half, 52.1 percent, of the family heads have parents who never left the farm. Another 18.2 percent of the fathers entered mill

12. In the Cromwell Mill, 45 of the 497 workers, 9.1 percent, lived outside Kent in the surrounding rural areas in September, 1948.
13. See George Simpson's Introduction to Lewis, *Blackways of Kent*, pp. xvii–xix.

work after having farmed.[14] Of the fathers 22.9 percent have done only mill work, and the remaining 6.8 percent have done other work, usually of a laboring nature. When asked during the interviews whether they preferred farm or mill work, these ex-farmers said almost unanimously that they liked the farm better. Because of the death of a father, or a severe drop in the price of cotton, or the inability to purchase machinery, they had had to leave the farm. The consensus was that it was much more difficult to make a living farming. A man had to own his land and his machinery before he could be successful. As tenants and sharecroppers, many of these ex-farmers said that they had worked from sunup to sundown without making enough to feed their children. Although mill life was not considered so free or so healthful, at least it gave a person enough to live on, and the hours of work were not so long as those on the farm. This statement by a former tenant farmer would be endorsed by many of his fellow millhands: "If a body could jus' git set up right on his own place with the right kind of help, he couldn't have no better life anywheres in the world."

Will Clayton is an example of those forced to leave the farm and enter mill work. He was born in Kent County at the time the first cotton mill came to Kent. When he was nineteen, a friend from nearby Blossom told him of job possibilities in the mills there. His father did not want him to go, although his farm was already overcrowded with Will's older brothers, but he agreed that Will might try it. Will was put on as a learner without pay, but he did not like the noise and stifling atmosphere of "inside" work. When the bossman tried to change his job from the one on which he had started, Will revolted, climbed out the window of the mill, went back to the farm,

14. J. J. Rhyne, *Some Southern Cotton Mill Workers and Their Villages*, p. 72, a study of North Carolina mill workers in 1926–27, found that 51.2 percent of the heads of families had farmed before entering mill work, while 62.6 percent of their fathers were farmers.

and did not return. A short time later he married and rented a farm of his own, three miles from Kent. For several years he ended up with nothing after paying the rent and other costs. His three small children were girls, and he said that he did not want to put them behind a plow. In spite of the warnings of his landlord that going back to the mill would ruin his health and corrupt his daughters, Will left the farm for a job in the Cromwell mill. Later his daughters went to work when they became old enough. Will is now in his twenty-sixth year at the Cromwell and has lived in the same house the entire time. His daughters have married Cromwell workers and are living near him. He says that he feels homesick for the farm at times but is convinced that going to the Cromwell was the only step he could have taken.

"Shorty" Moss has never been satisfied with his change from farm to mill work. In 1920 when he was a tenant farmer at Phillippi, three miles from Kent, a labor scout from the mill called on him. The scout told him that he was such a hard worker that he could make an independent living in the mill instead of just getting by on the farm. "Ignorant-like, I believed him, sold my chickens and cows, left the farm, and come to the mill. And I been livin' out of a paper poke ever since." "Shorty" always wanted to go back to the farm but could never get far enough ahead to buy property or equipment. He now lives at the Neilson village and expects to be there the rest of his life.

Mill workers who were born and reared in the mill village evidently do not share the preference of their elders for farm life. To them the farm is lonely and "dead," and they wonder what could happen if a doctor were needed in a hurry. Farm work is too hard and the return too meager to attract them. They enjoy brief visits to their grandparents' farms, but they say they would not care to live and work there.

The great majority of the heads of the Kent mill families surveyed were born within a radius of twenty miles from

Kent. Table 2 shows that 60.9 percent were born in Kent
County and that only 21.9 percent were born outside the state,
almost all of them in Piedmont State just to the north.[15] Among
all mill families contacted directly and indirectly, I discovered
only two persons who were born outside the South, both of
them women who had married Kent mill boys when they were
in the armed services.

TABLE 2. BIRTHPLACE OF 192 KENT MILL FAMILY HEADS * IN 96 FAMILIES, BY
MILL-VILLAGE SECTION

	Kent County		Old South State		Piedmont State		Other Southern States	
Village	No.	Percent	No.	Percent	No.	Percent	No.	Percent
Total	117	60.9	150	78.1	36	18.8	6	3.1
Cromwell	64	59.3	86	79.6	18	16.7	4	3.7
Locksley	17	65.4	22	84.6	3	11.5	1	3.8
Neilson	22	68.8	23	71.9	8	25.0	1	3.1
Townsend	14	53.8	19	73.1	7	26.9	0	0.0

* Includes both husband and wife in each family, even if one is no longer
living.

The Surrounding Subcultures

The Kent mill-village subculture contains both rural and
urban elements, yet it stands apart from the surrounding country and town to the extent that these two areas might be looked
upon as "foreign" cultural components in the mill subcultural
setting. The relationship among these three somewhat different ways of life will be discussed at length in a later chapter,
but a brief summary view of them in order to get a full picture of the setting in which the mill subculture operates will be
helpful.

15. Rhyne, *op. cit.*, p. 69, found that less than 2 percent of his sample of
500 southern cotton-mill families were born outside the South.

We have seen that in the rise of the cotton mills in the South, those who entered the mills frequently had been failures on the farms. Those who went into the cotton factories of Kent were not exceptions, and they carried their low status into the mill villages. The townspeople did not want what they termed "cotton mill trash" in Kent, and even today some townspeople speak of them as "those horrible people who came here fifty years ago." The editor of the Kent newspaper in 1898 felt called upon to defend the operatives as being different from those who carried the reputation of being morally and mentally inferior. He said that the little village at the Kent Cotton Mill was composed of a respectable group that knew how to treat people civilly, who demanded that treatment for themselves, and who tended to their own business.

The most successful farmers tend to look upon those who leave the farm to enter mill work as lacking in energy and industry. They feel that if the person who gave up farming had just expended enough labor, he too could have been a success. One prominent farmer complained that those sharecroppers who left the rural areas to enter the mill had never taken an interest or active part in the affairs of the rural community. "They just aren't," he said, "worth a damn."

Suffice it to say that town, country, and mill people all think of themselves as "different," and that both town and country look down upon the mill people and their way of life. It might be said, then, that the dominant white subcultures surrounding the mill subculture are unsympathetic and even hostile.

The third impinging subculture is that of the Negro. The Negro sections in Kent are even more segregated from the mill sections than these are from the dominant town and country areas. Just as they are looked down on by the other whites, so do the mill people look down on the Negroes. Mill people have very limited contact with Negroes, a point which will be discussed in a later chapter.

Of these three surrounding subcultures, the town's influence in modifying the mill-village subculture is strongest. The townways are being brought into the village sections through the school, the radio, movies, television, and newspapers. While the older mill people look nostalgically back to the farm as the ideal way of life, the younger mill people look toward the town for their standards. There is little doubt, then, that town influences will grow in strength.

Cotton Mill as King: Economic Life

CHAPTER 3   JUST AS IT rises above and dwarfs the mill houses, so the cotton mill dominates the lives of the mill workers. It was the mill which beckoned the workers from the soil, provided them with houses, and presented them with the all-important weekly pay envelope. It is the mill which determines their eating time, their leisure time, and to some extent their worship time. If the mill shuts down or curtails production, life in the villages is at low ebb. When mill business is good and wages are high, life in the villages is comparatively prosperous. Villagers feel dislike of the mill as a "prison" which restricts them, and at the same time they are thankful for it as the basis of livelihood. Mill children grow up in the shadow of the mill, knowing that it is the source of their food, clothing, and shelter, and realizing, subconsciously at least, that they will likely work there by the time they reach the age of seventeen or eighteen.

THE WORKER WITHIN THE MILL

Organization of Cotton-Mill Work

Because mill-village life is so intertwined with the manufacture of cotton yarn and cloth, we must have some understanding of the mechanical processes involved in cotton manufacture. The type of job a worker holds in the mill and the shift on which he works are among the most common means of identifying him in the village sections. One of the first things I did was go through the mills in order to observe their systems of production and organization. Each of the Kent mills goes through the following six basic steps in manufacturing yarn: First, the five-hundred-pound bales of cotton are opened and fed into machines which tear apart the compressed layers of cotton through the action of beaters and grid bars. Then the cotton is sucked up into the "picker" machines which clean the cotton of leaves, motes, and any other foreign matter. From the picker machines the cotton emerges on large aprons in thin, even sheets known as "lap." This lap is carried to the carding machines, each consisting primarily of a huge, revolving cylinder with more than a million small wire teeth. These teeth eliminate remaining trash and short, fuzzy fibers. At the same time they straighten out the long fibers so that they lie parallel. When the cotton comes from the carding machines, as a thin gauzy web about forty inches wide, it is gathered into a thick, soft rope, or "sliver." Next, sixteen slivers are combined and drawn out into one sliver by the "drawing" machines, thereby further paralleling the cotton fibers. In the fifth step, slivers from the drawing machines go to the "slubber," or roving frame, where the fibers are further drawn out and paralleled. This machine twists each strand of cotton and winds it into a "roving," or ropelike form, onto a bobbin. Finally, the roving is sent through a spinning frame which performs two operations: it draws the strands of roving out into smaller strands, and it twists them slightly to give them strength. This operation of twisting and drawing out produces the yarn used in weaving.

In weaving, which in Kent is done only at the Cromwell mill, the yarn to be used as filling or woof thread goes to the loom on the bobbins, or quills, on which it is wound by the frame as fast as it is spun. Other yarn is wound in strands running parallel to each other on a large cylinder known as the warp beam, or "warper." The warp thread is then taken to the "slasher" room, where it is starched and made ready for weaving. Both the filling and warp thread are connected to the looms, and, amid deafening noise, with the shuttles flying faster than the eye can follow, the cloth is woven. After being inspected in the cloth room, it is packed away and made ready for shipment to a bleaching and finishing company.

The basic role of intricate machinery in transforming raw cotton into cloth is obvious. The chief function of the mill worker is to tend the machines that have absorbed most of the skills required to produce yarn and cloth. It might be said that specialization is by task rather than by skill, and that the workers themselves tend to be interchangeable parts in a machine process.[1] It is true that the way in which the machines are tended and the deftness with which certain other jobs are handled determine to some degree the quality and quantity of the finished products. Yet most of the jobs in the mill, with the exceptions of weaving and loom fixing, are readily learned and become largely automatic. Most of them can be learned passingly well through observation of an experienced employee at work, followed by a few weeks of on-the-job supervision.

"Bossmen" in the mills include the superintendent, overseers, and foremen. The superintendent usually has had special training in textiles, either in college or by correspondence. The present superintendent of the Cromwell mill took courses at the Y.M.C.A. night school in Cromwell Town center of the Cromwell mill chain and in adjoining Piedmont State. Immediately under the "super," as the superintendent is often called, are overseers or "desk bosses," who are in charge of the main divisions of the mill—the card room, spin room, and weave room. These overseers are brought from outside Kent, as a

---

1. For an elaboration of the difference between specialization by skill and by task, see Ronald Freedman, et al., Principles of Sociology (New York: Henry Holt and Company, 1952), pp. 412–13.

rule, and have also studied textiles. They live in the best mill houses and are set apart socially from the other workers. Next in line of authority are the foremen, or "second hands," often called "walking bosses." Each department has three of these foremen, one for each shift. In addition, there are foremen for the slasher room, machine shop, yard crew, and cloth room. Most of the foremen are Kent millhands who have been promoted. Regular workers sometimes speak of them, somewhat in jealousy, as workers who have tried especially to please the big bosses and who "report" on other workers. The superintendents claim that the foremen are selected because of their ability, knowledge of and desire for the job, character, church membership, and loyalty to the company. The order of authority at the Cromwell mill of those above the operatives can be charted as follows:

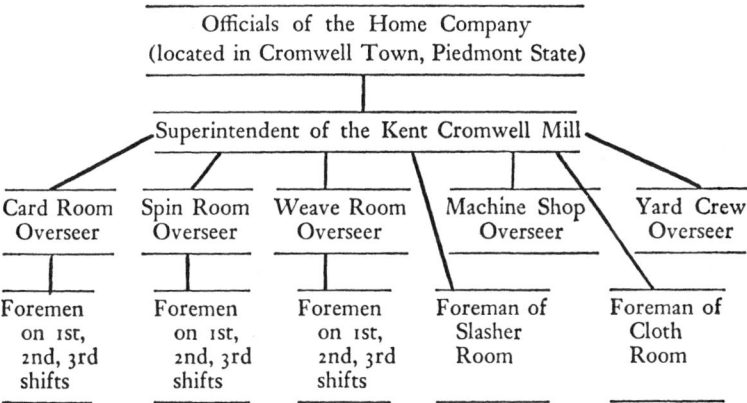

Officials of the Home Company
(located in Cromwell Town, Piedmont State)

Superintendent of the Kent Cromwell Mill

Card Room Overseer	Spin Room Overseer	Weave Room Overseer	Machine Shop Overseer	Yard Crew Overseer
Foremen on 1st, 2nd, 3rd shifts	Foremen on 1st, 2nd, 3rd shifts	Foremen on 1st, 2nd, 3rd shifts	Foreman of Slasher Room	Foreman of Cloth Room

Thus in a mill of 500 operatives, there are 17 "bossmen" positions, with 11 of them—the foremen positions—open to the regular operatives as possibilities for promotion.

The superintendent and overseers receive an annual salary, while all others in the mill are paid either by the hour or on a piece basis. Wages are paid each week, on Wednesday. Exact information could not be found on the salaries of superintendents and overseers, but it is estimated that the Cromwell superintendent made $125 a week and the overseers $85 a week in 1948, exclusive of bonuses and housing subsidy. Reginold bossmen are paid on a lower scale. Foremen at the Cromwell made $1.51 an hour, and regular operatives ranged from the minimum of 94 cents to $1.39 an hour in 1948. The minimum hourly wage at the Reginold mills was 75 cents for this same period. In 1948 the Reginold workers made about $35 a week on the average, while the Cromwell worker made about $45. On a yearly basis this would be from $1,800 to $2,400 a year for the average Kent textile worker. For Kent County as a whole, from July, 1947, to July, 1948, the average weekly wage for textile workers was $40. This indicates that the Cromwell mill is above average in its wage scale and the Reginold mills below average in the county.

It is the job that is paid for in the Kent mills rather than the man, for the length of time with the company and the amount of experience do not count in calculating wages. As workers grow old and are unable to keep up with the fast-moving machines, they are shifted to jobs requiring less speed, and consequently their wages are reduced. All strictly manual tasks such as sweeping, carrying bobbins, laps, rolls of cloth and other products from one machine to the other, opening bales of cotton, working with the yard crew, and cleaning machinery pay the minimum wage. Weavers, doffers, slubbers, and spinners are paid according to the amount of work accomplished.

In its earliest beginnings in England, and even in parts of New England, cotton-mill work was done almost entirely by women and children. Mills in the South, however, began to employ some men, because the housing system made it desirable to use all the labor available in a family. As more farmers were forced off the farm and as mill machinery increased in speed and complexity, men gradually increased in number in the mills. In Kent the number of men and women operatives is about the same. Only spinning has remained exclusively women's work, while the heavy manual labor is done only by men. Working conditions in non-air-conditioned mills are not considered pleasant. Entering a mill for the first time, a visitor will find it hot, moist, lint laden, and noisy. Air conditioning has been installed in very few mills in the South, and the Kent mills are not among them. The lint that fills the air and covers everything in the mill, so that sweepers and cleaners must be constantly at work removing it, makes breathing difficult. Moisture must be continually sprayed into the air to prevent the fibers from becoming dry, for when dry they become unmanageable from static electricity and tend to fly apart and cause sliver and even spun yarn to break easily. The hum of the spinning room and the clatter of the looms can be heard some distance from the mill, and inside the mill itself the noise is deafening.

Kent mill workers protest strongly the lack of adequate rest rooms and smoking lounges in the mills. Because of the lint in the air and the danger of igniting the cotton material, smoking is strictly prohibited inside the mill itself. At the Cromwell, workers may have one fifteen-minute pass per an eight-hour shift to go outside the mill to smoke, but some say that their work keeps them on the go so that they "hardly have time for a drink of water." But a few find time to patronize a soft-drink stand inside the mill. The workers have to eat their dinner or supper when they can, usually when they have "caught up to" their machines. These meals are brought to the mill by children, wives, or husbands. It is a common sight to see a small child carry a dinner pail and a fruit jar of iced tea to the mill gate and leave it there for his dad or mother.

Each of the mills has three shifts. The first is from 7:00 A.M. to 3:00 P.M., the second from 3:00 P.M. to 11:00 P.M., and the third from 11:00 P.M. to 7:00 A.M. Whistle blasts in the morning at 5:30, 6:00, and 6:30 rouse workers from sleep and warn them of the beginning of another workday. The mill gate is opened fifteen minutes before and fifteen minutes after the time of change of each shift, allowing workers free access to and from the mill. At all other times the gate remains locked, and no one may enter or leave without a pass from a bossman. This gives rise to the term "prisoners" applied jokingly by the workmen to the mill.

Everyone in each of the village sections knows the particular shift that neighbor or friend works. Often the shift is mentioned in the same breath with a person's name, for it determines in large measure the time a person is free. To some degree it also indicates status, for the first shift carries highest prestige and the third lowest.

Attitude of Workers toward Mill Work

We have seen that the millhands jokingly refer to the mill as the "prison"; they also call it the "sweatshop" and the "death hole." They do not appear to enjoy the work and often complain to each other about how it is taking years off their lives. A few quit the mill because of their strong dislike for "inside" work. Among them is a man who went back to the farm on which he would rather break his back picking cotton all day because "at least the air's fresh and I can feel the sunshine." Another is a woman who said that she tried to do mill work after she had married but the noise was so frightening, the heat so oppressive, and her blisters from sweeping so bad that she had to give up the work. The preacher at the Cromwell Baptist Church reflected the dislike for mill work when he said that he realized that most people did not like mill work, but it was at least a way to earn a living. He told of his own dislike of the work during the fifteen years he was in the mill and he contrasted it to the joy he found in preaching the Gospel. Yet mill work is largely taken as a common experience, and after "getting the slight of the work" the workers make their adjustment. The work does provide a weekly pay-check, and it is probably the best job they can get.

While millhands take pride in doing a good job on their assignments, they appear to make no special effort to outdo other workers. Women on piecework who have fallen below average production will sometimes go home, throw themselves on their beds, and "have a good cry." Men have told of encountering a problem in repairing machinery that they just could not solve. They became angry with the problem and with themselves, walked away from it for a while to do something else or go outside to smoke. Then, "after the mad spell passed," they tackled the job again, staying with it until it was successfully completed. But they all generally resent any attempt by a worker to push himself ahead of others, especially through special effort.

Such resentment is sometimes seen in the attitude toward local mill villagers who have become foremen, especially if they have made an obvious effort to gain promotion. Note the young worker living outside the town of Kent who, when asked what he did in his spare time, replied that he was studying textiles by correspondence in order to get ahead in the work—but hastened to add that the other workers should not be told this, "because they would run me out of the mill if they found out." One foreman has the nickname among the operatives of "Two-tongue" because "he has one tongue to lick the bosses' asses and another to lick the workers' asses." But the worker who is circumspect and who is pushed into the job of foreman by the superintendent (and the superintendents say they must frequently do this) does not become the object of resentment.

The workers hold special dislike for a bossman who has "learned it all from books." They agree that those who have had little actual experience in mill work itself, regardless of how much studying they have done, make poor bosses. Often held up as an ideal boss is the head of another chain of mills in the state. As a young man he worked as a millhand, although his father was a superintendent. He knows from experience how a mill should operate; he does not mind getting into his overalls to help with the dirtiest job, and often he dresses so that he cannot be distinguished from a regular worker.

Types of Workers

We have seen that some of the mill workers, about one-tenth of the total, live in the surrounding countryside and commute to and from the mills. They rent small farms which they work during the hours they are not at the mill. When they have sons to help them with the farming, mill work and farm work can supplement each other. More often, however, these workers do not attempt to farm, except to raise some of their own food. During World War II, when gasoline was rationed, the Reginold mills used station wagons to pick up these workers and carry them back to their homes. Generally they are the last hired and the first laid off, and they work most frequently on the third shift, the third shift being the first to be reduced in force in times of production curtailment.

We have seen that women preceded men as millhands, for historically it was a ready transfer for them from spinning yarn in the home to spinning it in the factory.[2] In 1891 a letter from the Stone Valley correspondent to the Kent weekly newspaper stated that many families were preparing to move from the country to town and place women and children in the cotton mills. The correspondent commented that as a general thing this was a bad omen, for there was scarcely anything for the men to do which was at all remunerative. This tradition of women's working in cotton mills has continued in Kent. As Table 3 shows, 84.9 percent of the wives questioned were mill workers, although at the time the survey was made only 70.3 percent were actually employed. The others had

2. Herbert J. Lahne, *The Cotton Mill Worker*, p. 103.

dropped out temporarily or had retired. It is generally expected in the mill sections that a woman who is healthy should work in the mill, regardless of how large a family she may have. The fact that women work is significant in husband-wife relations and in child rearing, matters that will be discussed in the next chapter.

TABLE 3.. MILL WORKERS * AND NONMILL WORKERS AMONG 86 KENT MILL WIVES, BY MILL-VILLAGE SECTION

Village	Number of Wives Who Are Mill Workers	Number of Wives Who Are Nonmill Workers	Percent of Wives Who Are Mill Workers
Total	73	13	84.9
Cromwell	36	6	85.7
Locksley	10	3	76.9
Neilson	13	2	86.7
Townsend	14	2	87.5

* "Mill Workers" are those working at the time of the survey and any others who have worked for a year or more after marriage.

Children under sixteen are prohibited from working in the mills, since they are required by state law to attend school until that age. The Cromwell has an additional rule prohibiting girls from working until they are eighteen. Consequently, more Cromwell girls than boys are finishing high school and going into other jobs. But most of the girls in the Reginold villages enter mill work at sixteen or seventeen, and the majority of boys in all the mill sections go into the mill as soon as they complete the compulsory term in school. The superintendents feel that they have a special obligation to provide employment for those children from families that have worked for a long time in the mill. Although the majority of mill children enter mill work, there has been no evidence of "mill daddies." [3]

3. Liston Pope, *Millhands and Preachers*, p. 65, n. 30. Mill daddies are defined as those who "carry lunches to their children at work in the mills, and this constitutes almost their only responsibility."

"Floaters" or "drifters" comprise another type of mill worker. They consist mostly of unattached men who work a few weeks in order to save enough money for a week of loafing and drinking and a bus ticket to the next mill town. Their status among long-time residents of the villages is low, as Chapter 9 points out.

MILL-VILLAGE ECONOMY

Ownership of Houses

Mill houses are supplied to workers as a part of the job. This is entirely the case in the Cromwell village and to a limited extent in the Reginold villages. Mill-owned houses rent for as little as seventy-five cents a week. The pattern of mill control of housing is changing in the South,[4] and in line with that change the superintendent of the Cromwell mill has suggested to Mr. Cromwell that the Kent mill houses be sold to workers. The superintendent argues that the small rental does not pay for the upkeep and insurance. But Mr. Cromwell wants to keep the houses in order to be able to provide workers with readily available places to live. This, of course, gives the company greater control over the workers at the same time. Union organizers claim that mill-controlled housing is one of the most powerful weapons that management has against organization attempts.

The superintendents have the responsibility of assigning company houses and apparently they are quite arbitrary, even though there is a waiting list. Some villagers think the bossmen play favorites, but the superintendents say that they must make the most expedient assignments to keep as many satisfied workers as possible (and, no doubt, to get as many workers from the houses as possible). Some families can be put off in

4. This is the thesis of Harriet L. Herring in *The Passing of the Mill Village.*

their requests for more living space because the superintendent knows they will not object strenuously. He also knows the size of each family, how long it has lived in the village, and how valuable it is to the company.[5]

When a family moves out of a mill-owned house, there is rarely only a single move to fill the house vacated. Usually there is a series of moves, especially if the house vacated is one of the more desirable. Typical of such a series of moves was that in the Cromwell village when Mrs. Hope left the house on New Hill where she had lived for twenty-four years—she and her family went to live in a new house built on Charlesville Street with insurance money received after her son's death in the war. The Clantons moved from across the street into the Hope house, which was larger and next door to relatives. The Penneys moved from Old Hill into the Clanton house in order to be on New Hill and nearer relatives. The Goforths moved from across the street into the Penneys' house, leaving behind a two-room house they had outgrown. A young worker and his wife and baby moved into the Goforths' house, after having lived in a single room with the husband's parents for a year and a half. Thus five families moved when the one vacancy was created.

The majority of mill workers would rather own their homes than rent from the company or from private individuals, for such ownership gives a feeling of independence and security.[6] There is an underlying resentment of the control of housing by the mill. As one worker expressed it, "If you own your own place, and they come around to tell you to get out, you can just tell them to kiss your ass."

The Wiltons of the Locksley village lived in the Cromwell

5. This is an example of the detailed knowledge the mill has of its people—and they of each other. Life in each village section consists largely of face-to-face contacts as in any small town. However, these contacts are even more intimate among mill people, because they are carried into the job.

6. This finding coincides generally with that in Herring, *op. cit.,* pp. 55–62.

at one time but preferred to buy a much less attractive place in the Locksley section when some of the houses were put up for sale. After four years they are finding it a struggle to pay for the house, but they are much more satisfied in their own place, they say. Mrs. Wilton claims that the tendency of the mills is to make the entire family leave a mill-owned house if any member quits his job. As her children grew dissatisfied with mill work, she feared all of them might eventually be put out of the house. According to Mrs. Wilton, "The house we got may be only a run-down shack, but at least it's our'n, and if'n we keep on payin' the payments, there ain't nobody can tell us to git out."

Willie Saddlemeyer at the Cromwell Old Hill has one of the most attractive lawns and flower gardens in any of the village sections, and he is very proud of them. At the same time he is sorry that he does not live where he could be sure that all the improvements he has made would be his permanently. The deepest regret of the Cromwell superintendent in retiring was that the house in which he had lived and reared his family would remain with the mill, and he would have to move. However, some of the younger mill workers prefer not to buy houses in the mill sections, if ever they do come up for sale. They prefer more modern housing.

The majority of mill families who move out of the villages do so of their own accord, either to homes of relatives or to other mill villages, and occasionally to places they have built themselves, as Mrs. Hope did. Sometimes, however, the company will have to force a family to move. This is likely to happen if one of the family heads is fired, especially if jobs and houses are scarce. For example, at the Cromwell village the Campbell family was told to leave because the male head of the family missed work on two Mondays in succession owing to drunkenness, the culmination of several years of irregularities. The entire family, including the wife and son who worked in the mill, were asked to leave. The Campbells were given a "reasonable" time to move but were so slow in making any attempt to do so that the company threatened to move their furniture into the warehouse if they did not go. Finally the Campbells found jobs at Blossom and moved up there. Repairs to mill houses are made by the company maintenance crews. If a screen is broken, or boards on the porch rot, or the roof leaks, the occupants of the house report it. This contributes to the attitude that appears to be prevalent among those who live in mill houses, namely that if anything goes wrong, the mill will take care of it. Teachers in the mill school claim that this is also reflected in the tendency of mill children to destroy property or to be careless in its use. They report that the children frequently say, "Let the mill take care of it; they've got plenty of money anyway."

Insurance

Mill workers in Kent believe strongly in insurance. During visits in over one-third of the mill homes, I found that better than ninety percent of the families carried at least one policy of industrial insurance, for which premiums are collected each week. Parents frequently take out a one-thousand-dollar policy on themselves and a five-hundred-dollar policy on each child. The most popular type is the twenty-year-pay. At least five companies have agents in Kent, and their collectors are often seen going from house to house in each village, collecting premiums and checking the insurance-payment cards, invariably hanging on a nail just inside the front door.

Each of the mills has also instituted insurance policies for its workers. Cromwell employees contribute forty cents a week from their pay, and the company adds a like amount, giving a one-thousand-dollar life-insurance policy and limited hospitalization protection. The Reginold Company charges fifty cents a week for an individual and seventy-five cents a week for a family, providing death and sickness policies. When the mills are shut down or a worker laid off, this insurance is continued and the premiums paid by the company, later to be repaid by the worker when his job starts again.

Unemployment compensation and old-age security—"rocking-chair money," according to the mill workers—have given a degree of financial independence. Formerly, when they became unable to do mill work, old people had to be entirely supported by their children. Now they receive enough from social-security payments to supplement the income of a household. Unemployment compensation has taken away part of the fear that comes with being laid off.

Before these insurance aids were instituted, the workers depended on the bounty of more fortunate relatives and on "purses" voluntarily made up by fellow workmen. Good friends of a person whose family had met with serious illness or death would "pass the hat" in order to make up a sum of money to help the unfortunate family. This is done far less frequently now. Relatives continue to rush to the aid of each other in event of distress, and neighbors help with cooking, washing, and child tending when a housewife is sick. But insurance is playing an increasingly important part in lightening the financial burden in times of crisis and in reducing financial insecurity. It occupies an important place in the family budget, as we shall see shortly.

Unions

The mills in Kent are not unionized. Both the Cromwell officials and the Reginold brothers are adamant against them, claiming that the union is divisive, pitting employee against employer. These company officials say they strive for a "family-like" relationship of harmony with their workers, whereas the unions "do not practice the golden rule" and cause "antagonisms" to develop. Furthermore, the officials say they do not want labor leaders telling them how to run their business.

Reginold workers often quote the Reginolds as having said they would close down their mills and remove all the machinery if their workers ever voted for the union. And the workers are convinced they would.

There have been two attempts at unionization in Kent. During the 1934 general strike in textiles, a "flying squadron" of cars from Piedmont State filled with union workers rode up to the Cromwell mill but were dispersed by armed mill guards, electrically charged fences, and a heavy rain. The first concerted effort at union organization was made in August of 1946 by the Textile Workers Union of America, a C.I.O. affiliate, with the Reginold workers. An organizer was sent over from Stone Valley, where the T.W.U.A. had been voted in by workers in several plants. This organizer signed up a majority of workers in a small rug mill operated by the Reginold brothers at that time, and he began to sign up workers in the Neilson and Locksley mills. But union participants began to be laid off, and the rug mill was shut down. When several workers were fired, the organization attempt was stopped. The T.W.U.A. filed a complaint with the National Labor Relations Board, claiming that the Reginold plants had resorted to unfair labor practices. The case was brought to trial in Kent two years later in 1948. The federal judge dismissed the union claim at the Neilson and Locksley Mills, but concluded that unfair labor practices had been used in the rug mill.

Kent mill workers were greatly interested during the trial. Many expressed the hope that the Reginolds would "get it this time," for they believed that the brothers had become rich by "cheating" their workers, paying them only as little as they had to. Others, apparently in a minority, felt that workers had no right to tell an employer what he could or could not do— if a worker did not like the job or the pay, he should leave to find one he did like. A number of the Reginold workers expressed gratitude to the Reginolds for having started the mills again and giving them employment, even though the wages were low. Those who talked in favor of the union did so only with people they knew they could trust. Mrs. Ross, one of the Neilson workers whose discharge was contested by the union, had not told her son, who lived and worked at the Cromwell mill, of her union affiliation for fear he would disapprove.

Few Cromwell workers attended the trial sessions, but many were anxious to know about developments. Some would ask how "their side" was getting along, identfying themselves with the union. A number of Cromwell workers felt that the Reginold mills really needed a union, because "the Reginolds squeeze their workers for all they are worth." At the same time they thought there was less need for a union at the Cromwell mill because they received "decent" wages and were shown some concern. However, the most outspoken workers at the Cromwell said that a union would not be a bad thing at their mill, for it would help prevent what they consider the arbitrary actions of management and stop "speed ups" and "stretch outs." Many agreed that if it were not for the unions, Mr. Cromwell would not have raised wages as high as the union minimum, nor would he have granted insurance and vacation benefits. They believe that if any worker is known to be strongly prounion and voices his opinions, he will be fired by the Cromwell mill, and they resent this. The fact that several plants in Stone Valley have been successfully organized and that some of the workers who live in Kent and commute to Stone Valley are union members has helped to bring about an understanding and acceptance of unions that did not exist among Kent mill workers before.

But as long as the Cromwell company raises wages when union mills do and suppresses any apparent interest in unionism by its workers there seems to be little chance of the growth of unionism among its workers. And the Reginold mills are so irregular in production that attempts at organization can be stifled by what might appear to be a regular, periodical closing of the plants. Therefore, the development of unions under these conditions appears unlikely.

Use of Money

The monthly expenditures for five different mill families were analyzed in detail. They had much in common and seem to be reasonably typical: The Mooney family of the Neilson village had an income of $225 during the month of March, 1948. The father drew $20 a week from his unemployment compensation, the mother made $30 a week as a spinner at the Neilson mill, and Mrs. Mooney's mother, who lived with the family, drew $25 during the month in old-age insurance. The Mooneys' four children ranged in age from one to twelve. The family income was spent approximately as follows:

Rent	$12	
Food	150	
Insurance	25	(all seven members of the family have policies)
Telephone	4	(one of the few telephones in the Neilson village)
Water	1	(from a single spigot in the kitchen)
Electricity	3	(for lights only)
Clothing	15	(bought very irregularly)
Miscellaneous	15	(including coal, garden seeds, an occasional movie)
Total	$225	

Only the water, electric, and telephone bills were actually paid by the month. The other items were paid by the week. The food budget broke down into the following items: $10 a week for "rough rations," or staples, including flour, meal, coffee, lard, fatback, sugar, salt, evaporated milk, margarine, syrup, kerosene (for the stove), ice, and soap; and $25 a week for fresh vegetables, meats, eggs, dried beans, and peas of various kinds. These items were charged at a nearby store that caters to mill workers. If the Mooneys owned their home, they would be putting an amount equivalent to rent into payments for the house and into repairs. If their wages were higher, the additional amounts would be put into payments for a washing machine or electric refrigerator or secondhand car, all of which they would like very much to have. If times were to get harder, the Mooneys would give up their telephone, reduce their insurance, stop buying clothes of any kind, and have the electricity shut off. Food would be the last item reduced. Had the Mooneys attended church, they might have put as much as $25 a month into church contributions.

These expenditures were not budgeted in any sense, and they could be ascertained only after considerable probing. Like other mill workers, the Mooneys usually spend their money as soon as they receive it, reflecting the generally prevalent attitude that money is something to be used as soon as it is received, or even before. Mill people do not think highly of "tight-fisted" persons or of those "who have kept every penny they ever earned."

Yet it does not appear true, as townspeople seem to believe, that mill people are suckers for any door-to-door salesman that comes along. Some mill workers do buy shoes, medications, clothes, and gadgets in this way, but when they are able to, most invest in such substantial goods as stoves, refrigerators, inner-spring mattresses, linoleum rugs, and washing machines. During the period of high wartime wages, when the mills ran six days a week as a rule, a number of workers were able to buy modern appliances and house furnishings. Among them was Clyde Watson, a Cromwell worker who spent $1,200 of his wartime earnings to modernize his kitchen completely; his wife spent an equal amount in furnishing their home. During this period he and his wife earned together an average of $90 a week, or more than $4,500 a year for a four-year period. With the sharp reduction in the number of working days in the spring of 1949, their earnings dropped to $55 a week. Clyde and his brother had bought lots on Charlesville Street and had dug the foundations for their new homes, but construction had to be postponed indefinitely because of the decrease in earnings.

A number of mill workers borrow money from week to week. There are moneylenders in each of the mills, and they charge weekly rates of interest as high as 15 percent per week. At the Cromwell mill a loom fixer reportedly makes considerably more from lending money than he does from working in the mill. The Cromwell mill itself does not lend money, but it allows the lending business to go on and even sends workers to this "official" lender when they need money. The lender is allowed to attach the paychecks of the workers in order to be sure of being paid. Many of the workers condemn such garnishments when "the worker's children have to do without bread," and they resent the amount that has to be paid as interest. But more than a few find it necessary to borrow, and at the time are glad they can do so.

Transportation

About one-third of the Kent mill families surveyed owned automobiles (see Table 4). In contradiction to what some

TABLE 4. NUMBER AND MAKE OF AUTOMOBILES IN 96 KENT MILL FAMILIES, BY MILL-VILLAGE SECTION, IN 1948

Village	Number of Families	Number Owning Autos	Percent of Families Owning Autos	Average Year of Model	Most Popular Make
Total	96	33	34.4	1938	Chevrolet
Cromwell	54	25	46.3	1939	Chevrolet
Locksley	13	4	30.8	1939	Chevrolet
Neilson	16	3	18.8	1937	Ford
Townsend	13	1	7.7	1931	Chevrolet

townspeople say, mill people do not spend much money on cars. An automobile is not essential, since the majority live only a few blocks from their work, but mill people would like to have automobiles, especially for going visiting, hunting, and fishing. Car owners share their cars with neighbors, by taking them along to hunting and fishing grounds, when all pay the cost of the trip, or simply by carrying them to and from town. Mill people driving to town always stop to pick up fellow villagers who are walking. They never appear in too big a hurry to stop, and they always seem to have room for an additional passenger.

There is no public bus in Kent, and mill people without cars rely on taxis. The charge for a taxi ride to any place in town is 25 cents for each passenger, and mill people complain that this is too high. Those living a mile or more from the mill in which they are employed sometimes arrange to be carried to and from work every day for a set amount, usually $2.00 a week, and parents of young mill children have them taken by taxi to and from school in town for a fixed sum per week. Taxis carry more mill people than townsfolk, and becoming a taxi driver is one of the alternative occupational patterns followed by mill workers. Three Cromwell workers own taxis, which they operate while not at work in the mill.

Summary Characteristics of Economic Life

From this description of certain details of economic life in the mill-village sections, several salient characteristics emerge.

Paternalism

One of the most readily recognized characteristics of the economic system is its paternalism. We have seen how this paternalistic system developed historically when poor, dispossessed farmers were "saved" from pauperism by "benevolent" mill owners, and how they were brought into village life controlled almost completely by the company. The owners of the Kent mills have continued to maintain a high degree of control over their workers. They claim that they "take care of" their workers by spreading the work out during periods of curtailment and by admonitions to them on conduct when they get into trouble. The owners pride themselves on the family-like relationship that exists between employer and employee, and one of their objections to unions is that union organization would break down this relationship.

In this paternalistic setup the owners attempt to maintain a personal relationship with each worker. Mr. Cromwell himself has let it be known that any worker can write directly to him whenever something goes wrong. This is rarely done, since there are more than nineteen thousand workers in the Cromwell chain of mills and since a plant superintendent would not like one of his workers to go over his head. The local superintendent stated that he was proud that such appeals have not been made, since this indicates that the workers are satisfied with him.

The paternalistic attitude of the Reginold brothers was brought out during the National Labor Relations Board trial. Workers who had joined the union reported that the particular Reginold brother directing the mill in which they worked came to them objecting, "What have I done that you don't like? Haven't I always treated you right? If there's anything wrong, you come to me rather than to those outside union fellows." The Reginolds give Christmas parties for their workers and present each with gifts of fruit, candies, and clothing. If their people get into trouble with the "law" the brothers often bail them out, scold them, and make them promise to behave. Reginold workers who joined the union complained bitterly about those who "worshipped the Reginolds like gods and bowed down and kissed their feet," and who were afraid to speak up for themselves "no matter what the Reginolds did to them."

Kent mill people seem generally to approve of this paternalistic care if the benefits are great enough. Often the Waters mills, a chain with plants in other towns of the state, are held up by Kent workers as ideal, because "Mr. Waters does so much for his workers." He has built brick houses in some of his villages, installed plumbing, provided playgrounds, and constructed cottages at the beach where workers can spend weekends. Mr. Waters maintains strict control of housing and of every phase of hiring and firing. Like the Cromwell company, Waters pays the union minimum wage, raising his wages whenever union mills raise theirs.

One concomitant of paternalism is that the workers do not know in advance about actions of management. Rumors run rife through the mill and the villages. Cromwell operatives seldom get as much as one day's advance warning of a curtailment or increase in work load, and Reginold workers sometimes find their mills shut down when they report for work. Since they are told so little in advance, workers try to predict what will happen from certain "signs" they see. For example, several loom fixers were put to checking cloth, and the workers concluded that something was wrong with the cloth and that the company was preparing for drastic changes. When I asked for a list of workers who lived outside Kent, the bookkeeper went through the mill asking these people for their addresses. A rumor developed and was generally believed that all of those so questioned were to be laid off. Workers agree that "you jus' can't believe none of them rumors you hear all the time in a cotton mill."

In one sense paternalism can function to reduce anxiety in its emphasis on taking care of the worker. The workers know that if they are loyal to the company, cooperate with the bossmen, and do a reasonably good job in the mill, they can be sure of their jobs and their houses. Many of their problems are solved for them if they submit to the system. Furthermore, severe competition is avoided, for there is little emphasis on bettering oneself and one's position. We have seen that workers exert pressure to prevent individuals from trying to forge ahead of the group. Their common occupation insures essential equality of wages and housing, so that economic status is generally the same for all. The desire for economic betterment is present, but the mill people seem to feel that there is little the individual can do to accomplish it. Their income is determined by mill conditions, a situation that affects all alike and over which they have no control.

Hereditary Occupational Group

Most of the children of Kent mill workers enter cotton-mill work. Among the ninety-six mill families surveyed, 65.4 percent of the children who had jobs were employed in a cotton mill (see Table 5).[7] There are several third-generation families in the village sections, especially in the Cromwell, and the superintendents are very proud of this.

TABLE 5. NUMBER OF WORKING CHILDREN IN 96 KENT MILL FAMILIES WHO WORK
IN A COTTON MILL, BY MILL-VILLAGE SECTION

Village	Number of Working Children	Children Working in a Cotton Mill	
		Number	Percent
Total	162	106	65.4
Cromwell	92	54	58.7
Locksley	20	14	70.0
Neilson	22	16	72.7
Townsend	28	22	78.6

This tendency toward establishing an inbred occupational group serves to solidify differences between mill people and the rest of Kent. At the same time it promotes the feeling of *esprit de corps* and security among the mill villagers. Mill work might be a social stigma so far as many townspeople are con-

7. In her study of a mill-village section in Greer, South Carolina, S. W. Hutton found that 71.2 percent of the working children work in a mill. This is reported in her unpublished master's thesis, Social Participation of Married Women in a South Carolina Mill Village, p. 27.

cerned, but it also acts as a reinforcement of in-group feeling among mill workers. It makes placing a person a simple matter, for he is either one of the group or he is outside the group, depending on whether or not he works in the mill. A mill worker knows just what actional patterns to follow with another mill worker, while he is uncertain just how he should act with a townsperson or anyone outside the mill group.

Week-by-Week Basis of Economic Existence

Kent mill workers live on a week-by-week economic basis. Their wages are paid each week, and with them they pay for groceries, rent, insurance, installments on furniture and electrical appliances, all by the week. They say that they would not like to live on a monthly basis because "a working man just can't afford to plunk out a big pile of money at the end of a month." There are seven grocery stores in the village sections where the mill people do most of their buying. These stores are operated by independent merchants, although one of them is on Cromwell property and partly controlled by the company. Each of them allows charge accounts and delivers groceries, and most mill families use these services. But because of such services and their small size, these stores have higher prices than the chain stores in town. Grocerymen say that it is customary for mill people to take care of their bills for the past week on payday and then get fresh supplies of groceries which they charge and pay for the following week. As a rule the mill worker spends his money the same day that he receives it, and Kent merchants claim that unless workers are seen on payday, it is difficult to collect a bill.

This hand-to-mouth existence, so deplored by townspeople, appears to be the result of several factors. Wages in textiles are low, and, after paying for the essentials of food, clothing, and shelter, mill people often have nothing left to save. The paternalistic system of taking care of the worker does not promote the feeling of the need for thrift, and, besides, there is a deep-seated distrust of banks as town institutions that might cheat the mill person. Thus thrift and economy are not established drives among mill people as they are among townspeople. If mill workers have money, they spend it, and if times are hard and money is scarce, they do without. Their attitude is one which directs them to accept whatever comes their way, whether times are good or bad. Apparently they accept week-to-week existence with comparatively low wages and uncertain income as a part of their lot, and it does not seem to bother them much. They believe that in one way or the other they will always make out.

Kinship as Security: Family Life

CHAPTER 4   GETTING MARRIED and rearing a family are considered essential goals for a normal person in the Kent mill-village sections. According to estimates, less than 3 percent of Kent mill people over twenty-five years of age are single.[1] Being single limits a person's participation in mill culture, and bachelors and spinsters are thought of as "queer" and often pitied for missing an area of life considered very important.

GENERAL DESCRIPTION OF COURTSHIP, MARRIAGE, AND FAMILY CUSTOMS

Courtship

Mill boys and girls are teased about their "sweethearts" very early, and boys as young as two and three are urged to hug little girls their age and "give them some sugar." Open interest in boys develops among young girls throughout grade school, but the reverse situation is much less obvious in boys

---

1. These estimates were made by two persons in each of the villages who knew their sections well, and they were checked by my own observations and visits with the ninety-six mill families. Some of those not married have physical disabilities. One bachelor is subject to epileptic seizures, while another has been partly crippled since birth. One of the old maids is "not right bright," and another has devoted her life to rearing her deceased sister's children.

during this period. Girls' groups and boys' gangs of grade-school age discuss sex, and some of the boys and girls engage in sex experimentation. Dating begins late in grade school and continues steadily and more seriously throughout high school. The earliest form is unplanned and informal. Two or more boys the same age will happen along and meet several neighborhood girls. They will decide to go to a movie, or to Pop's Place, the favorite hangout for mill boys and girls, where they have cokes or milk shakes and listen to the juke box.

One of the favorite meeting places of teen-age boys and girls is at church during evening services. In such cases boys drop by the homes of their girl friends and walk with them to church, or else they meet them immediately after the service and walk them home. Since mill homes are small and crowded, they offer little space or privacy for dating. Some young couples have trysting places in the woods near each of the villages, and one couple reported having to use the cemetery as a rendezvous. When boys and girls begin to reveal interest in each other by taking greater pains with their personal appearance and showing each other a great deal of attention, they are subject to good-natured teasing by those older than they.

After mill young people leave school and start making their own money, courtship begins in earnest. One of the incentives for entering mill work early is making enough money to take girl friends to movies and buy them presents. Mill parents seldom make enough to give their children sufficient spending money to do these things. Much of the serious courting and eventual marriage continues to take place between fellow workers, although there is probably less of this now than formerly. A typical courting experience involved a man of twenty-one who used to weave on the same shift as the girl he married—they walked to and from work together and managed to go to the refreshment stand in the mill at the same time; they would attend Sunday night church services together, and go to movies and dances. After six weeks of steady courtship, they were married at the home of a justice of the peace in a nearby town.

Kent mill young people generally marry within Kent mill sections, or the mill sections of Blossom or Stone Valley or some other nearby mill town, or the surrounding rural areas. Kinship lines are tightly intertwined within each village section, and they also cross among all four villages, attesting to this fact that Kent mill people marry each other. And relatives of Kent mill workers are frequently found in Blossom and Stone Valley and in the surrounding hamlets of Phillippi, Corinth, Shalem, and Dan. If the ability of mill workers to own automobiles increases, marriage outside Kent, with mill and farm people, will probably increase.

Premarital sexual experience is more or less expected of mill boys.[2] Groups of young men in their late teens and early twenties sometimes go to Stone Valley on weekends to visit prostitutes, occasionally after having had "respectable" dates with their Kent girl friends. The majority of boys in the mill apparently have had sexual experience by the time they are in their mid-teens although their parents do not approve of such behavior. "Boys will be boys" is the way that parents generally condone such action. However, a boy expects to marry a "decent" girl, that is, a girl who has not run around "loose" too much. Couples who go steady usually have sexual intercourse, often with the understanding that they will marry "soon." One young mill worker spoke of breaking off with his girl friend because she would not give him "some" when he asked her. She said that such relations were wrong until people married and that he would have to marry her first. But he felt that she was prudish, for they had been going together for over a year. Premarital chastity is considered the ideal for

2. Findings in this and other areas of sexual activity generally agree with the data for lower social-class groups presented by Alfred C. Kinsey, et al., *Sexual Behavior of the Human Male* (Philadelphia: W. B. Saunders Company, 1948), chap. 10, especially.

girls, but according to more than one person, "you find very few girls today who ain't been out to the woods with one or more boys."

There were at least four cases of premarital pregnancy that came to my attention during the year I lived in Kent.[3] In only one of these did the boy involved marry the girl, and in another the young mother was widely believed to have smothered her illegitimate offspring and thrown it into the outhouse pit. Little stigma seems to be attached by mill people to children born out of wedlock, nor is the mother herself censured severely. As a rule, she has little difficulty in marrying later. Her illegitimate child is taken into the family and given his stepfather's name, although in at least two cases illegitimate children of mothers who have later married have retained their mother's maiden name. Some of the mill people gossip about such offspring, but the majority say, "It's nobody else's business." Children known to be illegitimate are accepted by the village simply on personal merits.

Marriage

Kent mill people marry at a comparatively early age. A justice of the peace who marries many of the mill workers gave the average age of girls as 18 or 19 and that of boys as 20 or 21.[4]

3. Rhyne, *Some Southern Cotton Mill Workers and Their Villages*, pp. 187–88, found no higher rate of illegitimacy among cotton-mill girls and women than among the rest of the white population of Gaston, North Carolina. However, in Kent it is higher among mill workers than among townspeople, according to the doctors, who say that official records are inaccurate.

4. This compares favorably with the findings of S. W. Hutton, Social Participation of Married Women in a South Carolina Mill Village, p. 22: "...young girls at Victor [a mill-village section in Greer, South Carolina] may expect to marry in their later teens or early twenties. Among the women interviewed [from 75 families], 92 per cent married before they were twenty-five years of age, and 64 per cent married before reaching the age of twenty. The average age of the group that married before reaching the age of twenty was seventeen.... The husbands as a group tend to be a little older than the wives: 81 per cent married before reaching the age of twenty-five, with only 20 per cent marrying before twenty years of age.... The young person

Cases were found where girls had married as early as 14, one of them in 1949, and boys as early as 16 and 17, but these were unusual. Reasons for early marriage are not difficult to find. Boys usually go to work in the mill when they are 16 or 17, since mill work requires no more than a minimum of schooling, and girls work too, making about as much as the boys. A couple's joint income will initially be as high as they can ever expect it to be, for a person makes almost as much as he will ever make on first entering mill work. Further, a mill couple is not required to set up a separate household, for it is expected that they will live with relatives, usually parents, until off-spring appear and a house is assigned them. Thus with the occupational, economic, educational, and residential require-ments so readily fulfilled, marriage can be entered into early and without extensive preparation and planning.

Parents allow their children almost complete freedom in choosing a husband or wife, although some fathers "run off" boys who are reputed to be of low character, boys who are known to drink and gamble to excess and who cannot hold a steady job. The requirement, so all-important among town people, that a mate must come from the "right" family, does not apply among people in the mills, for there is no anxiety about marrying out of one's "class." Marriage is not forbidden between first cousins, and such marriages are not uncommon, although some mill people believe that defective children come from such a union.[5]

Once a couple decide to marry, the ceremony is arranged and performed quickly and quietly. Couples' decisions to "make it next Thursday" or even to "make it tomorrow" are

at Victor, at least one who intends to remain in mill work, tends to marry someone who lives in the village, another mill village, or in a surrounding rural area."

5. A child of one first-cousin marriage who is defective in intelligence and bodily formation is quietly "accounted for" by the nearness of kin of the parents. However nothing is said about two other children in the family, who appear to be quite normal.

indicative of the speed with which the marriage date is set. There are almost no preliminaries in the way of an announced engagement, an engagement ring (although it is becoming customary to give one later in married life), or prenuptial parties. Marriage is regarded almost as a private affair between the couple, and the couple prefer to surprise everyone with the news of their marriage. The degree of surprise is a matter of prestige comparable to making the headlines. In more than one case couples out riding with friends have decided to stop at the office of the justice of the peace to be married, although they had said nothing to each other beforehand about being married on that particular day.

Within the last few years some cotton-mill operatives have begun to announce their marriages in the Stone Valley *Bugle*. A typical announcement and the way it is arranged would be this:

Mr. and Mrs. A. B. Harris
of Kent
announce the marriage
of their daughter
Emma Lou
to
Roy H. Taylor
of Kent
at 10:30 in the morning
Saturday, January 15, 1949
Kent, Old South State

Below this stylized announcement is an article which says that the ceremony was performed by the Kent judge of probate in his home. The dress of the bride is described ("an aqua dress with black accessories and a corsage of red rosebuds"), and the name of the attendants given (a brother and sister-in-law of the bride). The future residence of the couple is stated (with the bride's parents), and the place of work of both the bride and groom are given. Sometimes a picture of the bride appears with the announcement. Not many years ago, such announcements would not have been carried by the paper, according to informants, and only the "better class" of mill worker makes the gesture now. This new practice is evidence of the influence of town customs, and it is perhaps an indication of the changing social status of the mill worker.

Most marriage ceremonies are conducted by a justice of the peace or judge of probate, either in Kent or in one of the nearby county seats. Until the state passed a bill in 1947 requiring a waiting period of twenty-four hours between the time the license was obtained and the marriage ceremony performed, couples from adjoining Piedmont State flocked into Kent to be married. The Kent County probate judge is renowned in the area for the number of marriage ceremonies he has performed, and Kent has come to be known as a place where people go to get married. According to the probate judge, more and more Kent mill people are being married by preachers, either in the home of a relative or in the parsonage. Church weddings are a rarity and looked upon as ostentatious.

The following wedding is an example of one held in the home, and it also demonstrates the speed with which weddings are undertaken. A twenty-one-year-old worker had been going for two years with a girl who also worked in the mill, and he decided it was time they were married. He insisted one afternoon that they be married that night, although the girl objected since she had a church meeting to attend. He said that they could be married after her church meeting. Preparations were made at the home of the groom's brother, the Wesleyan Methodist preacher was asked to officiate, and the license was secured (at that time, no waiting period was necessary). The groom drove by the church, picked up the girl when her meeting ended, and took her to his brother's home, where they were married before a few close relations who could be rounded up on short notice. No rings were given, because the Wesleyan Methodist Church, a holiness group, does not believe in wearing rings of any sort. The groom gave the minister a five-dollar bill, but the minister returned it, saying the groom needed it worse than he did. A wedding supper was held at the brother's home, and the couple spent their first night there, moving into the home of the bride's parents later.

Honeymoons usually consist of two or three nights spent in the homes of the parents, often alternating between the two if both have a room they can provide for the couple. Since weddings generally occur over the weekend, no time is lost from work.

Wedding presents are not usually given to the couple, nor are silver and china patterns chosen by the bride, as is done in town. The mill community pays little attention to the weddings of its members, partly because of the speed and secrecy with which they are carried out. However, this might well change as the mill begins to follow town practices more closely. But it shows great interest when a child is born to the union and when the couple move into a house of their own. When it is known that a mill woman is pregnant, particularly for the first time, elaborate stork showers are given in which baby gifts are presented to the mother-to-be. And when the couple and their offspring leave the house of their parents to move into a house assigned them, or to one they have rented, house showers are given. Kitchen equipment and other household furnishings are presented the wife on this occasion. These parties are recognition by the community that the husband, wife, and children are an established unit-family, an integral part of the village.

Mill people believe that "marriage is what you make it." They say that if husband and wife work together and pull in the same direction, everything will be all right. But once they start pulling in opposite directions, the marriage will not be a success. Couples should always act toward each other "jes' like when they was a-courtin'." The ideal husband and father is one who provides for his children and shows an interest in them, stays at home part of the time, does not abuse his wife, does not drink excessively, and does not fuss or complain continually. The ideal wife and mother, in addition to helping with the family income by working in the mill, takes primary responsibility for the children, and does cheerfully and well the cooking, washing, ironing, and house cleaning, and is patient and understanding.[6] While few marriage partners embody all these ideals, the vast majority look upon their union as a permanent one. Both religion and strong social approval give heavy sanction to such permanence.

The fact that most wives work and have their own sources of income can in Kent be a factor in strengthening the marriage bond or it can be an underlying element in its severance. It can strengthen the union by making for a more democratic relationship, somewhat in contrast to the male dominance in rural life. While the wife works, the husband must help at home, if no female relatives are available, which demands close cooperation and mutual respect. In most cases the incomes are cooperatively disbursed. The wife generally uses her income to buy food, clothing, and furniture, while the husband pays for rent, electricity, repairs, fuel, and the car, if the family happens to have one. Most spouses appear highly loyal to one another in such divisions of responsibilities. On the other hand, for couples who do not get along, this independence and difference in working hours can provide opportunities for liaisons with others, and such an arrangement can prevent man and wife from having close companionship during the week.

Married couples are not demonstrative in the traditional way in the presence of others, for "honeying in public" is frowned

6. The story is told in the villages that a man could not decide between two girls he was thinking of marrying, so he gave to each a ball of badly tangled string, asking her to untangle it for him by the next day. When he returned, he found that one girl had become disgusted with attempting to untangle the ball and had thrown it aside. But the other had removed all the knots and tangles and rewound the cord to make a perfect ball. The man, of course, married the girl who had shown the greater patience and dexterity.

upon. During daily greetings and farewells, kissing is rarely in evidence. But open signs of affection are not lacking, for couples tease one another before others, apparently an approved way of showing affection, and the more demonstrative "hug each other's neck" after being separated for a few days. And as seen from the following letter, they are not reticent about writing in affectionate terms. Mill people do not often write one another, and only two or three letters came to my attention, so it is not possible to know how typical this letter is. It was written at Christmas time by a mill worker to his estranged wife, separated from him, he says, because her family did not approve of him. In the letter, he asks that his wife and their two young children, who were in Stone Valley, meet with him for a Christmas celebration at his sister's home. The letter was written on lined tablet paper in pencil.

Dear Wife and Children. Thought I would drop you a few lines. To let you know I am well. Hope this will find you the same. I know Ralph [his son] is laughing his head off by now I know Ronald [another son] is knocking at the door saying you got company. And take care of my little woman for me. Daddy hopes Santa will bring her lots for Xmas and make her well. I really wanted to go home with you the other day But the way things stood I just couldn't. If you every write to any of my people Dont say nothing about anything for they dont know nothing. I just told them what kind of settlement we made. And they think that was the right thing I should have done. I dont forget to say goodnight to you and the baby every night. Mary [his wife] I was just wondering if you have made any plans. So I could spend Xmas with you and my babys. Mary Mamma told me they had all got together and have got lots of things for the children. She said that Ella [his sister, with whom he is staying] had git more than any. That what she had. Has get her for about a Hundard dollar. And I realy dont want to dispint them if there is any way we can get together and write and let me know one way are the other. And where will you be at. I will get some boday to come after you. If you think it will be safe. But I dont want to get no one else in trouble. If its all right with you. I would rather spend it [Christmas] at Ella's. For Mamma said she had told her that she sure was hoping we could spend it with them. That she was expecting to surprise every one of use. You remember what a happy Xmas we spent last Xmas. And I am hoping to spend another one like it again. As for drinking I dont entend to drink a drop. I have done with out it so far. And I espect to. So you sure wont have that to worrie about. That is a sure promise. I have been laying around the house all day. My asthma is giving me some trouble since it has been so cloudy and damp. But I know I am not going through half as much as you are. For I truly love you and hope you will soon be out of it. If you can come we can spend three or four days to talk things over. If you will stay that long. Tom [Ella's son] said he wonted to play Santa Claus. I thing he will be dispointed and all the rest if you dont come. I saw Tom the other day and he told me he wonted to see them get in their things and tare them up. Well I guess I had better close. So good night darling. With all my love to you and the children. From your husband. p. s. I am sending you paper and envolpe stamped. So please answer soon.

The marriage bond holds, as a rule, despite the strain placed upon monogamous love by the leniency regarding extramarital relations. One young husband summed up what is apparently the view of many of the men in saying that while newly married couples are faithful to one another for the first year or so, "nine out of ten begin to look around again" after that. Most of this "looking around" is done by men, and evidently it tapers off as the couple passes middle age.[7] Couples past fifty appear strongly devoted to one another in almost every case. Sexual expression, particularly among the younger men, is looked upon as one's due, and if such expression is not allowed at

---

7. This again is in accord with the general findings of Kinsey, *op. cit.*, pp. 587–88, on sexual behavior in lower social levels. Just the opposite is true of those in the upper socioeconomic brackets, according to Kinsey, for here extramarital intercourse tends to increase with age, reaching its highest point at age fifty.

home with one's spouse when desired, the husband, especially, feels justified in looking elsewhere. Kent townspeople tend to exaggerate the extent of sexual promiscuity in the village sections. For example, I heard the story related at a dinner for town men that the reason a Neilson worker left his wife was that he grew tired of repairing his bedroom-window screen, broken out continuously by his wife's bed companions escaping when he came home from working at night. But some of the incidents told by mill workers themselves of third-shift escapades are much more likely to be true. A Townsend worker said that while he was single and boarding at a house where the husband worked on the night shift, the landlord's wife slept in a room adjoining his, and after her husband left for work she would disarrange her bed as though she had been sleeping in it and then get into bed with him. When her husband returned from work, she went to the door to let him in and then together they went into their bedroom. She and the boarder were able to keep up their sexual liaisons for over a year, until the husband changed shifts. During the war, three Neilson women had children by other men while their husbands were overseas, and one long-time resident of the Neilson section said he knew of only one wife in the entire village who was completely faithful to her husband overseas. He added that probably none of the men who went overseas were faithful to their wives.

No indication of the stability of the marriage bond could be ascertained from figures on divorce, for up until 1949 divorce on any grounds was illegal in Old South State. People in town resorted to out-of-state divorces when they desired legal termination of the marriage bond. In some cases, according to both town and mill people, they would establish residence in Piedmont State by renting a room in Metro City and leaving laundry or a suit of clothes there, thus qualifying themselves for a divorce from Piedmont State. But mill people would not bother to go through this complicated and expensive arrangement. Desertion has been the most common method resorted to by mill villagers in severing the marriage tie. Twenty-two cases of desertion among the approximately three hundred mill families came to my attention, and undoubtedly there were more.[8] Some of those spouses separated by desertion had, as the mill people termed it, "shacked up" with a new mate, an arrangement whereby a person legally married to someone else cohabits with another individual on a long-time basis. Fairly typical is the Townsend worker who when asked for the name of his wife replied that the woman with whom he was living was supposed to be his wife, but that they had never actually married. They had "shacked up" several years ago, after he and his legal wife, now living in another state, had separated. Mill workers say that shacking up is not the proper way to live, but their attitude of "it's nobody's business but theirs" modifies severe condemnation.

Bachelors, widows, and widowers are given more leeway in sexual relations than are those who are married and whose spouses are alive. The Cromwell woman who had a child after she had been a widow for several years was not censured, partly because "she kept everything out in the open." However, as in other phases of living, a double standard of morality is in force in the villages. Women's conduct is expected to be on a higher plane than that of men. It is generally considered worse for a woman to have extramarital relations, regardless of her marital state, than it is for a man. Boys will be boys and men will be men, but girls and women are supposed to be circumspect.

It is also worse for a woman to curse, to drink, and to smoke than it is for a man. In a sermon at the Cromwell Baptist Church

8. This is a considerably higher rate than that found by Rhyne, *op. cit.*, pp. 191–92, who discovered only four cases of divorce or desertion among the five hundred families he studied in North Carolina. However, he studied only those families that had not been completely broken up and therefore had a highly selective sample, so far as this particular measurement is concerned.

against profane language, the preacher said that it was bad enough for men to curse, but it was much worse for a woman to use bad language: he had been told about a woman who had cursed on a certain occasion, and he told the congregation with great emotion, "I think she should have been so ashamed that she ought to have pulled a hat down over her eyes so that she would never have to look anyone in the face again." An elderly couple listening to a young woman in an adjoining house using profanity said that she was a disgrace to womanhood for speaking like that and had no right to be called a woman.

The Family

The family, including the kindred group [9] of aunts, uncles, cousins, grandparents, and in-laws, is of fundamental importance in the organization and activities of the Kent mill-village sections. Only a few nuclear families were found which were not related to any other family in Kent. Common sayings such as "almost everyone in the village is related to everyone else, so you have to be careful what you say to anybody about anyone" indicate how ingrown the group is. Kinship charts become so involved that they are difficult to draw, for almost any person chosen at random can be shown to be related to almost any other person along either consanguine or affinial lines, although the relationship may be quite distant. There is the tendency in each of the mill sections for kindred groups to rent houses in close proximity. In the Neilson village a woman of sixty-five lives within sight of the homes of all ten of her children, eight of whom are married and live in separate houses. A few family names dominate each village, and these names are almost always found in the other villages as well.

9. Gillin, *Ways of Men*, p. 435, uses the term "kindreds" to refer to groups of relatives. On pages 428-42, he places this term in context with others that designate kinship relationships.

One example, somewhat extreme, of such overlapping is a 29-year-old man in the Locksley village who has sixty-five relatives, not counting his wife and children, about half of whom live in his village and the other half in the Neilson and Cromwell villages. They include both of his parents, 3 brothers, 1 sister, 3 aunts, 2 uncles, 15 first cousins, 7 nieces and nephews on his side of the family, 23 nieces and nephews on his wife's side of the family, 5 brothers-in-law, and 4 sisters-in-law. One of his brothers-in-law is married to an aunt, and a brother recently married a first cousin.

The kindred group gives a strong feeling of security to mill people. Neighbors help in times of illness and stress, but do not feel the responsibility that relations do. Mill people are very loyal to their family groups, and such statements as "I'm downright selfish only when it comes to my family" are frequently heard. A child has so many cousins, uncles, aunts, and other kinsmen around him who provide him with playthings and food treats that he feels he is on friendly ground. Because the mother must work again shortly after the arrival of a baby, parental surrogates appear when the child is very young, and he spends almost as much time in the homes of his relatives as he does in his own. This makes for difficulties in discipline, as the next chapter will indicate, but it does give broad security. The lines of kinship are continually reinforced by visits, family reunions, stork and house showers, hunting and fishing trips, and funerals. Continual marriage among near neighbors and nearby relatives, plus the restriction of the line between town and mill, strengthen the in-group nature of the mill sections and the dominance of a comparatively few large kindred groups. This strength of the in-group based on kinship does not, however, imply that there are no discords. Some relatives are not on speaking terms with each other, and there are preferences for some kinsmen over others. Also, a few children have had to be sent to children's homes following the death of one or both parents. This has happened when the nuclear family has had so many children that they could not be absorbed by the kindred group. But this is rare and occurs only when the kindred group is small. The concept of "mother" is highly idealized by mill people. Many of their hymns contain the idea of meeting mother in heaven, and on the walls of their homes are found maxims demonstrating veneration and love for mother, the comforter, the healer of all woes, the maker of the home. Mother's Day is celebrated by special church services. At such a service at the Cromwell Baptist Church in 1949, two girls with trays stood at the door at the beginning of the service to supply each worshipper with a flower, a red one if his mother was living and a white one if she was dead. The sermon paid special tribute to mothers, and at the close of the service corsages were presented to the oldest and to the youngest mother present.

Table 6 gives an indication of the size of nuclear families of Kent mill workers. The ninety families include those in the survey on whom data on family size were complete. The average number of children is 4.7 and the modal number 3. Completed families, in which the mother is over 44 years of age, average 5.8 children, while those families in which the mother is not past the child-bearing age average 2.9 children. Evidently the farm pattern of having as many children as physiologically possible was at first continued in the mill village, where children became an economic asset as early as ten years of age.[10] Often by the time they were fourteen, they could make as much as an adult. But with the passage of child-labor laws and the raising of the compulsory-school age, children remain economic liabilities for a much longer period of time. Older parents admit that the restrictions on child labor are good things, but at the same

10. Lahne, *The Cotton Mill Worker*, p. 64, shows that, in the beginning, owners of southern cotton mills required each home to supply a certain quota of workers, usually one for each room in the house. A circular issued by one mill in seeking workers stated, "We want families with at least three workers for the mill in each family." This put a premium on child labor and on large families.

time they are sorry that their children cannot help with the family income as they (the parents) had been able to help when they were children.

TABLE 6. NUMBER OF CHILDREN IN 90 KENT MILL FAMILIES, BY AGE OF MOTHER

Number of Children	All Families	Families in Which Mothers Were Under 44 Years of Age	Families in Which Mothers Were Over 44 Years of Age
Total	90	36	54
0	4	3	1
1	7	5	2
2	12	8	4
3	15	10	5
4	9	3	6
5	11	2	9
6	10	3	7
7	8	2	6
8	6	0	6
9	3	0	3
12	3	0	3
13	2	0	2
Children per family			
Mean	4.7	2.9	5.8
Mode	3	3	5

There are strong indications of a continuing trend in the reduction of family size among mill families. It seems safe to say that families of eight or more children will be exceedingly rare in the mill sections in the future. This can be deduced both from the figures in Table 6 and from the attitudes of young mill parents, who do not hesitate to say that they want only two or three children.

As a means of maintaining control over the number of off-spring, contraceptive devices are becoming generally known. Kent doctors say that some of the mill people, especially those at the top of the mill scale, resort primarily to the use of condoms and withdrawal. However, among some of the mill people there seems to be some sort of religious injunction against them. On two occasions reference was made to such "non-Bible" ways of conception control. One mill worker of fifty was critical of the tendency to limit the number of children through the use of contraceptive methods: "When a couple ain't having no kids, you can be sure the wife's holding out or the man's covering up."

Married women in the village sections lead strenuous lives, for they not only do the housework and attempt to look after the children but also work eight hours a day in the mill. Mrs. Penney, who lives in the Cromwell section, is not atypical in her work schedule. She works on the third shift and her husband on the second. When she returns from work at seven in the morning, she cooks breakfast, bathes the three youngest of five children, cleans the house, prepares lunch, goes to bed at three in the afternoon, rises around six to feed the children and to send her husband supper, returns to bed, and gets up to go to work in the mill at ten-thirty.

The fact that mothers spend eight hours a day in the mill has several important effects on the family. One is that they have little time for supervising and disciplining their children. A large part of such supervision is left to relatives, neighbors, and older siblings. No figures could be obtained on juvenile delinquency of children from Kent textile families, but social workers in Stone Valley said that almost all the children with whom they had to deal were from textile homes.[11] These children were detained by juvenile authorities for not attending school, for stealing from stores, for breaking out windows and street lights, and for sexual misconduct. Nevertheless local authorities say that they "rarely" have encountered a mill child who is so incorrigible that he must be sent to a state institution.

11. In his study of textile operatives in Gaston County, North Carolina, Rhyne, op. cit., p. 181, found that "apparently the textile communities do furnish more than a proportionate share of delinquent cases of both sexes when based on comparisons made from the proportion of gainfully employed in each occupational distribution."

Nor could data be found on the effects of mill work on the health and longevity of mothers and their offspring, but other studies indicate that children born to working mothers are not so healthy as those born to nonworking mothers and that they have a higher death rate.[12] The tired and dogged look on the faces of many Kent mill women reveals the strain of constant work. They seem to become old before their time. A Kent lawyer who has advised some workers in marital difficulty said that one of the principal reasons for such difficulty was that husbands tired of their wives who appeared "worn out" at about thirty or thirty-five.

Another effect, almost impossible to measure, is that mill women have very little leisure time for educational or aesthetic pursuits and therefore do not stimulate their children in those directions. The question might be raised whether mill women would spend their time in such pursuits if they did not work. But many of them say they like to read and are fond of music but have no time for either.

Old Age and Death

As mill people approach old age, the roles they play in the mill subculture diminish in importance, but they continue to have a place in the group. At the mill they are shifted to jobs requiring less speed, and by the time they are sixty or sixty-five they are usually no longer able to do mill work. They are reluctant to leave their mill job when finally forced to, although there is less reluctance now that they receive old-age benefits at the age of sixty-five. The loss of a job in the mill means the loss of a house in the Cromwell village, and in each of the villages retired people go to live with their children as a rule. There they make themselves useful by taking care of grandchildren, sewing, cooking, doing housework, and working in the garden. Old people are not especially honored but they are shown re-

12. Lahne, *op. cit.*, p. 105.

spect, and their offspring feel obligated to take care of them. Most villagers agree that "after all they've done for their children, their children should be willing to take care of them when they are too old to work." Mill people are reminded that they will be old some day and will need the care of their families.

Apparently young people make sacrifices gladly for the old —note the young Cromwell couple who after struggling for two years to get a house to themselves gave it up almost as soon as they had become settled in order to take another place in which the wife's parents, retired from mill work, could also live. Some people look forward to the time when they can draw their "rocking-chair" money and spend more time hunting, fishing, visiting, and loafing. However, the majority seem neither to look forward to nor dread old age. They accept it, as they do the rest of life, as a matter of course, never expecting very much from the future and consequently never being very disappointed.

Funerals are the most elaborate rituals among Kent mill people. They are religious and social events, but above all they are times for a gathering of the kindred group and a reaffirmation of family unity. An old person can expect a "good" funeral if he has life insurance and many relatives, and the survey found no old person in the mill villages who did not have both of these. Mill people are very much aware of and are awed by death. There seems to be a fascination with knowing and repeating the details of a death.[13] "Viewing the body" is a standard practice, and pictures are taken of the deceased in the coffin. Undoubtedly, the religious emphasis on the imminence of death and on the unpredictability of the return of Jesus lead people to expect death at any time. To some extent death is looked upon as a release from the trials and tribulations

---

13. For example, one elderly lady saves all the *Bugle* articles pertaining to deaths and burials, even though she does not know any of the people written about.

of a life of toil and trouble, because of the religious promises of "a mansion on high." Mill people view death with a fatalistic attitude, for "when your time's up, you go," and no one ever knows how much more time is allotted him.

When the news of critical sickness or death is made known, relatives who are not too far away are expected to stop whatever they are doing and rush to the stricken family member. It is best if they can arrive before the actual death, but if this is not possible, they must attend the funeral. One of the most severe criticisms possible by mill people is "he didn't even attend the funeral of his own blood kin." No matter how estranged two members of a kindred group may be, when one of them dies, it is expected that the other will "bury the hatchet" and attend the funeral.

According to Kent funeral directors, funeral customs followed by mill families closely resemble those held in rural areas. There is a large gathering of relatives, an all-night vigil over the body, many wreaths of flowers, displayed publicly by "flower girls" chosen from among the relatives, and a strong expression of emotionality at the church service and in the cemetery. One of the more elaborate mill funerals in 1948 was that of Mrs. Alma Moss Montgomery, who lived in the Townsend village but who had relatives in each of the villages. She was over 73 at the time of her death and had 10 living children, 53 grandchildren, and 48 great-grandchildren, most of whom lived in Kent County. The night before the funeral, the body was on display in the casket at the home of one of her sons. Wreaths of flowers, many of them artificial, were displayed around the casket, and name cards were prominent on each wreath, so that those who had given flowers might be known. If Mrs. Montgomery had been working in the mill at the time of her death, there would have been wreaths from the department of the mill in which she worked and from her bossman. Sandwiches and iced tea were served throughout the night of watching and on into the next morning before the body was removed to the church. During that time relatives met and chatted with one another, the women tending to occupy one room and the men another. Everyone talked in hushed tones. The funeral service was held at the Church of God, where Mrs. Montgomery had been a faithful member. The entire middle section of the church was reserved for relatives, and the seats in both side sections were filled with friends long before the 2:00 P.M. service began. A few minutes after two, a group of great-grandchildren, carrying floral wreaths, entered the church, and one of the funeral directors helped arrange the wreaths in front of the pulpit. Next, two directors of the Kent funeral home entered, followed by the Kent and Stone Valley Church of God pastors. Pallbearers, who were grandsons of the deceased, brought in the casket. All were wearing white carnations in their buttonholes and had on coats and ties. The majority in the audience were dressed in what were apparently their best clothes. After the casket had been placed at the foot of the pulpit, about 150 descendants and other relatives of the deceased entered the church and filled the center section to overflowing. A number of people stood in the doorway and rear of the church, making an audience of over 250.

The service began with a selection by a sextet from Stone Valley, especially engaged for the occasion. Their song was a highly sentimental one about shaking hands with mother up in heaven. The Stone Valley preacher read the Twenty-third Psalm and then gave a funeral sermon praising Mrs. Montgomery as one who had died in the Lord and who would go to her reward where there would be no pain, no sorrow, and no parting. Next, the sextet sang, "When Those Saints Go Marching In" in typical "swingy" Church of God style. Then the local preacher said that Mrs. Montgomery, like Saint Paul, had fought a good fight, had run the race, and was now communing with the saints and with Jesus in heaven, and if her kin would live as she did, they would see her again up there. As the singers sang "Safe in the Arms of Jesus," the audience passed by the coffin, which had been opened for a last glimpse of the deceased. As the group filed by, some stopped, several shed tears, and a few broke down, sobbing, "Oh, Jesus, Blessed Jesus." Two persons (sisters of the deceased) threw themselves on the corpse and kissed the lips of the deceased. They were gently pulled away by the attendants. Everyone looked very sad and many had their handkerchiefs to their eyes. Even young children were crying.

The flower girls marched out first with their wreaths; then came the pallbearers with the casket, followed by the pastors. The funeral procession of cars with headlights turned on and with police escort went directly through the main street of town, although it would have been shorter to have used another route to the cemetery. Townspeople later commented that it must have been a big funeral because of so many automobiles. At the cemetery the open grave was covered by a canopy and was surrounded by artificial grass. The casket was placed on supports over the grave, and the nearest relatives sat under the canopy in chairs. The visiting preacher read from a manual of the promises regarding the resurrection, the Kent preacher pronounced the benediction, and the casket was lowered into the grave. The pastors and the head funeral director shook hands with those seated, and the crowd slowly dispersed. Almost immediately, Negro gravediggers began covering the casket with dirt. Most of the relatives of the deceased went back to their homes, but some from out of town gathered again in one of the Townsend homes.

The funeral cost slightly over $400, plus the cost of flowers, another $150 or so. The expense was fully covered by the $1,000 life-insurance policy carried by the deceased, but in the event that she had not had such a policy, her relatives would have provided the money. Mill people spend more on funerals than do those in town, on the average. In 1948, the average cost of a funeral in Kent was $278, and the majority of mill funerals were above this amount, according to the Kent funeral director. Burial insurance has recently been introduced and is making a strong appeal to mill people. It should be added that a minister always conducts a funeral, for no matter how non-religious the deceased may have been, some of his relatives are connected with a church and arrange for a religious service, at the funeral parlor if the person was not a church member.

It is customary for an announcement of thanks to be inserted in the Stone Valley *Bugle* a few days after the interment, headed "Card of Thanks":

We wish to thank the many friends and neighbors for the beautiful flowers and heartfelt sympathy shown us in the death of our beloved wife and mother, Mrs. Martha Lou Workman White, who passed away on Wednesday morning, February 9th.

Husband, R. S. White
and children
Joyce White
James E. White
Ida Bell Herren
Edward Lewis White

Summary Characteristics of Marriage and the Family

Several characteristics of courtship, marriage, and family life stand out in the foregoing description, and they will be given added emphasis in the following brief summary.

Central Place of Family and Kindred

The nuclear family and kindred group have a place of central importance among Kent mill workers, similar in some respects to that of the family in the folk society. Almost all mill workers have relatives in one or more of the village sections, and there is a tendency for kindred groups to form small "colonies" in each of the villages. Relatives expect and give each other strong loyalty and mutual support in time of stress. Kindred groups form the basis for much of the social life in the mill-village sections, for relatives frequently visit one another, hunt and fish together, and exchange meals with each other. They seem to be as much at home in the houses of their relatives as they do in their own, and children are often cared for as much by grandparents and other relatives as by their own parents.

The kindred group, especially if it is large, gives long-range security that mill work does not give. If members of a nuclear family lose their mill jobs and their mill houses, they can crowd into the home of a relative, at least temporarily. If sickness or death or other misfortune comes, there are almost always relatives who will help. If a nuclear family is broken by death or desertion, it is the kindred group which most frequently helps with the children. The majority of mill-village people seem willing to make almost any sacrifice for relatives in distress.

Customs at funerals, family reunions, and other family gatherings reinforce the kindred group and reaffirm its unity. This, in turn, adds to the security given by the kindred group and also tightens the in-group feeling that contributes to separation of mill from town.

The number of children per family appears to be decreasing sharply, and this will no doubt decrease the importance of the kindred group. But the average of 5.8 children per completed family is, for the present, high enough to ensure the dominant place of the kindred group. Also significant in its continuing importance is the fact that many of the mill families have relatives with large families in the rural areas of Kent County.

In-Group Marriage

In the description of courtship and marriage, we have seen that Mill children date each other and often marry within their own village. The marriages now taking place are primarily between mill workers, either from Kent or other nearby mill towns. But there is also a continuation of marriages between those of mill families and rural families of lower socioeconomic status, for the older Kent mill couples come primarily from farm backgrounds, and strong ties between poorer farmers and mill workers, especially between relatives, remain. Comparisons of the family backgrounds [14] of wife and husband (in the ninety-six Kent mill families surveyed) show that mates have been chosen almost entirely from farm or mill background (see Table 7). Of course, this sample is selective of

TABLE 7. OCCUPATION OF FATHER OF WIFE BY OCCUPATION OF FATHER OF HUSBAND IN 96 KENT MILL FAMILIES

Occupation of Father of Wife	Total		Occupation of Father of Husband					
			Farm		Mill		Other *	
	No.	Percent	No.	Percent	No.	Percent	No.	Percent
Total	96	100.0	54	56.3	35	36.4	7	7.3
Farm	46	47.9	36	37.5	8	8.3	2	2.1
Mill	44	45.8	16	16.7	25	26.0	3	3.1
Other *	6	6.3	2	2.1	2	2.1	2	2.1

* "Other" includes carpenter, sawmill worker, machinist, store clerk.

those persons who have entered mill work,[15] and those who leave the mill might marry in other patterns. However, the indication is that about the only eligible mates for Kent mill people are other mill people, either in Kent or nearby towns,

14. The background is according to the occupation of the father and is a reformulation of the data contained in Table 1, p. 22, with the categories "farm-mill" and "mill" combined under "mill."

15. The conclusion by S. W. Hutton quoted in n. 4, pages 57-58, is of interest here: "The young person at Victor, at least one who intends to remain in mill work, tends to marry someone who lives in the village, another mill village, or in a surrounding rural area."

or poorer rural people. The line against marriage between town and mill is drawn almost as tightly as that between Negro and white,[16] and it is also most unusual for a member of a well-to-do farm family to marry a mill person. Parents give very little direction in the selection of mates, but just who is and who is not eligible is well known to mill children. Parents have little to do directly with the marriage ceremony itself, which is often arranged quickly, even secretly. They do not customarily attend wedding ceremonies of their children, although this is changing as more weddings are held in the home and are conducted by ministers.

Comparative Freedom of Sexual Expression

Sexual expression appears to be less repressed and restricted than in American middle-class society in general. While marriage is the only overtly approved outlet for such expression, premarital and extramarital sexual experiences are common among mill people. A Kent doctor who treats many of the mill families stated it in this manner: "There's a great deal of neighborly 'screwing' going on in the mill villages, even by men who have passed fifty." Although sex is generally tabooed as a subject of conversation in mixed company, men talk freely to each other about such matters, and it is often the butt of their jokes. In rare cases a man might tease a woman in sexual terms in front of others, as, for example, when a man of fifty-five told an unmarried girl of twenty who had a cold early one spring, "You should have knowed better than to lay around out in the woods when the ground's still cold like it is."

There is tacit acceptance that under certain conditions men, especially, will express themselves sexually outside of the mar-

16. Ralph C. Patrick, Jr., in an unpublished paper entitled A Cultural Approach to the Stratification System of a Southern Town (read at the 51st Annual Meeting of the American Anthropological Association in Philadelphia, December, 1952), elaborates the distinction between town, especially "Old Kent," and mill, indicating the castelike line that exists.

riage bond. This is condoned in cases where the wife is not cooperative. It is believed that men, particularly, must "get it," and if it is not "ready" when they want it, they are justified in going to other sources, either professional prostitutes or "girl friends." Men speak quite frankly of the sexual function of marriage, saying that a man who marries late "misses a good many years."

Learning the Millways: Education [1]

CHAPTER 5   THE PARENTS of a Kent mill child, other relatives, older siblings, playmates, the school, and the church all share in the process of teaching the child mill-village patterns of behavior. Together they help produce a person with habits, traits, interests, and attitudes similar to others who live and work in the mill-village sections of Kent.

Attitude toward the Birth of Children

It is generally expected that couples who marry will begin having children within a year or two. Children follow from marriage almost as inevitably as one season follows another. Formerly the coming of children was left largely "in the hands of God," and farm people who first entered the mill-village sections had as many children as was physiologically possible. However, we have seen that techniques for conception control are gradually being adopted by mill couples, particularly younger ones. While they still want children, many young couples prefer to limit them to two or three and to space them more than their parents did. Boys seem to be more generally desired than girls; mothers say that boys are less trouble to

1. Much of the material in this chapter on child rearing is based on the information gathered by Barbara Chartier in interviews with a cross section of twenty Kent mill mothers and written as Weaverton: A Study of Culture and Personality in a Southern Mill Town (unpublished master's thesis, University of North Carolina, 1949).

rear, and fathers prefer sons with whom they may go fishing and hunting. By mill custom a man's co-workers tear his shirt to shreds upon the arrival of his first son or grandson, but there is no comparable recognition for the arrival of girls. Some men have the attitude that a man has to "pay for" the pleasure of sexual relations in marriage by having children whom he must support and care for. A man of fifty who had had children so rapidly that "one chased the other from the tit," hearing that a recently married worker was about to have a child, grumbled, "He's gittin' ready to pay for something he done nine months ago." On the other hand, a twenty-eight-year-old mill worker said that his marriage meant more than ever when his son was born. "When I come home from work and he meets me and puts his little arms around my neck, there's nothing better in the world." Younger women, especially those in the Cromwell New Hill section, at times express their dissatisfaction when they find themselves pregnant, for this curtails their work, interferes with their recreation, and adds expense. At the same time, a group of mill workers strongly condemned a woman who had induced an abortion.

Regardless of parental attitudes before the birth of a child, once he arrives, he is accepted and loved with great affection, especially during infancy and early childhood.

Birth and Care of Infants

Until a local hospital was established in 1943, mill children were born at home. Now almost all mill women go to the hospital to have their babies. Physicians attend the few remaining births in the home, just as they did before the hospital was built. Women stop work at the mill two or three months before the baby is born, and, especially among the younger mothers in the Cromwell village, stork showers are very popular. Women place themselves under the care of a physician as soon as they realize they are pregnant, but according to the Kent doctors, they are not careful to follow the advice given them. Certain traditional ideas concerning prenatal influences still remain. For example, a 14-year-old boy's inordinate fear of the dark, of water, of sleeping alone, in fact his general "scariness," is attributed by his grandmother to his mother's having attended so many "scary movies" during pregnancy.

Mothers return to their work in the mill five weeks to six months after the birth of a child, depending on how much help is available for tending the child and how badly the mother's earnings are needed by the family. If a grandmother is living with the family or nearby (as is often the case), the mother can go back to work after a few weeks, but if a Negro maid must be hired (rarely), the mother takes care of the child herself for a longer period. None of the Kent mills has a nursery in which working mothers may leave very young children. Some of the mothers complain about this lack.

After the mother starts work again in the mill, the care of the child is shared by older siblings, relatives, neighbors, and, only occasionally, Negro women. Fathers are supposed to help to some extent, especially while their wives are at work, but they are not made fully responsible for the care of very small children as a rule. Child care is considered a woman's task. Mill babies are handled a great deal by their mothers and mother surrogates. Infants will be passed around a circle of friends and relatives, each of whom will pat and "love" the baby. Mothers are pleased to say of a child "He has never knowed a stranger," and this continual handling by neighbors, relatives, and brothers and sisters helps to develop easy interpersonal responses in the child. As the child becomes old enough to crawl and walk around, the lap of his mother or grandmother becomes a favorite resting place, and here the child is rocked back and forth. This rocking motion becomes so automatic with mill women that they employ it even when sitting on sofas or straight-backed chairs. Since cribs and play-pens are practically nonexistent, mill mothers carry their infants across one arm while cooking and doing other household tasks. Children as young as three or four are allowed to carry a younger sibling. Mill children are fond of their grandparents, particularly their grandmothers, and often spend much time with them. Grandparents are more indulgent than parents in their treatment of children, and some mothers admit that their children would rather stay at their grandparents' house than at their own. In four cases that came to my attention, children live by choice with their grandparents, although their mothers live only a few blocks away.[2] Children may sleep with their grandparents long after they would be expected to leave their parents' bed.

Feeding

Mill mothers have no strong preference for either breast or bottle feeding. But infants who "are swung from the breast," as breast feeding is called, are shifted to the bottle soon in order that mothers may return to their work in the mill. The standard formula for milk in bottles consists of two parts of water to one part of evaporated milk plus Karo or sugar syrup. Digestive disturbances are treated by a change in formula upon the advice of a doctor. Although infants are put on a three-hour schedule in the hospital, this is soon dropped after the mother returns home, and the baby is allowed to nurse whenever it seems hungry. Nursing is often used as a pacifying technique whenever the baby cries, and this may continue until the child is three or four. Since children sleep with their parents for at least the first year, night feedings, particularly for breast-fed babies, are readily available. Some mothers ob-

2. In two of these cases, the children are illegitimate and dislike their stepfathers, and in another there are so many siblings that the mother would find it difficult to care for all of them. Three of the children have assumed the last name of their maternal grandparents and for all practical purposes have become full-fledged members of their grandparents' families.

serve taboos on eating the flesh of wild animals during lactation, but this taboo is not widely followed.

At three months, nursing is supplemented by orange juice, cod-liver oil, and Pablum. By five months baby foods and soft foods from the table are fed the child. A few high chairs are used, but most mothers place children in their laps to feed them. No attempt is made to force the child to eat, nor are there many restrictions upon the time, method, or type of food chosen for feeding.

Mothers say they wean their children at one year, but the average age at weaning is nearer two. Often children of three or even four are seen with a bottle, and some mothers express concern lest their children take their bottles to school with them. In cases where mothers have great difficulty in getting children to drink from a cup, the child is allowed to nurse as long as he likes, and local doctors encourage this. Several methods are employed to accomplish weaning. Shaming a child is common: "You're a big girl now, and the bottle is for baby sister." "Aren't you ashamed to let this man see a big boy like you sucking out of a bottle!" Sometimes weaning is accomplished by putting the bottle out of sight.

With breast-fed babies, weaning is a somewhat more difficult process. Some mothers resort to blackening the breast with soot or something "hot," like pepper, or they have the child spend a few days with its grandparents. Many mothers still follow astronomical signs as indicated in the almanac and wean their children when "the sign is in the knee and going down." To wean them when the sign is in the stomach or above will cause the child's bowels "to be all tore up." Mothers abiding by these signs sometimes apologize for them as superstitions, but they uniformly report no trouble in weaning as long as they do adhere to them. Apparently weaning is not a traumatic experience, since it occurs when eating habits are well established and at a time which does not coincide with walking or toilet training.

The indulgent attitude toward nursing is carried over into later eating habits. Children are allowed to eat between meals, and few restrictions are placed on what they may or may not eat. Biscuits from the table and candy from neighborhood stands are eaten throughout the day, and there is little objection if children do not eat at regular meal time.

Sleep

Babies sleep with their parents, and baby beds are almost never used. The night bottle is frequently resorted to as a means of inducing children to go to sleep and is persistently clung to after nursing has been given up during the day. When a new baby arrives, the one just older is forced out of its parents' bed into a bed with siblings or sometimes with a grandmother. Siblings sleep as many as four in a double bed, and brothers and sisters sleep together until they are eight or nine years old.

Making way for baby brother or sister in the parental bed is symbolic of giving up the favored position as the baby of the family. It is the youngest child that is petted and made the most of. Just what the effect is of being pushed out of the spotlight of love and attention so suddenly is not clearly known. Perhaps it is related to the attitude among mill people that good things will not last and that it is unrealistic to expect very much from the future.

Cleanliness Training

From birth to eighteen or twenty-four months, children wear diapers. Sphincter training is begun when the child is about a year old and is usually accomplished by placing the child on a slop jar immediately upon his awakening in the morning. Mothers say that children soon learn to indicate a desire for the release of colon tension but that urethral control is more difficult to induce and is usually not completed until after the third year. Since the mother is away much of the day and is busy with other children and with household duties when at home, it is not likely that she has the time or energy to institute consistent training. Bed-wetting is abhorred by parents and severely criticized by older siblings with whom the offending child sleeps. Children are scolded, shamed, and even whipped for this habit.

Children continue to use a slop jar in the house until they are four or five years old, although they are allowed to urinate in the back yard during the summer. Mothers are afraid to let their children use the outhouse when they are younger for fear they will fall in or be bitten by spiders. At night, slop jars are kept in bedrooms for use in an emergency or in case the weather is too bad to get to the outhouse.

Pain and Illness

The services of four town doctors are available to mill families, and the doctors are freely called on, particularly when wages are high. But when times at the mill are not good, mill people attempt to get by with home remedies until they are forced to call a doctor, often making their illness more protracted and serious than if medical help had been sought sooner.

Kent doctors say that the incidence of contagious diseases is slightly higher in the mill-village sections than elsewhere in the county. A few cases of typhoid, with one death, in 1943 have been attributed to the lack of sanitation, and an epidemic of diphtheria broke out in one of the village sections in 1946. Scabies is more prevalent at the mill than elsewhere, and more complications result from tonsilitis because mill people tend to neglect it. With so many children living close together, childhood diseases such as whooping cough, measles, mumps, scarlet fever, and chickenpox spread rapidly, and mothers assume that their children will catch whatever is "going around." Mill people have been slow to adopt immunization and inoculation measures, mainly because they have not understood them. But most of their children are now receiving preventive shots through the free facilities offered by the county in the public schools.

Since playpens and cribs are almost unknown in the mill sections, as soon as a child can crawl he has free access to the three or four rooms comprising mill houses. Each house has a wood or oil cookstove and a coal or oil heater for winter use, usually with a teakettle of boiling water within easy reach. These stoves constitute a danger to children, but apparently the lesson in avoidance is learned early, for there is seldom need to warn a child away from a heater or stove. Only a few families at the top of the mill scale have homes furnished with overstuffed furniture and breakable whatnots that can be reached and pulled down by young children. In such cases, the living room is shut off from the children and used only with company. The vast majority of homes are so furnished that few restrictions are placed on a child's exploratory activities, nor are there many objects, with the exception of the stove, with which he can injure himself. Gates are sometimes placed on the porches of mill homes to prevent young children from falling down the steps. But when they are old enough to walk around outside the house and to ride tricycles and bicycles, children receive their full quota of cuts and broken arms.

Death and illness appear to be very close to mill people, and women, particularly, seem to enjoy talking about the details of illness and death, including those of their children. Grief at the death of a child is intense and the deceased child is continued in thought as a member of the family. In cases where one or more children had died, queries about the number of children in a family were invariably answered like this: "Six— four living and two dead." When the ages of the children were asked, those of the deceased were given as though they continued to live to the present time. The age at the time of death had to be asked for specifically. That children are also concerned with sickness and death is illustrated by the fact that over half of the mill children in the Cromwell elementary school answered the question "What is the worst thing that could happen to you?" by mentioning death, illness, or injury. Of the ninety-two mill children in the consolidated school questioned about the saddest thing that happened to them when they were small, 74, or 80.4 percent, replied by telling of a personal illness or injury, or the death or illness of a relative or pet animal.

Discipline

Punishment of children is done almost entirely by "whuppings" by either parent using a "hickory." Any slender, flexible twig off a bush or tree serves as a "hickory," and the "whupping" is usually administered by switching the legs. The father sometimes uses a belt or razor strop or his hand and spanks the child on the buttocks. Often just the appearance of a switch or belt, or even the threat to get one, will serve to make the young child do what his parents want him to do. Parents believe firmly in the adage "Spare the rod and spoil the child," although some mothers believe that too much whipping will make the child "mean" and that it is also necessary to talk gently at times. Most parents do not believe in slapping a child; "Don't strike a child in the face, for God has made a better place." Mothers find it harder to punish children than do fathers and will sometimes "have a good cry" after switching one of their children. In general, the fathers punish the boys, and the mothers the girls, because the men are too "rough" and might hurt the girls. Punishment by fathers, though usually not so frequent, is surer and more severe, and they are called in by the mother when a son has been discovered in "meanness." One boy reports that when he was caught cursing and smoking, "I had to take my clothes off and get the blood whipped out of me by my Dad." Of the ninety-two mill children reporting on childhood experiences, eighty, or 87.0 percent, said they were whipped or spanked whenever they did wrong, and the others said they were punished by being made to stay in the house rather than play, not being allowed to go to a movie, and not being given candy. Frequency of whipping varies from once a day for some children to only once a month or so for others, and this method of punishment may continue until a child is well along in his teens.

Young children are punished most often for "slipping off" to play with a neighbor or relative when their parents have told them to stay in the house or in the yard. They are also disciplined for fighting, especially with siblings, for using bad language and tobacco, for stealing and lying, and for "talking back."

Frightening is also used to bring forth the "right" response. The child is told that unless he behaves in the way his parents desire, "buggers" will get him. "Buggers" include a host of vague, indefinable creatures, sometimes specifically linked to "niggers," ghosts, skeletons, animals (including gorillas hiding behind trees), and fieldworkers in anthropology. The parents put themselves up as protectors of the child, promising him that if he does what he is supposed to, they will save him from whatever "bugger" happens around at the moment. One is reminded of the Hopi Indians and their use of "kachinas," supposedly supernatural beings (but really members of the tribe dressed up in frightening costumes) which scare children into obedience and at the same time reinforce their feelings of dependence and loyalty to parents. Sometimes frightening appears to be teasing for adult amusement, and older children seem to enjoy scaring younger children. The ninety-two Kent mill children reported being frightened during childhood by insects and animals of every description, by older relatives in sheets, by the dark (especially when alone), by ghost stories, and by storms. These fears seem to be carried over into adulthood, for many adults think they hear noises at night under the house or in the yard or on the porch and are frightened. They are apprehensive about Negro burglars, about being left alone in a house after dark, and about storms and other natural phenomena. These anxieties persist in spite of the fact that by the time children are six or seven, they have been fooled so much by their elders and older siblings that they are skeptical about almost everything with which they are threatened, for by that time they have caught on to the methods of frightening and teasing.

In summary, discipline of mill children seems to be inconsistent, haphazard, and authoritative when administerd. We have seen that one or both parents must be absent for a large part of the day or night, and the necessity for mother surrogates means that discipline will be administered differently by different persons. Grandparents are allowed to punish but are not so strict as parents. Older siblings and Negro nurses may not punish directly but may report misbehavior to the parents. The child does not know quite what to expect because of the irregularity of the discipline practices of the various disciplinarians. Authority, when it is enforced, is often of an absolute, unreasoning kind, and a child is told to do something for no other reason than that the parent gives the command. Obedience is expected to be unquestioning at this point.

Sex Typing and Games

At an early age, little boys are taught, especially by the male members of the household, to be "manly." A boy of two might be taught to flex his muscles, sing "Slap her down again, babe," and whistle and wave at girls. Although boys are scolded at the time for "rough" speech, speech often an imitation of the males around them, parents later brag about such talk to friends. This is demonstrated in the following incident. A two-and-a-half-year-old boy at supper with his parents and grandparents kept helping himself to the pinto beans, which he liked very much. Each time his grandfather told him he had had enough and must stop, the boy replied, "I ain't done it." Finally, the grandfather removed the beans from the table so the child could not eat any more. Thereupon, the little boy stood up in his chair, beat on the table with both fists, and shouted, "Goddammit! Gimme some more beans." The grandfather in telling the story would laugh with pride and brag, "Now ain't that a *real* boy for you!"

Boys and girls of preschool age play the same games, often in the same group. Among the favorite games are hide-and-seek, tag, froggie-in-the-millpond, drop-the-handkerchief, London Bridge, and ain't-no-bears-out-tonight. Parents make swings for their young children, using long pieces of twisted cloth from the mill as strands. As they grow older, boys prefer rough games like capture-the-flag, cops-and-robbers, fox-and-hound, hickory man, throw-the-tin-can, baseball, and football. They are sometimes taken fishing and hunting with their fathers and older brothers. Fathers tend to identify themselves with their sons, and they are quite hesitant even to be seen at play with their daughters.

Boys' gangs begin to form around the ages of six and seven and are based on neighborhood and closely delineated age groups. Membership in these gangs overlaps, with the youngest members of older gangs being leaders in younger gangs. It is through this overlapping of membership that much information and misinformation on varied subjects are passed down the line from group to group. In them boys learn about sex, for mill parents say they cannot bring themselves to teach their children about such matters, although they realize they should. The bolder members tell of their "exploits" with girls of their age, and from these boys younger ones learn about masturbation. These groups have a strong influence on boys, and by relentless teasing and restricting of the younger boys from group activities unless they overcome their "sissy" ways, the older boys help mould them into the "boy-type." Mothers despair of these gangs and the "meanness" their sons learn through older members. But fathers tacitly accept them, for they believe it is "natural" for boys to get into a certain amount of devilment and go through certain sexual experiments.

Girls are kept under closer surveillance than boys, and their mothers do not approve of their keeping company with boys' gangs. Girls have their own play groups, but their games are ones that are "suitable" for girls, that is, they are more gentle than boys' games. To call a girl a "tomboy" is not a compliment, especially after the age of eleven or twelve. Girls play hopscotch, jump-rope, dolls, volleyball, dodgeball, and playhouse, in which they act out the roles they will later assume as wives and mothers. One of the main responsibilities of girls is to mind younger children as well as help clean house. Much of this must be done in the mother's absence, and, by the age of twelve, the majority of girls are able to run a household. They have less time to play than do boys. Boys and girls of ten and over get together for kissing games of spin-the-bottle and post office, apparently without the knowledge of their parents or else with their tacit approval. Girls' play groups are also centers for spreading information about sex and about what words, expressions, and acts are considered "bad." Many of these ideas come from older sisters and other older girls in the neighborhood. These things are discussed in detail by girls with each other, never with boys, and rarely with parents. One mother reported, "My girls know lots, and I know they know lots. But as long as they don't talk around me about it, it's all right."

Induction into Work

By the time they are five years of age, children are helping around the house by sweeping, making beds, bringing in wood, drying dishes, and caring for younger siblings. They run errands, especially to the store, and take lunches to their fathers and mothers in the mill. As they grow older the duties of boys and girls diverge. Girls take over housecleaning and cooking, helping their mothers with these tasks. Boys bring in coal, chop kindling, cut grass, help in the garden, and feed the chickens and hogs, if there are any. Children are taught that it is a "good" thing to help with the house and with younger brothers and sisters. Of the mill school children reporting on the good things they did as children, over three-fourths mentioned some form of household duty. Parents reward children mainly with money, giving it in varying amounts from a penny to a dollar, depending on the child's age and the work done. Some give praise only, while others reward with candy, new clothes, and permission to go to the movies or to visit a favorite cousin.

Children of 12 and over begin to earn extra money in various ways. Boys have wider opportunities than girls. They can throw papers, deliver groceries, and work at the moving-picture theater, while girls are limited largely to caring for children. After dropping out of school, girls of 16 and 17 work in the five-and-ten-cent store, in drugstores, and in dress shops. By the time they are 18 or 19 many of the mill children are doing mill work. This is something they appear to drift into because it is the type of work most readily available and pays more than any other work they can enter at that age.

Although children have numerous chores to do around the house, parents who were reared on the farm say that in comparison their children have far fewer tasks than they had at that age. Some feel that children reared in the mill village "ain't worth a damn for nothin'." They point out that a dog must be trained from the very first or there is no use in trying to train it, and they say that too many children are allowed to play and roam the streets with not very much to do. Another difficulty, so these parents report, with trying to raise children in the mill village is that they see other children doing things they are not allowed to do and in this way learn bad habits. A number of parents demonstrated ambivalent feelings about child-labor laws. In general they approved, but they regretted that their children could not work in the mill during the summer and that they had to go to school so long that they could not be of financial help to the family, while they themselves began working in the mill when they were so small they had "to stand on boxes to fill the batteries" to add to the family income.

Schooling

Kent mill children attend two different schools. Those living outside the city limits on Cromwell Old Hill go to the Cromwell Elementary School, while those living in the city attend the town school, consisting of an elementary division for Kent children and a consolidated high school for Kent and the surrounding towns.

The Cromwell school has seven grades taught by three women teachers, all of whom are from the town part of Kent. According to teachers, parents, and children, this school is inferior in many ways to the school downtown. Facilities are limited, stimulation from other pupils is low, and the children do not learn as much as do those in the downtown school. Consequently, those who attend the Cromwell school have a difficult time when they enter the downtown school.[3] Mill parents who live outside the city limits may send their children to the downtown school before they reach the eighth grade if they pay an extra fee, and a few parents do this. Most of the

3. S. W. Hutton, Social Participation of Married Women in a South Carolina Mill Village, p. 27, points out that the reason many mill children in her study stopped school at the end of the seventh grade was that it marked the division between the mill and town schools. This is similar to what happens in Kent to those who have their early schooling in an all-mill school. However, the majority of Kent mill children enter the downtown school, but drop out after a few years upon finding the work too difficult or after losing interest.

mothers on Old Hill would welcome the abolishing of the mill school if they did not have to pay to send their children downtown. The older children express their dissatisfaction with the school by saying that all they learn is fighting and that they need men teachers to keep order. The teachers, on the other hand, say that parents do not cooperate in disciplining children who are unruly in school. In fact, the teachers claim that parents encourage their children to fight by urging them "not to take nothin' off'n nobody."

Teachers in both the Cromwell and downtown schools say that mill children, as a general rule, make poor students. Every now and then a mill child will do quite well in his studies, but this is rare. These children frequently present problems in the classroom because they do not prepare their lessons, show little interest in class discussion, and play hooky from time to time.

The homes of the mill children do not provide the kind of setting that would encourage academic success. They are crowded and afford little chance for quiet study. The parents have had only a few years of formal education, on the average, and can do little to stimulate their offspring to study. Most of the mill parents realize the advantages of formal education, saying that they would like their children to have more education than they had. They realize that times have changed and that education is much more important than when they were growing up. But, actually, parents do little to encourage their children to learn, and they do not take much interest in their children's school work. Often they are embarrassed by being unable to answer their children's questions about school lessons.

The attitudes of mill children vary widely toward school. Most of them apparently do not like it but feel that it is something necessary, though not very pleasant. Among the ninety-two compositions that mill children wrote, the following comments on their feeling about school indicate the variance in attitude:

"I don't like any subjects at school and hate all of them."

"At school my life is very miserable because I do not like school."

"This is my senior year and about thirty more days I will be out of school for good. And now it can be told; the thing I like best in school is the last day. What I liked least was the day it started."

"I like lunch most of all, then health, and last but not least, the bell to go home in the afternoon."

"I like all my subjects at school and do not like any of them least. I study every one and try to make good grades on them. . . . I like health best of all because you can play and take exercise. I do not like anything least at school."

"The best thing I like about school is that I have fun and at the same time know more about things you should know."

"I like school because you can have fun, meet all of your friends, and have good times together."

Mill children are beginning to take a greater part in extracurricular activities in the downtown school. The captain of the Kent High School football team in 1948 was from Cromwell New Hill, and mill boys were among the outstanding athletes on each of the varsity teams. In 1948 a girl from the Cromwell village won the school beauty contest, and another Cromwell girl was judged to be among the most neatly dressed girls during that year. But the social lines between mill children and those from the town and country are still tightly drawn. Even though a mill child is successful as an athlete or beauty-contest winner, his social relationships with other children do not extend beyond the school campus. Town people were greatly concerned in the spring of 1949 when one of the outstanding leaders in high school, a boy from the Cromwell village, began going "steady" with a girl classmate from town, and they feared something "serious" would result. They displayed great relief when the romance broke up, and the girl married the son of a prominent Gilead farmer in the summer of 1949.

The teachers estimate that about 90 percent of the mill children complete grade school and enter high school, but only about 10 percent of those entering high school complete the twelfth grade. More mill girls than boys finish high school, since girls in the Cromwell village cannot begin work until they are eighteen years of age. In the Reginold villages few boys and girls complete more than the tenth grade of school, since they are both eligible to go to work in the Reginold mills at sixteen. Thus Kent mill children, on the average, are getting about three more years of schooling than their parents.[4]

But regardless of the amount of schooling they are getting or what their attitudes toward school may be, the great majority of mill children want to complete high school and to continue their schooling beyond that. Of the 92 mill children who wrote compositions on "The Story of My Life," 85 responded to the question asking how much longer they wished to go to school. The results are shown in Table 8.

TABLE 8. THE AMOUNT OF SCHOOLING DESIRED BY 85 KENT MILL CHILDREN IN THE SEVENTH THROUGH THE TWELFTH GRADES OF THE DOWNTOWN KENT SCHOOL

Amount of Schooling Desired	Total		Girls		Boys	
	No.	Percent	No.	Percent	No.	Percent
Total	85	100.0	54	100.0	31	100.0
Less than High School	3	3.5	0	0.0	3	9.7
High School Only	15	17.6	5	9.3	10	32.3
High School, Special Training (nursing, etc.)	35	41.2	31	57.4	4	12.9
College (4 Years)	27	31.8	18	33.3	9	29.0
College, Professional Training	5	5.9	0	0.0	5	16.1

4. In her study of a mill village in Greer, South Carolina, Hutton, op. cit., p. 27, found results comparable to these: "The children who have finished their formal training average 9.1 years of schooling completed, compared to an average of 7.6 years of schooling for their parents."

Only 3.5 percent said they wanted less than a high school education, while 78.9 percent indicated that they wished to go beyond high school. Obviously there is a sharp difference between what mill children say they would like in the way of schooling and what they actually get (or, rather, what they have obtained in the past). Several of the children indicated that they might not be able to fulfill their ambition. One Cromwell girl observed, "I would like to go to College, but my family doesn't have that kind of money." Also, they mentioned often that education was an important thing to have: "It is a great thing to have lots of education."

These desires of the mill children, then, seem to reflect a dominant American value more characteristic of the town sections than the mill sections of Kent. It is logical to suppose that the mill children modify their ambitions in the face of hard realities. Their parents simply do not have enough money to send them to college, and most of the mill children are such poor students that they are not encouraged to go ahead by their teachers.[5] Even for mill children to go away to nursing or secretarial schools is too difficult a burden for most families in the mill sections. For their part, the children can observe the tangible rewards that come from working in the mill, and also, such work is usually readily available. To seek training beyond the time they may work in the mill means that they continue to be dependent upon their parents and that they miss the advantages that come with having one's own income. Although mill parents want their children to have more education than they had, most of them think that a high school education is sufficient and do not encourage their children to continue further.

5. Apparently very few mill children have gone to college in the past. During my twelve months' stay, I learned of only seven mill children who had ever attended college. Most of them were children of foremen and were helped by the government through the G. I. Bill of Rights. None of them plan to return to Kent.

Kent town and rural-farm children in the seventh through the twelfth grades also wrote compositions on "The Story of My Life" and gave answers to the question of how much schooling they would like to have. Their responses are shown in Table 9, with the categories, "Less than High School" and "High School Only" combined into the category, "Not Beyond High School."

TABLE 9. THE AMOUNT OF SCHOOLING DESIRED BY 247 CHILDREN IN THE SEVENTH THROUGH THE TWELFTH GRADES OF THE DOWNTOWN KENT SCHOOL, BY MILL, TOWN, AND COUNTRY (RURAL-FARM) AFFILIATION

Amount of Schooling Desired	Mill		Town		Country	
	No.	Percent	No.	Percent	No.	Percent
Total	85	100.0	79	100.0	83	100.0
Not beyond High School	18	21.1	7	8.9	18	21.7
High School plus Special Training (nursing, etc.)	35	41.2	17	21.5	24	28.9
College (4 Years)	27	31.8	34	43.0	36	43.4
College plus Professional Training	5	5.9	21	26.6	5	6.0

The mill children are much closer to the country children in their ambition for schooling than they are to the town children. Far fewer of the town children would be content with just finishing high school, and considerably more want to go to college and beyond. When chi square is computed for the mill and town figures, it is found to be 21.3712, with a probability of less than .001 that such differences could be due to chance. On the other hand, chi square for the mill and country answers is .3593, with a probability greater than .95 that the differences could be due to chance.

Closely related to the amount of schooling desired is the kind of occupation the children would like to enter. In the composition directions for writing "The Story of My Life," the children were asked to tell "What I would like to be when I am grown." Of the mill children eighty-five responded, and their answers are shown in Tables 10 and 11.

TABLE 10. OCCUPATIONAL PREFERENCES OF 54 KENT MILL GIRLS IN THE SEVENTH
THROUGH THE TWELFTH GRADES OF THE DOWNTOWN KENT SCHOOL

Occupation	No.	Percent
Total	54	100.0
Secretarial Work	23	42.6
Nursing	12	22.2
Teaching	8	14.8
Religious Work	4	7.4
Airline Hostess	2	3.7
Beautician	2	3.7
Entertainer (Actress, Singer)	2	3.7
Housewife	1	1.9

TABLE 11. OCCUPATIONAL PREFERENCES OF 31 KENT MILL BOYS IN THE SEVENTH
THROUGH THE TWELFTH GRADES OF THE DOWNTOWN KENT SCHOOL

Occupation	No.	Percent
Total	31	100.0
Mechanic, Carpenter	6	19.4
Farming	5	16.1
Doctor	4	12.9
Professional Athlete	4	12.9
Armed Forces	4	12.9
Cotton-Mill Work	3	9.7
Religious Work	2	6.5
Civil Engineer	1	3.2
Lawyer	1	3.2
Undertaker	1	3.2

Note that only three, or 3.5 percent, of the children indicated cotton-mill work as their preference, yet a majority of mill children enter mill work, or at least they have in the past. We see that the occupational preferences of girls and boys differ to the extent that two separate lists of occupations emerge. The only point at which the occupations overlap is in the category of religious work, and here the boys stated they wished to be preachers and the girls missionaries or religious education directors. There is greater consensus among the girls in occupational preference, with almost two-thirds of them hoping to do secretarial work or nursing. The boys are much more widely scattered in their preferences.

As with the amount of schooling desired, the question arises how the mill children adjust their vocational ambitions to the realities of life, granted that many of them will enter mill work. Presumably the reconciliation here is similar to that made to the amount of education that could be obtained. It is possible, of course, that these ambitions are not stated seriously but are merely the types of answers written on compositions or given to curious adults. On the other hand, it is also logical that adjusting what one would like with what one can get is not easy for the mill child. Just how the adjustment is made would be a fruitful area for further research.

Millways and Townways

The schooling experience for the Kent mill child is not only a matter of learning the fundamentals of reading, writing, and arithmetic. It is also an encounter with a somewhat different way of life. Teachers in the mill school, as well as in the downtown school, come primarily from middle- and upper-class families, some from the town section of Kent itself. These teachers hold up before the children what are essentially town standards, and the mill children discover that much of what they have learned in their homes is inadequate or even incorrect. They find that their speech is substandard, their cleanliness habits insufficient, and their information on matters that are important in school inadequate. Their teachers attempt to pull them away from the standards they have learned in their villages, thereby implying the inferiority of such standards.

Some of the children try to adapt themselves to these new standards, but this can complicate the adjustment at home. On the one hand, the American value of "getting ahead" beckons them, and the majority seem to want to get sufficient education to improve themselves economically and socially. But on the other hand there stands the well-known mill village with its familiar, noncompetitive way of life. To try to "get ahead" would mean a sharp break with the mill village, and as we shall see later, apparently few are willing to pay the price that would take them away from the safe confines of the village. Yet of all the influences making for change in the mill-village sections, none is stronger than the public school.

Sin and Salvation: Religion

DEVELOPMENT AND DESCRIPTION OF
ORGANIZED RELIGIOUS GROUPS

CHAPTER 6   THE TENANT FARMERS and sharecroppers who made up the bulk of the cotton-mill workers first entering the Cromwell village had not been very active in their rural churches. When they belonged, few held positions of leadership, even in the poorer Baptist and Methodist churches. It is true that these ex-farmers had a strong religious heritage, especially a faith in the Bible, but they had fallen to the bottom of the rural social scale and their church connections had grown tenuous. For those who had remained active in rural churches, mill environment offered a new situation. Working hours were long and debilitating, and time, energy, and transportation necessary for continuing contact with rural churches were not available. The incentive of going to church for social reasons was greatly weakened in the village, for there one saw his neighbors every day, especially while working in the mill, in contrast to the comparative isolation on the farm.[1]

Twenty years elapsed after the Cromwell village had been founded before leadership developed among the mill workers to the extent that they formed their own church, the Charles-

---

1. Of interest in this connection is Grace C. Leybourne, "Urban Adjustments of Migrants from the Southern Appalachian Plateaus," *Social Forces*, 16 (December 1937), 238–46.

ville Street Baptist, later to become the Cromwell Baptist Church. Until that time an interdenominational chapel, erected by the Company, had been used for religious services. The downtown Baptist, Methodist, and Presbyterian churches would send their ministers and laymen to take charge of these services. Evangelists were called in occasionally to conduct campaigns of conversion. The founding of the Charlesville Street Baptist Church greatly decreased the importance of the chapel. Today the chapel has one evening service a week, on Sunday, with the town Presbyterian and Methodist ministers alternately in charge.

In 1944 the site and name of the Charlesville Baptist Church were changed. A new brick church was built on land given by the Cromwell Company, located on Cromwell Street, and named the Cromwell Baptist Church. It is attended almost exclusively by Cromwell mill families, with 85 percent of its membership of 214 from the Cromwell village. The rest of the members come from nearby farms and from the Locksley and Neilson villages. No town person is a member.

During the depression of the early thirties, the Kent mill villagers felt the impact of the Church of God movement. A woman evangelist set up a tent near the Cromwell chapel and began to "pack them in." Before many weeks a number of mill people had become converted and had joined the Church of God. "They nearly wrecked the Baptists," one informant reported. This group moved into a garage and after a few years built a long frame structure near the Cromwell and Neilson villages. At one time its membership equaled that of the Cromwell Baptist, but it has slowly declined to about 125 members, well divided among the four mill-village sections.

The third mill church, the Wesleyan Methodist, came into existence in 1938, first in the form of a revival meeting conducted in a tent at a point focal to the Neilson, Locksley, and Cromwell villages. The high wartime earnings of the

forties made possible the construction of a small brick building to replace the tent. The Wesleyans attracted people who
desired Holiness doctrine but felt that the Church of God was
too undignified, and who, at the same time, did not like the
"coldness" of the Cromwell Baptist Church. This church has
about eighty members, largely from the Neilson and Locksley
villages.

Some of the mill families maintain church membership in the
downtown Baptist, Methodist, and Presbyterian churches, but
few of them attend regularly. Most of the mill people do not
feel comfortable in the town churches—the congregations dress
too "fancy" to suit them.

A third type of church to which mill people belong is the
rural church, usually the one they grew up in on the farm.
But unless these members are particularly energetic and have
transportation available, they rarely attend their rural churches.
If they do not affiliate with one of the mill churches,
they usually drop out of the church altogether. Often the children of the members of rural churches, and to some extent the
children of the members of town churches, become active
with one of the mill churches' young people's groups.

Sporadic attempts are made by individuals or by dissatisfied
groups to form a new church. Tents are set up and special services held. People attend for a while, but after a few weeks
enthusiasm and curiosity wear off and the movement dies.
During the summer of 1948, a snake-handling cult, led by a
mill worker from a neighboring town, set up a tent in the
Locksley village and attracted attention for four or five weeks
before disbanding (see pages 129-31).

The survey of ninety-six mill homes asked the husband and
wife whether they were church members, and if so, where
and how often they attended. The results are tabulated in
Tables 12 and 13. It should be remembered that the children
in the ninety-six families are not included in these results and

they go more often than their parents, on the average, to mill churches, particularly if the parents are members of town or rural churches.

TABLE 12.　CHURCH MEMBERSHIP AND ATTENDANCE OF 177 KENT MILL FAMILY HEADS IN 96 FAMILIES,* BY MILL-VILLAGE SECTION

Village	Number of Heads	Number of Church Members	Percent of Church Members	Number Attending Regularly †	Percent Attending Regularly
Total	177	125	70.6	73	41.2
Cromwell	96	79	82.3	54	56.3
Locksley	26	19	73.1	10	38.5
Neilson	29	18	62.1	5	17.2
Townsend	26	9	34.6	4	15.4

* Information was not obtained for 15 husbands and wives, some of whom were deceased.
† By "regularly" is meant at least every third Sunday.

TABLE 13.　PLACE OF CHURCH MEMBERSHIP OF 125 KENT MILL FAMILY HEADS, BY MILL-VILLAGE SECTION

Village	Mill Churches		Town Churches		Rural Churches	
	No.	Percent	No.	Percent	No.	Percent
Total	65	52.0	31	24.8	29	23.2
Cromwell	48	60.8	20	25.3	11	13.9
Locksley	7	36.8	7	36.8	5	26.3
Neilson	7	38.9	4	22.2	7	38.9
Townsend	3	33.3	0	0.0	6	66.7

Church and Sect

There are sharp differences between the Cromwell Baptist Church and the Holiness churches (Church of God and Wesleyan Methodist), as well as between the mill churches and the town churches. These differences can be delineated by making use of the terms "Church" and "Sect." These "ideal types," or "polar types," were formulated in detail by Ernst

Troeltsch in his *Social Teaching of the Christian Churches*.[2] Troeltsch defined the "Church" as an institution into which members are born. It is highly conventional, conforming to and helping maintain the norms of the upper social classes upon which it is largely dependent. It is primarily conservative in outlook. The "Church" accepts the secular order, and is, indeed, an integral part of it. The religious authority of the "Church" is placed in the hands of an established ecclesiastical hierarchy which relies largely upon the precedents of tradition in making its decisions. The "Sect," on the other hand, separates itself from the secular order and is even antagonistic toward it. The "Sect" is a small, voluntary group, aimed at inward perfection and is sufficient unto itself. Members are from the lower classes,[3] and they enter the group as a result of a personal decision. Insead of putting authority into the hands of a tradition-oriented clergy and a hierarchy of officials, the "Sect" appeals directly to the Scriptures for its authority. It demands rigid adherence of its members to its doctrine and regulations, and it criticizes the "Church" for having fallen away from the original ideas of Christianity.

Liston Pope elaborates upon the Troeltsch distinction,[4] showing that these ideal types may be thought of in dynamic terms. There is constant movement of the "Sect" toward the "Church." Pope works out a scale of twenty-four indices, indicating transitions from "Sect" to "Church." As the "Sect" becomes more formalized and develops a larger stake in secular society, it begins to embrace the "world" which had once re-

2. See especially Vol. I, pp. 331–49 (translated by Olive Wyon; New York: Macmillan Company, 1931). Max Weber had developed and utilized "Church" and "Sect" as "ideal types" earlier in his *The Protestant Ethic and the Spirit of Capitalism* (translated by Talcott Parsons; London: Allen and Unwin Company, 1930).
3. Russell Dynes, in an empirical study, gives support to the assumption that socioeconomic status and the degree of acceptance of "Church" or "Sect" characteristics are associated. See his "Church-Sect Typology and Socio-Economic Status," *American Sociological Review*, XX (1955), 555–60.
4. Liston Pope, *Millhands and Preachers*, pp. 117–24.

jected its members, who in turn had rejected the "world." If a line representing a continuum from "Sect" type to "Church" type is drawn, various churches may be placed in position on it, depending on how near each type they are. The continuum, then, becomes an ordinal scale and can provide a useful framework for gaining an over-all view of how the churches in Kent are related to each other:

		Mill			Town		
Snake Cult	Church of God	Wesleyan Methodist	Cromwell Baptist	First Baptist	First Methodist	Presbyterian	Episcopal

SECT   CHURCH

The Cromwell Baptist Church

The Cromwell Baptist is more formal and conventional than the Holiness groups. The most prominent mill people, including several foremen and one overseer, make up its membership. It is the church considered most respectable and helpful in the mill community by the officials of the Cromwell Company. The Company demonstrated its support of this church by giving it land on which to build and by contributing to its building fund. I was advised by the mill superintendent when I first arrived at the Cromwell village to line up with the Baptist Church, for, he claimed, "you'll find the best element among the mill workers there."

The Cromwell Church is frequently criticized by members of the Holiness groups for its formality and "coldness." One young Church of God member expressed it in this way: "Those meetings at the Baptist are *dead*. The preacher is draggy, and if you ever said 'Amen' there, everyone would crane their necks trying to look at you." And a Wesleyan Methodist member complained, "Why, when I visited the Baptist, not more than three people bothered to speak to me."

Although it is less "Sect"-like than the Holiness groups,

the Cromwell Church has little, if any, more relationship with the town churches than do the other mill churches. When a serious dispute split the First Baptist Church into two factions in 1947, the group that was ousted went to the Unity Baptist Church, four miles out in the country, rather than to the Cromwell Church, which was much closer. The town-mill distinction overrides any similarity the two Baptist churches may have because of their common denominational affiliation.

The Cromwell Church is a two-story brick structure with the church auditorium occupying the upper floor and the Sunday School rooms the lower, semibasement floor. A wide flight of cement steps leads from the sidewalk to the church auditorium. This auditorium, seating about three hundred, has a hardwood floor slanting down toward the front, frosted glass windows, plastered walls with a sound-proofed ceiling, stationary pews, carpets along the aisles, and a carpeted pulpit platform flanked by two sections of pews for the choir. Concealed below the pulpit platform is a baptismal pool, which is opened by removing a part of the flooring. Two doors lead from the rear of the auditorium to a vestibule with a Sunday School room on either side. Above these rooms is located the pastor's study. A flight of stairs leads from the vestibule down to the ten Sunday School rooms below, with cement floors, plastered walls, and sound-proofed ceilings. A furnace room on this lower floor provides central heating. A two-story, brick pastorium next to the church is the most expensive house in the mill villages.

These two structures cost slightly over $30,000 in 1943-44. The members of the church are very proud of their buildings. Much credit is given the preacher for his success in the building campaign even at a time when prices were considered high and building materials scarce. The Cromwell Baptist buildings are more expensive and imposing than those of the Holiness groups.

There is better attendance at Sunday School than at the two

Sunday services. Parents either send or take their children to Sunday School, and both parents and children often leave directly afterward. The preacher often complains about this lack of church attendance, saying that no one will mind if the children stay and that if there is a choice of services, "preaching" should come first. Sunday School begins with an assembly of all classes. This service is in the charge of lay members who direct hymns, lead prayers, read the Bible lesson for the day, and make announcements. Classes are divided according to age and sex, and each class member is provided with a Sunday School quarterly containing the lessons. The teacher is given a special magazine with aids for presenting the lesson. Few if any of those attending prepare their lessons, and the teacher presents the lesson in lecture style without group participation. Lessons are made up of Bible studies, usually in a series of connected expositions on some phase of Jesus' life or some book in the Bible. Envelopes are used for the offering, and on them may be recorded the name and "score" of the member. This score is based on 100 points: 20 for attendance, 10 for being on time, 10 for bringing a Bible, 10 for an offering, 30 for studying the lesson, and 20 for attending church. The average score seems to range between 40 and 60, for almost no one carries a Bible or studies the lesson, and many do not stay for church.

After Sunday School is over and the members go outside to chat and smoke, very rarely if ever is the lesson just heard discussed. The men talk of baseball, the weather, or recent happenings in Kent or in the nation, especially as they have been rumored around the village or have appeared in the Sunday edition of the Metro City *Mirror*. The preacher does not approve of the men's smoking on the church lawn, but he does not explicitly forbid it. The women remain in church and talk about families, gardens, and local rumors.

The morning church service follows ten minutes after Sunday School is dismissed. Men and women tend to sit in separate groups, following the Sunday School groupings from which they have just come. A mimeographed order of service is prepared each Sunday on the inside of folders issued by the Baptist Bulletin Service. Already printed on the outside are news of the Baptist world and exhortations to Christian living, along with the pictures of Baptist leaders, prayers, and short homilies.

The order of service usually follows this form: Prelude (a hymn played on the piano); Call to Worship (short prayer by the pastor); Hymn (from the *Broadman Hymnal*, of which there are enough copies for the congregation as well as the "choir," a voluntary group gathered before each service and directed by a lay song leader; hymns are chosen to fit in with the sermon topic, and favorites include: "My Faith Looks Up to Thee," "There Is a Fountain Filled with Blood," "Are You Washed in the Blood," "When He Cometh to Gather His Jewels," "Jesus Calls Us," "Work for the Night Is Coming"); Prayer (in the morning by the pastor and in the evening by a layman called upon without advance notice, the one offering the prayer standing, while the congregation remains seated, no one kneeling or saying "Amen" during the prayer; such prayers follow the same general form: asking for forgiveness of sins, healing of the sick, thanksgiving for blessings, an entreaty that "he who brings the message may be filled with the Holy Spirit, so that he can bring lost souls to Christ"); Offering (taken by deacons regularly assigned as collectors and accompanied by piano music); Hymn (sometimes special music by a quartet, rarely by a soloist); Sermon (takes forty minutes of the sixty-minute session and is composed largely of expositions of Bible texts applied to everyday life); Hymn (an invitation is given to anyone wanting to join the church, either by confession of faith or by transfer of letter; rarely does anyone respond to such an appeal, for almost everybody attending belongs to the church already); Benediction (prayer by a layman while the preacher walks to the rear of the church to shake hands with the congregation when they leave).

Evening services follow the same form. As a rule these services are better attended than the morning ones, since home duties interfere less with the attendance of women and since boys take their girl friends, or at least meet them there. Greater expectations are felt for the evening service with its evangelical fervor.

One of the principal themes followed by the pastor of the Cromwell Baptist in his sermons has been the insistence on being humble, on not coming to church to show off clothes, and on not trying to depend too much on one's own strength and therefore leaving the Lord out. The mill people themselves appear to be characterized by attitudes of humility, lack of self-confidence, and nonaggressiveness. The sermons, then, along with their emphasis on the authority of the Scriptures, give sanction and support to these important character traits of mill people.

An example of the type of sermon delivered is "The Vision," in which Isaiah 6:1-13 was read as the Scriptural basis. The preacher began by commenting on each verse. Isaiah saw the seraphims near the throne of God, and therefore those who attend church should sit near the front rather than occupying the rear pews. The seraphims were reverent, since they covered their heads, and those in church should be reverent, although it is not necessary for heads to be covered (most of the Cromwell women do not wear hats to church). They should go to church to worship and not to show off clothes or to gossip with neighbors. Isaiah was humble because he recognized himself as a man of unclean lips; we, too, should be humble. These verses reminded the preacher of seven "C's," on which he next expounded: (1) Conception: Isaiah saw the Lord; (2) Conviction: Isaiah was convicted of his lack of cleanliness and of the uncleanliness of those about him; (3) Confession: he confessed his uncleanliness; (4) Cleansing: this was done by means of fire; (5) Calling: "Whom shall I send?"; (6) Consecration: "Here am I. Send me." (7) Commission: God told Isaiah to go and preach to the people. The congregation sits apparently unmoved during these sermons, which seem to be primarily a juggling of verbal symbols and an exercise in semantics without visibly touching those listening. In contrast to his congregation, the preacher is highly emotional, talking in loud, quivering tones much of the time. He walks back and forth, continually waving his arms and emphasizing points by beating his fists on the rostrum. Even apparently inconsequential statements are made in this loud, strained voice: "I'm not a-saying you aren't reverent. Sometimes thar's papers a-rattling and children being noisy, but that's not what I'm a-talking about." No attempt is made to use loudness and intensity to build up to a climax. It is expected that the preacher will do some shouting. A large electric clock behind the preacher and in full view of the audience keeps everyone informed of the time, and if the preacher goes beyond the noon hour in the morning or beyond eight o'clock in the evening, he apologizes.

After the offering at the evening service, a board which hangs on the wall back of the pulpit and on which is recorded attendance and offering is removed and the figures for that Sunday posted. Attendance and offering are compared with those of the previous week, and the weekly budget is given so that it is possible to tell whether the offering has been sufficient. The posting of a weekly budget is in keeping with the weekly basis on which mill people conduct all their financial affairs.

Prayer service is held in the church each Wednesday evening and is attended by about fifteen core members of the church. The preacher constantly exhorts more members to attend, and he prints squibs in the mimeographed folder to that effect. Of course, those working on the second shift are not free to come. At these prayer services a book in the Bible is studied, or a particular theme is followed over the course of several Wednesdays. The pastor lectures during these sessions, while members are called on to pray at the start and at the close of the service. The same form of prayer found in the Sunday prayers are present in these prayers, though the latter are longer and more fervent.

Revival services are held twice a year, in the fall and spring, and an outside evangelist is brought in to lead these services. He might be a preacher in a nearby town who has a reputation for "saving" people, or he might be a professional evangelist who goes from revival to revival. Revival is a time for stirring up the people and for bringing new members into the church. Even the children of members are usually "converted" during revival services and join the church, as a rule, at that time. The belief is that each person must be "born again," the result of an inner conviction, hence joining the church is a deeply personal matter. There are no pastor's classes to explain to would-be members the doctrines of the church, for salvation is an emotional rather than an intellectual thing. Most of those "saved" during the revival meetings are children nine to fourteen years of age whose parents are members of the church. A few members are taken in by transfer of letter when mill workers move in from other communities. But the membership is largely self-perpetuating through the continual joining of the children of members. The young children who are "born again" do so at approximately the same age, at a time when it is expected by parents and other church members. However, if a child has not experienced this by the time he is thirteen or fourteen, something is considered amiss, and the pastor makes a call to bring pressure to bear on the family and the individual who has not joined.

As with the Sunday church services, almost all who attend the revival meetings are already members of the Cromwell Church. The evangelist consults with the pastor after each meeting is underway to find out whether anyone present is "unsaved." If all present are Christians, the evangelist at the close of the sermon will call for some sort of overt demonstration on the part of those present to indicate their promise to lead a more Christian life. At one meeting, he called for bowed heads and a show of hands of all those who wanted the Lord to fill their "fruit basket" with the Christian fruits of love, joy, faith, temperance, etc. On another night he called for all faithful members of the church to come forward and shake the hand of their pastor. On nights when non-Christians were present, he stressed the need for salvation *now*, for tomorrow might be too late. After an intensely emotional sermon on the urgency for accepting Jesus as Lord and Saviour, one evangelist left the pulpit and walked directly to a non-Christian, put his arm around him and begged him to go to the altar at once. He whispered, "You do want to be saved, don't you? This might be your last chance, for we never know when the angel of death might come. Won't you come and give your heart to Jesus, now, tonight?" In this case, the non-Christian, a boy of fourteen, did not yield to the plea, and, in fact, refused to attend any more of the revival services. He said that the evangelist made him feel uncomfortable and did not help him make up his mind. The only thing keeping him from joining the church was the fear of being pushed under water when he was baptized. More than one Baptist evangelist stated that it was becoming increasingly difficult to convert people, something that they attributed to the growing power of the Devil.

Various organizations for children, young people, and adult women meet at the church during the week, have programs, and conduct projects such as making scrapbooks for those who are sick and collecting clothes for Christian converts overseas. Once a month, all of these groups and the adult men gather at the church for a supper, supplied and prepared by the Woman's Missionary Society, and for a program, usually a play or a series of recitations put on by the children or young people. These church organizations and meetings are an outlet, particularly for the mill women, who are more limited in the types of activities open to them than the men.

The Holiness Churches

The Church of God and the Wesleyan Methodist Church are closer to the "Sect" type than is the Cromwell Baptist. These churches attract the poorer mill workers, especially those from the Reginold villages, and they do not have any foremen or many from the "New Hill" part of the Cromwell village in their membership. They are on a lower level economically.

This economic difference is obvious in the contrast in the types of buildings. The Holiness churches are smaller and less expensive, and neither one has space separate from the church auditorium for Sunday School rooms. Both have movable benches for pews, plain glass windows, and carpetless floors. Coal stoves in the auditorium supply heat. The Church of God is larger than the Wesleyan Methodist, but it is a crude wooden structure without plastered walls, while the Wesleyan Methodist is a small but relatively new brick building. Both churches have in the front quarter of the auditorium a platform for a pulpit with pews for a choir on either side. As in the Cromwell Church, these choir sections are filled by volunteer members. However, unlike the singers at the Cromwell Baptist, the Holiness choirs leave the platform and take their seats with the rest of the congregation when the sermon begins. The Holiness churches have attendance and offering records hung in conspicuous places.

The dress of the members and the number of automobiles they own further mark the economic differences between the Holiness groups and the Baptists. Holiness men seldom wear coats and ties, and the women dress much more simply than those at the Cromwell Baptist. Children at Holiness meetings often wear overalls or blue jeans, something never done by Baptist children at their church. On the other hand, the Holiness groups are more aggressive in seeking new members than the Baptist church. They pride themselves on the warm welcome they give strangers. The Church of God purchased a school bus which goes around to the various mill-village sections both Sunday morning and Sunday evening to gather those who want to attend. In this way the Church of God has been able to get people from each of the Reginold villages. Within each Holiness church there is competition to see which class has the largest attendance, which class gives the largest offering, and what person has brought the most people to church. On special Sundays, such as Easter, Christmas, and Rally Sunday, pencils inscribed with "Jesus Never Fails," tin crosses, church buttons, and other souvenirs are given to all who attend.

Sunday School dominates the Sunday morning services, just as it does at the Cromwell Baptist. There are about as many children and young people as adults at the Holiness meetings, although many of those in the younger group do not attend "preaching" on Sunday morning. Sunday School is conducted in much the same way as at the Cromwell Church. All classes meet in a general assembly, sing hymns, listen to a Bible reading and a prayer. In their classes they have a single sheet of printed lesson material published by the denomination. The lesson is composed of Bible text, Golden Text, brief commentary on the text and questions on the lesson. Classes are taught in lecture style by church members, and lessons consist of Bible studies: "God's Promise to Abraham," "God Calls Moses," "Joseph and His Brothers," "Ananias, Disciple at Damascus." Sunday School ends with the classes' parading by the altar and dropping in their offerings, which have been put into envelopes with the giver's name on each.

The church services have little formal organization. There

are no mimeographed programs or even a set order of worship. Informality is a basic characteristic, and children are allowed to go in and out of the church auditorium, almost at will. The service is opened with a group of songs, sung almost entirely by the "choir," since they are the only ones who have song books. A song leader, one of the church members, directs the choir, and the preacher attempts to pep things up by clapping his hands in time to the music and urging the congregation to do the same. There is more of such clapping and tapping of feet at the Church of God than in the Wesleyan Methodist, and the hymns are more jazzy, but the favorite songs of both groups emphasize the rewards and glory of the life beyond the grave: "When We All Get to Heaven," "Walking on the Streets of Gold," "When You Get to Heaven, Come to See Me in My New Home," "We're Going to Have a Good Time in Heaven." In addition to the glories of heaven, the songs tell of the love of Jesus in having saved sinners and brightened the world: "When the Master Reached Down His Hand for Me," "I Love Jesus," "Where Could I Go but to the Lord?" A song often sung in the Wesleyan Methodist is typical:

The windows of heaven are open; the angels are happy tonight;
There's joy, joy, joy in my soul, since Jesus made everything right.
I gave him my old tattered garments; he gave me a robe of pure white;
I'm feasting on manna from Heaven, and that's why I'm happy tonight.

The music of these hymns, especially in the Church of God, have a definite beat and a fast, swingy rhythm. Most of the songs are "happy" but a few are reminiscent of the blues; for example, "If Ever You Leave Me, Jesus, I'll Die." Others tell a story in ballad fashion, almost mountain style. The pianist plays all of these hymns in a jazz manner, with numerous offbeats, runs, and trills. Invariably during the singing the preacher stirs the people to activity and full participation by such exhortations as "Let's show tonight just how happy God's people are"; "Don't be afraid to be joyful before the Lord"; "Let's get a blessing out of this meeting tonight." At one Church of God meeting the pastor began exclaiming about the glories of God and asked the people to give a round of applause to show just how much they thanked God for being so wonderful, whereupon the congregation clapped loudly. During the singing of the hymns, the preacher will shout, "Amen," "Glory," "That's true, brother," but members of the congregation rarely throw out such exclamations. The lay song leader plays a passive role, only announcing the hymn number and singing in a perfunctory manner without trying to induce more participation from the choir and congregation. Apparently he leaves it up to the preacher to do this.

After several songs, interspersed with an announcement or two and a prayer and an offering, the preacher will say, "Well, that's about enough singing, I guess," and this is a signal that the members of the choir are to leave the platform and take their seats among the congregation.

The prayers at the Holiness meetings are group prayers in which almost everyone present prays aloud at the same time. The preacher announces, "We'll go to prayer at this time." And he asks if there are any requests for prayers. Such requests are shown by raised hands, and a few will speak out to tell of someone in their family who is not saved or who is sick. The preacher assures the people that God will answer all the requests, and he calls on one of the members to lead the prayer—rarely women, although they usually outnumber the men at the meeting. Almost everyone kneels, using the seat of the bench as a place for resting the arms, rather than the back of the bench ahead as in Episcopal style. The leader's voice is scarcely audible above the noise from the prayers of others. Such a group prayer lasts for four or five minutes. The voices suddenly subside, and the leader is heard clearly as he brings the prayer to a close.

Members of the Holiness groups are strict tithers, giving at least one-tenth of their incomes to the church. In addition to the regular tithe, special offerings are taken: for the visiting evangelist, for repairs to the church bus, for the electricity bill, or for delegate expenses to a conference. These special collections are highly dramatic, especially when they are for the revival leader. At one meeting the preacher announced that they needed a good offering for their evangelist, and he held up a dollar bill he said he was contributing, claiming it to be his last. He said he was giving it to increase his bank account in heaven where it would be safe from moth and rust and thieves. And he said he was sure he would be going up there one day to collect it with interest. He then asked those who would like to make a loan of one dollar to God to raise their hands. Several members raised their hands, and the preacher left the pulpit, took the bills personally from each giver, thanking him warmly. He almost broke into a run as he went up and down the aisles gathering the bills and asking, "Are there any more?" And if a hand was raised, "I see you, brother; hold on, I'll be right there." The people chuckled during these antics of their pastor and seemed to enjoy the collection. When no one else would give a dollar, the plate was passed for loose change. Then the entire amount was counted aloud and was found to be just short of forty dollars (about eighty people were present). The pastor then asked the congregation to give a little more to make the sum an even forty dollars, and enough quarters, dimes, and nickels came in to make up the desired amount.

Sermons in the morning are less emotional than those at the evening service, which is referred to as the "evangelistic" service. Morning sermons are more akin to teaching, according to Holiness members, for no attempt is made to save and sanctify as at the evening service. At one typical morning service at the Church of God, the preacher promised not to keep the congregation long and began to read random verses from the Bible and to expound upon them. At one point, he began talking in a loud voice and jumped up and down, saying, "I'm beginning to really feel like moving," and he shouted, "Glory, hallelujah. I feel like evangelizing, not waiting until tonight." And he began to punctuate each phrase with a clap of his hands. The Scripture he was reading concerned the promises of God to Abraham and his seed, and the preacher showed that this was clear proof that the Jews rather than the Arabs would take over Palestine. He said that if people had the faith of Abraham, they could move mountains. But, he added, most people were like the woman who prayed that a mountain be moved, but arose the next morning to find it still there and exclaimed, "Just as I thought." The trouble was, said the preacher, she didn't believe it in the first place. The preacher said if we have faith enough we need not call a doctor—he apologized for having sent for a doctor once after a long siege of hiccups, but on another occasion, when he cut a deep gash in his head, he did have enough faith and refused to call for medical aid and his head healed without any trouble. Faith is certainly needed, for "we sure can't save ourselves." He spoke of heaven as a definite place, saying that he would be able to see Jesus as clearly as he could see anyone present at that moment. Then he left the pulpit and began to shake hands with several of those near the front, saying he would do the same with Jesus when he went to heaven, thanking him for all he had done to save people here on earth. All during his sermon he would ask the congregation, "Isn't that right?" and the reply would come, "That's right," "That's so." The preacher dismissed the group shortly before twelve, urging them to return for the evening service and to pray that souls would be saved and sanctified that night.

The Wesleyan Methodist preacher usually takes a single text and elaborates upon it, rather than giving a verse-by-verse treatment. He spoke one Sunday morning on "What does it profit a man if he gain the whole world and lose his own soul?" A line of demarcation was drawn between the world on the one side and the soul on the other. The two were contrasted, showing that devotion to material things of the world led to eternal punishment in everlasting fire. The big question was not how much we own here on earth but how much we own up above. On another Sunday he spoke on the evils of habit, which he equated with bad habit. He gave a series of graphic illustrations of the treachery of habit, comparing it to the spider web woven about a fly, a pet boa constrictor growing up and crushing its trainer to death, small insects worrying to death a man partly buried in the ground as the result of "African torture." The only sin he referred to specifically was drinking, claiming it to be the worst of habits and a false release from trouble, and he cited an incident in Stone Valley where five men sought such release by drinking paint thinner, and "all died and went to hell with no one to plead their case before God."

The evening services at the Holiness churches are much more lively and are better attended than those on Sunday morning. They are so much like the revival services that these two types of service might well be described together. The main difference is that revival meetings are in the charge of special evangelists. The evangelist stays in the home of one of the members of the church, and other members send over food to help share the living expense. It is considered an honor to put up the evangelist. Special music, usually songs by a church trio or quartet accompanied by an accordion or guitar, is also offered at the revival services. The Holiness churches have four or five revivals each year, more than twice as many as the Cromwell Baptist.

Testifying is a part of the evangelistic services. Members are urged to stand and bear witness to the goodness of the Lord, and many do, usually the same ones time after time. These testimonies follow set forms and include such phrases as: "I thank the Lord tonight that I'm saved, sanctified, and washed in the blood"; "I'm happy tonight because that I'm a Christian and that my sins are under the blood and washed white as snow"; "I'm glad tonight to stand up and say a word for Jesus, how he picked me up when I was despised and rejected by the world"; "I may not have much of this world's goods, but I don't need none, for I have Jesus, and He's enough for me." Some become intensely emotional and are so moved during their own testimony that they begin to sing and shout, skip up and down the aisles and wave their arms. A middle-aged woman at the Wesleyan Methodist Church became "happy" one night, jumped to her feet, and broke forth with: "I thank God for Jesus Christ tonight. He's washed away my sins, and I feel light as a feather. Hallelujah! Whoopee! I'm happy to-night, and I want all you people to know what the Lord has done for me and how wonderful it is. The Devil, he tried to keep me away from this meeting tonight, said I wouldn't get nothing from it. But I come anyhow and now the Devil's mad but I'm glad. Hallelujah, praise the Lord." She skipped up and down the aisle, and her voice, loud pitched in the beginning, grew even louder. The congregation seemed pleased with such an overt demonstration, and the evangelist said that it was a good sign for her "cup to overflow," because it meant that the Holy Spirit was at work in a special way.

The sermons at these revival services emphasize the imminence of the Day of Judgment and the need for salvation. Unless someone is saved or sanctified or filled with the Holy Spirit during the evening, the meeting is considered a failure. On Saturday and Sunday nights the services may last until after midnight in the attempt to get someone saved. The sermon is directed toward inducing sinners and backsliders to come to the altar and receive the "rapture." One particular revival that I attended at Wesleyan Methodist Church demonstrates how converts are sought, although the meeting was somewhat unusual in that no one came to the altar. The visiting evangelist spoke on "The Judgment." He depicted in vivid language the finality of that Day in which "the sheep will be divided from the goats *forever*, and there will be weeping, and wailing, and gnashing of teeth.... It's gonna be awful, mothers separated from sons, families all divided, parents never to see their precious dead babies who died in Christ!" He spoke of the horrors of eternal punishment and asked throughout the sermon, "Are *you* ready to face the Judgment? Do you want to see your loved ones again? Get right with God, now." Then he gave those who were not ready to die a chance to accept Jesus as their go-between when they faced God at the judgment bar. He urged and pleaded that sinners come down to the altar and repent, as the hymn "Only Trust Him" was sung. When no one responded from among the sixty present, tears came into the evangelist's eyes, and he begged the unsaved to come forward. "Someone is holding this meeting up. Someone is stopping the Spirit. Is it you? Don't you feel that tug at your heart? Answer that call and be saved." Some of the most faithful members came to the altar and said that if they were the ones holding back the Spirit, they prayed that God would forgive them. Then some of these "saved" members of the congregation went over to friends and relatives who were not Christians, begging them to go forward and be saved. But those approached steadfastly refused to respond. The evangelist came down from the platform and asked each individual in the congregation personally if he were saved. When he found someone who said he was not, he pleaded with him to take the step now rather than wait another moment. Still no one came. The evangelist said he would try one more thing, and he asked Christians to kneel silently by the side of their loved ones who were not saved, praying quietly that they go to the altar. Several did this. The preacher's wife knelt by the side of a young girl. A man went over to his young brother's side. A young wife cried silently at the feet of her husband.

Nothing availed, and no one was "saved." The evangelist asked, "What more can I do? Do you still love me? I love you." The pastor then stepped forward and said it was the saddest meeting he had ever attended, when no one was saved for Christ. He urged all Christians present to redouble their efforts to arouse people for Jesus, for the Devil was becoming stronger in the world, "and we have had evidence of that tonight."

During a series of revival meetings at the Church of God, an evangelist was brought from a large textile town a hundred miles away. One typical night about 90 were in attendance, including approximately 40 adult women, 35 children under fifteen, and 15 men. The evangelist took his text from the twenty-fourth chapter of Matthew, which tells of the suddenness and unpredictability of the return of Christ:

> Then shall two be in the field; the one shall be taken, and the other left. Two women shall be grinding at the mill; the one shall be taken, and the other left. Watch therefore: for ye know not what hour your Lord doth come.... Therefore be ye also ready: for in such an hour as ye think not the Son of man cometh.

The evangelist was highly dramatic, both in voice and gesture. Frequently he would make movements with his arms and hands without saying anything, looking as though he were going into a trance. He would take off his glasses and wipe his forehead with a handkerchief with great solemnity during strategic pauses. More than once he closed his eyes, threw back his head and uttered something that sounded like, "Oh, Kiminoshia. Oh, Kiminoshia. Oh, Allaharra. Oh, Lagskodra." This was "speaking in unknown tongues." He said that Jesus was coming back at an unexpected moment, perhaps before the sermon was finished. Would all those present be ready, or would they be like the five foolish virgins and have the door shut in their faces when the bridegroom came unexpectedly? On that final day of tribulation the saints are to be snatched up into the sky to meet Jesus. A sinner will find his wife gone; his children who had learned to speak in unknown tongues and who had died will disappear from their open graves. Of two men working in the mill, one will suddenly disappear, leaving the other mystified. At the close of the sermon, he asked that several of the "saved" sing softly while he invited those who wished to receive the "rapture" to come and kneel at the altar. One girl of about eighteen went immediately; a few minutes later a man in his thirties knelt; then three or four boys and girls in their early teens went. When it appeared that no others would come, the most active members went forward to help those kneeling to receive the "rapture." The men worked with men and the women with women. The helpers began to pray aloud, clap their hands, pat the one kneeling, shouting rapidly in his ear, "Glory, glory, glory...." The prayers and clapping of hands would increase in mounting crescendo if the one on his knees could be seen trembling, jerking, and crying as though he were "coming through." Sometimes it would take almost an hour for a person to "come through"; others might receive the "rapture" in far less time. Those who did "come through" were completely exhausted, their faces swollen from crying, and their hair and clothes dishevelled. Usually they would have to be laid out along a bench with a coat over them until they were able to walk again.

The actions and reactions of those receiving the "rapture" appeared to follow the same pattern. And it was evident that the young children were learning how it was done. When the backsliders and sinners knelt at the altar, children went up to observe, standing quite close to watch the actions and expressions of those being "brought through." Children as young as eight and nine years of age have been saved and sanctified and filled with the Holy Ghost, and later they have been re-saved when they backslid by going to a moving-picture show or by smoking. One of the lay leaders of the church told me that most of those who went to the altar had already been saved and sanctified numerous times previously. They had slipped into sin, and instead of praying their own way out, they had felt themselves lost and in need of the help of sanctified persons. He implied that they were of weak character. The Holiness churches hold prayer meetings two or three times a week when revival is not going on. In addition to the regular Wednesday prayer meetings at the church, there are "cottage prayer meetings" held in the homes of the most devout members. These are intimate gatherings of the most faithful. All participate, and prayers center around the events of importance at the time: a revival, an illness, a building fund, Rally Day, and so on. There are almost no formal organizations comparable to those at the Cromwell Baptist, but the young people's groups have outings and parties, and the entire church has an occasional picnic supper.

Snake-Handling Cult

During the warmer months of the year, representatives of a religious cult sometimes pitch a tent on an empty lot and attempt to gain converts. This was done during one summer of my stay in Kent. An evangelist named Tinkle came up each evening from the town where he worked in a cotton mill. He put up a tent on a vacant lot across from the Locksley mill, covered the floor with sawdust, set up crude wooden benches, and used an amplifier to attract attention to the meeting. Tinkle claimed that his "church" was the Church of Jesus Christ and was completely independent of other groups. He and his coterie of three handled snakes to prove their faith to be the true one, taking as their Scriptural basis Mark: 16:17–18:

And these signs shall follow them that believe: in my name shall they cast out devils; they shall speak with new tongues; they shall take up serpents; and if they drink any deadly thing, it shall not hurt them; they shall lay hands on the sick and they shall recover.

The reference to "they shall take up serpents" is singled out as a means of testing and demonstrating belief in Jesus.

The tent stayed up for five weeks in spite of the criticism from the Church of God and Wesleyan Methodist members and close surveillance by the Kent police force. It closed abruptly when the leader was bitten by one of the snakes and almost died. The services were not well attended, and the mill people who came seemed more interested in observing the handling of the snakes than in any other part of the service. They often milled around outside the tent until the word came that the snakes were being brought out, and then they hastened in to watch. The order of service resembled that at the Church of God: jazzy hymns, group prayer, testimonies, and sermon. The latter emphasized that those who could handle snakes were the true believers, and the climax of the meeting came when a wire-covered box of snakes was brought out and opened. The snakes were picked up by Tinkle and his assistants and held above their heads with the cry, "In the name of the Lord Jesus." Those watching were told that if they had enough faith, they could handle snakes without being harmed. But only Tinkle and his group did handle them, for the Kent mill people were unwilling to test their faith in that way.

At one meeting the Church of God minister was present and engaged in an argument with Tinkle. The dispute concerned the interpretation of the word "serpent." The Church of God minister said it was used figuratively and really meant the "Devil." The cult leader said that he took the Bible exactly as it was written, and he asked the Church of God man either to sit down or to leave and to quit "knocking" his faith.

The mill people appeared to be spectators rather than participants in the tent revival. They attended as though seeing a sideshow, and the "show" was largely the doings of one man who apparently had been unable to find leadership roles in established churches. One Church of God leader said that Tinkle had been "kicked out" of several groups and was a "fanatic" and a "bum." When Tinkle was bitten, jokes were passed among the villagers that his faith must have slipped or perhaps he forgot to pull the fangs out of the snake. Yet no one doubted that the true Christian should be able to handle snakes or the Devil, as the interpretation might be, for "it says so in the Bible."

BASIC RELIGIOUS BELIEFS AND PRACTICES

Religion and the Bible

Of the patterns of belief that emerge from observation of and participation in mill-village religious life, none is more striking than faith in the Bible. The Bible is accepted as the ultimate authority in all religious matters, and to some extent in secular matters as well. True religion, even for the unchurched, is "living according to the Bible," and a Christian is "a man of the Book." Literal acceptance of the Bible is the cornerstone of belief in the mill churches, and the Book is taken as a basis for making decisions in political, educational, recreational, and scientific, as well as religious, areas of life.

The fact that churches and individuals find quite different sanctions for actions and beliefs does not lessen the faith in the authority of the Bible. In the case of the snake-handling group, the mill people were somewhat disturbed by Tinkle's claim that true Christians should be able to handle snakes without being bitten, for Tinkle did have a Biblical basis for doing so. This matter was discussed at length by some of the mill people. They concluded that the Bible really means God will protect you from snakes only if you meet them in line of duty, in much the same way that St. Paul had met them on the Island of Cyprus. Paul was not bitten, but at the same time he did not go out of his way to handle them. The Bible also says, "Thou shalt not tempt the Lord thy God," so there is no guarantee that God will protect you, even if you are a Christian, if you deliberately expose yourself to danger. On the other hand, if you encounter a snake under your bed or crawling along the path, God will not let it bite you if you are a Christian. When Tinkle himself was bitten, they felt their interpretation justified.

In his argument with the snake-handling cult leader, the Church of God preacher did more than introduce another verse of Scripture to combat Mark 16:18. He got a parallel Greek, English, Hebrew translation of the Bible and showed that the English translation "serpent" was from a Greek word meaning "serpent-like person." In other words, the believer will be able to handle people who are like serpents but not necessarily be able to handle live, crawling reptiles. Thus, even in this disturbing passage the authority of the Bible itself was never questioned, for as long as something is in the Bible, it is true. But at times it must be interpreted and thought over carefully in the light of other verses of Scripture.

No higher praise can be given a minister than to say, "He preaches the Bible," or "He sure knows his Scripture." In the dispute with Tinkle, the Church of God preacher said that there were no references to "the Church of Christ" in the Bible. Tinkle shouted that there were and began frantically to search for a passage to prove it. The Church of God minister then said calmly that the reference was to "the Churches of Christ," and to this Tinkle agreed, reluctantly. Whereupon the Church of God preacher turned to the congregation and said with pride, "I *know* my Bible." This defeat for Tinkle was voiced around, and the prestige of the Church of God minister was enhanced.

Not only the preachers, but anyone who has knowledge of the Bible is highly respected. The story is told by mill villagers of "Cyclone Mac," a famous evangelist who swept through the Piedmont not many years ago. In a certain town in which he was conducting a revival, there was a man who did not go to church but who read the Bible and led a good life. Members of the church were unable to get the man to attend church services, and they asked Cyclone Mac to speak to him. Mac did so, but the nonchurchgoer asked questions on the Bible that Mac himself could not answer, showing his superior knowledge of the Book. Mac was put to rout and asked the church members to leave the man alone.

One need not belong to a church or even attend one so long as he reads the Bible and accepts "Christ as his Lord and Saviour." Even church members say, "There's about as many good people outside the church as in it." Indications of such goodness are found in the way a person lives (does not drink, smoke or chew, or have affairs with someone else's wife or husband) and in his belief in the Bible. The church might help a man live as he should, but it is his belief in the Bible and in Jesus that is fundamental to salvation.

Even those who are apparently uninterested in religion and who have never belonged to a church accept the Bible as a fundamental guide for life, at least in theory. George Mooney and Walter Lake, men in their thirties, are characteristic. One of them attended Sunday School in his youth, but neither has been inside a church for the last fifteen years. They defend themselves by saying that some people who go to church are even worse than some who do not belong. And those who go to church on Sunday but who "drink and carry on during the week are just hypocrites and worse than those who do not go." When asked what church he would join if ever he decided to do so, Lake said he would join the Baptists, "because it says in the Bible that Jesus came up out of the water after John baptized him, so he must have been immersed and not sprinkled." Mooney said that the proper way to bring up children, especially girls, is to send them to Sunday School and get them to believe in the Bible. His three daughters attend Sunday School at the Wesleyan Methodist Church regularly. Another mill worker quotes the Bible to support his non-attendance at church. The Bible states that false prophets and preachers are coming, and this worker says that they must be here now because of all the hypocritical preachers in the world today. (He probably had in mind the fact that a mill preacher in Kent had recently been dismissed from his church after being accused of improper relations with several young women of his congregation.)

The following letters to the editors of newspapers published in towns near Kent are not from Kent mill workers, but they would certainly be approved and subscribed to by them. These letters indicate the application of the Bible as an authority on any subject and were written in the fall of 1948:

... How is one to know what is right outside the Bible? ... The fact is that there has never been any treatise on any subject that is worth reading, the truth of which was not found in the only Book that is truth. Each painting and all art, all philosophy, science, ethics and history come from the Bible. They all stem from the Book....

And on the Bible as a guide in political problems:

I see in a number of articles where the States' Rights and the Progressive Party leaders want to come back to the National Democratic Party. I want to say to the voters and to the National Democratic Party leaders not to let them come back.

Jesus said in I John 2:19, "They went out from us, but they were not of us; for if they had been of us, they would no doubt have continued with us; but they went out, that they might be made manifest that they were not of us." The Bible says that they would come to us in sheep's clothing but inwardly they would be ravening wolves. These wolves and old he-goats will come back to the party when they want to run for office again.

But I want to ask you to do as the Bible says in Romans 16:17 —"Mark them which cause divisions among you and have no fellowship with them!" Now when these old he-goats and wolves come out for office, then is the time to mark them off your ballot. Put them out of the Party and keep them out.

In the fall of 1948 an amateur scientist made the claim that unless the ice pack gathering around the North Pole were broken up, it might some day cause the destruction of the United States and possibly the world. He advocated that atomic bombs be used to break up this huge clustering of ice. The Metro City *Mirror* and Stone Valley *Bugle* carried this news and the comments from readers about it for several issues. The item caught the imagination of the mill workers, and they discussed whether it could be true. In one discussion a sixteen-year-old boy, who does not "think much of the church," said that such a claim could not be correct, "for it says in the Bible that the next time the world is destroyed, it will be by fire and not by ice." The rest of the group agreed.

This stress on the importance of the Bible as the authority, not only in religion but in other fields as well, does not imply that the mill villagers quote Scripture often, nor indeed that they spend much time reading their Bibles. Quotations are relied upon when one wants to make a point, for support from the Bible lends strength to any argument, even that of condemning States'-Rights backers in a strongly pro-States'-Rights state. Those opposing the sentiments of the anti-States'-Rights letter recorded above might marshal other Bible verses to support their cause or argue that the writer has made incorrect application of the Bible verses. Yet they would never question the fact that the Bible could be used as a basis of argument in politics. Any person who did question the authority of the Bible would be severely criticized by the religious and the nonreligious alike in the mill villages.

Religion and Salvation

Another strongly held religious belief is in a life after death, either in a heaven of happiness or in a hell of pain. Religion is primarily a means of saving people from eternal punishment after they die and assuring for them a place in a glorious heaven. Unless a person's sins, as defined by the particular church, are overcome—and everyone is considered a sinner—he will be condemned at the bar of judgment. Salvation from certain punishment can come only if the sinner accepts Jesus as his Lord in this life and as his Saviour in the life to come. The doctrine often stated in the pulpit and accepted by the people is that Jesus sacrificed himself in order to appease God's anger caused by the sin of Adam. The Church of God minister expressed it this way: "The Devil kidnapped man when Adam sinned, but Jesus paid the ransom with his own life so that man might once again be with God." It is the "blood of Jesus," i.e., his death and sacrifice, that can wash away the sins of the world. An evangelist at the Cromwell Baptist told the story of a Sunday School teacher who asked whether anything were impossible for God. A small boy said that he knew of something: "God can't see my sins when they are put under the blood of Christ." Such salvation cannot be gained by good works or by paying for it with "all the jewels and all the cotton mills in the world." It is free to those who "accept Christ as the Son of God." The rich and the poor alike may have it free, but it is more difficult for the rich because of their tendency to depend upon wealth rather than upon God.

Hell is a place in which there are all sorts of torture, especially fire. The Cromwell Baptist minister believes there are varying degrees of heat, however, with the hottest reserved for those who have had an opportunity to hear about the Saviour but have not heeded him. There is less severe punishment for the ones in China and elsewhere who have never had a chance to hear about Jesus. Heaven, on the other hand, is a place where there is singing and people enjoy themselves forever. There are mansions for the faithful on streets paved with gold (the Baptist minister says we should not wonder about this, for God is surely powerful enough to turn base metal into gold; the Holiness ministers need no such explanation). No one will have any infirmity in heaven; everyone will have happiness, for there will be no sorrow; there will be no very old people, no different races, no cripples, no blind. Everyone will be just the right age and will never suffer pain of any kind. Best of all, Jesus will be there, and the Cromwell Baptist minister stated that for the first one thousand years in heaven, "I want to sit at the feet of Jesus, look into his glorious face, and ask 'How could you have loved me so?' "

Those who do not attend church and who do not live as they think they should are worried about their life in the next world. They are aware of their "unsaved" condition. One mill worker had to leave the Church of God because he could not give up smoking, and he said that if he died now he would go straight to hell and he knew it. However, he said, one of these days he would change and get right with the Lord.

Religion and Sin

A strong puritanical emphasis permeates mill religion, and morality is made almost synonymous with religion, especially in the Holiness churches. These have rigid rules in certain areas of conduct, including taboos against using tobacco in any form, drinking, dancing, applying make-up, bobbing the hair, wearing rings, going to movies, and (for women) appearing in public without stockings. Because of such definite and, for many, difficult rules, the Holiness churches have backsliders who must be saved and sanctified again and again, and also there are numerous expulsions from the church.

The Baptist Church has this puritanical element to a smaller degree. There are strong feelings against smoking by women and against drinking by any member. Many of the older members do not think it right to attend movies, and the minister could not attend the movies without raising a storm of protest among his parishioners. My own color slides could not be shown in the Sunday School because some of the members associated them with moving-picture shows. Five of the seven men on the Board of Deacons at the Cromwell Baptist Church smoke, but none would approve of the preacher's smoking. And the Cromwell minister himself does not approve of smoking by preachers. He resented it when the pastor of the First Baptist Church, at a Kent ministerial meeting, not only smoked but commented as he did, "I have no lace on my drawers."

More than one mill worker not in the Church of God said that it is all right for Church of God members, both the married and unmarried, to have sexual relations. It is only when they have such relations with those outside the church that they are condemned. Jokes and stories about the promiscuity among Holiness people were passed around by men in the villages, but when asked if the incident related happened in Kent, the one reporting the story always said it occurred somewhere else. It is true that the Holiness people classify all sin on much the same basis, putting sexual laxity on a par with smoking and drinking. The Wesleyan minister said that of course his church considered adultery and fornication to be sins, but at the same time, he said, there is no difference in the "quality" of sin—for example, between the sins of adultery and drinking—for "sin is sin."

The strict observance of Sunday as a day of rest reflects this puritanical orientation. Most mill villagers feel that it is wrong to do any work on that day other than essential household tasks, and Christians are not supposed to play games or engage in other amusements on the Sabbath. As a demonstration of how this ban on Sunday work operates, a member of the Cromwell Baptist Church was "tempted" to do some harvesting on Sunday on the small farm that he had in addition to his mill work. Sunday was a beautiful day after a long siege of bad weather, and he said he would certainly like to go out on the back hill and cut some hay. A fellow church member advised him against it, for, although it sounded sensible, "What's most important is what God writes next to our names up there on the Big Book." And the taboo against playing on Sunday was seen when a group of young girls were attempting to be quiet at a large family gathering. One of the girls suggested they play hide-and-seek, but another objected—they could not, because it was Sunday. The other little girls reluctantly agreed. Breaks are beginning to occur in the strict observance of the Sabbath, however. Some village boys play football and baseball on Sunday without overt disapproval, some men go hunting and fishing then, and a few mill families ride up to Metro City to see a movie. These breaks are regretted by older mill people who are staunch church members. While watching a game of horseshoes being played on Sunday, an elderly mill-hand remarked, "Used to be God's day was better kept than that. The law would put you in jail for sich as that when I was a boy, or at least you would have to pay a fine."

Separation from the "World"

Many religiously oriented mill people, especially those in the Holiness churches, pride themselves on being different from the majority. Instead of doing "worldly" things, such as drinking, dancing, gambling, smoking, and going to movies, a person who attempts to be "holy" is interested in "godly" things, like attending church, becoming sanctified, being led by the Spirit, praying, and reading the Bible. Mrs. Fannie Hall, devout member of the Wesleyan Church, said that when she first became a Christian she saw no harm in using make-up. But a fellow member explained to her why she should not, the reason being that if she did so she could not be distinguished from worldly people. To Mrs. Hall "that made sense, and I haven't used none since."

Not only must worldly habits be given up, but sometimes one's friends and even one's family must be forsaken if one is to become a Christian, particularly a Holiness Christian. The Wesleyan Methodist minister several times referred to the necessity of leaving his friends and their worldly activities when he became a minister. His four closest friends tried to dissuade him from joining the Holiness people, but without avail. "The last I ever saw of any of them," he said, "was when one came by my house to pick up a necktie he had left there." The Church of God pastor said that he had to leave his family when he became a member of his church. His mother objected strongly to his joining with "that ignorant class of people down at the Church of God." But the preacher said he listened to God rather than to his family.

Key Bible verses used by the Holiness groups as a basis for separation from the world are found in II Corinthians 6:14-18, 7:1:

> Be ye not unequally yoked together with unbelievers: for what fellowship hath righteousness with unrighteousness? And what communion hath light with darkness? And what concord hath Christ with Belial? or what part hath he that believeth with an infidel? And what agreement hath the temple of God with idols? for ye are the temple of the living God: as God hath said, I will dwell in them and walk in them; and I will be their God, and they shall be my people. Wherefore come out from among them, and be ye separate, saith the Lord, and touch not the unclean thing; and I will receive you. And will be a Father unto you, and ye shall be my sons and daughters, saith the Lord Almighty. Having therefore these promises, dearly beloved, let us cleanse ourselves from all filthiness of the flesh and spirit, perfecting holiness in the fear of God.

Holiness members take the command "Be ye not unequally yoked together with unbelievers" to mean that they should not join organized groups outside their churches. Even taking out membership in a community concert series is thought to violate this injunction. An example of the importance and application of this directive is found in a story in the March 13, 1949, issue of the *Sunday School Banner*, a weekly paper for young people published by the Wesleyan Methodist Publishing Association. A young girl, Lola, wanted to marry a man who was not a Christian (as defined by the Wesleyan Methodists) and who drank occasionally. She was dissuaded from doing so by a neighbor whose unfortunate experience with a husband who was not a "born-again Christian" led her to poverty and unhappiness. In deciding not to marry the non-Christian with whom she was in love, Lola said, "I will obey my Lord who knows best, and will not be unequally yoked with an unbeliever."

Rejection of the world makes Christians unpopular with worldly people, and those seeking to be unworldly reflect what might be termed a persecution complex. From his pulpit the Church of God minister stated, "Some people thinks us Holiness people is ignorant and shout and carry on too much. But it don't take no college education to love the Lord, no sir, and we shout and sing because we love the Lord. They's some of the ignorantest people ever I seen in the fine houses in Kent, that is, ignorant in spiritual things." The Wesleyan preacher has said more than once, "Nobody that walks close to God is well liked by the crowd. The Lord's people are not very popular nowadays, but one of these days we're gonna rule the world."

Role and Status of the Preacher

The preacher is a man called of God. This "call" is the result of an intense, personal experience when the person hears God speak directly to him, telling him to preach the gospel. The Baptist preacher had been working in cotton mills for fifteen years when he received his call: "It was like when God spoke to Elijah, not in the whirlwind, nor in the lightning and thunder, but in a still, small voice. Satan spoke to me, too, and asked whether or not I was sure it was God and not someone else calling me. He asked me, 'Supposing you do go ahead and preach but find out when you die that God hadn't called you after all?' I told Satan that even if I went to hell for it, I would go ahead and preach. And Satan hasn't bothered me none since." The authority of the preacher to speak to the people comes from the belief that God continues to direct him, just as He did in the "call." Sermons are not written out beforehand, for it is believed that if the preacher reads the Bible and listens for God, he will be told what to preach.

The preacher has a status different from that of anyone else in the villages. All of the preachers in the Kent mill churches at one time worked in a cotton mill, but their "call" set them apart as "the Lord's anointed." They dress differently from the average workmen by wearing a coat, white shirt, and tie, even on weekdays. They are dignified and use no curse words, and their very presence is a signal for good behavior on the part of others. A group of mill workers told with great relish how on a fishing trip one of them forgot that the Wesleyan minister was along and broke forth with, "Goddamit, I tore hell out of my ass on that damned old nail." The others immediately quieted him, reminding him of the preacher's presence, and he was greatly embarrassed. The Baptist preacher, complaining that women in the church were beginning to smoke, told of how he visited a fourteen-year-old girl who was sick. She had not expected the preacher and was smoking a cigarette when he came into the room. "She turned as red as far [fire]," the preacher said, "and almost set the bed on far trying to hide the cigarette."

"The Lord's anointed" is not free from criticism, however. Some of the older mill people think it is wrong for him to be paid for preaching. They recall how in former days the preacher supported himself by farm or mill work, just as Saint Paul and Jesus worked for their living. The older people also criticize present-day preachers for relying too much on education. A man of about seventy had this to say: "I believe in a man preaching what God tells him to preach. He has to feel the Spirit calling him, and he can't get that out of no book. Nowadays, preachers is taught like learning a trade, and they preach without having real religion. But our preacher is a good preacher even though he's educated." He was speaking of the Baptist pastor, who had had two years of high school and special courses by correspondence.

If preachers ever break religious-conduct taboos, they come under severe censure. One Holiness minister was caught "squeezing" one of the teen-age girls during an outing of a young people's group. Several members of the church, led by the girl's father, demanded the removal of the pastor, and he had to take a church in another town. Another Holiness minister had not paid his rent for several months and his landlady demanded her money. He told her with great indignation that she had insulted one of God's angels, whereupon she replied that if he were one of God's angels, she would certainly hate to meet someone who was a devil. The mill people strongly criticized this preacher for not paying his bills, and he too had to leave his church.

Satan and Evil

Members of the mill churches believe that the Devil or Satan is the personification of evil and is as much alive and at work as God. The world is a battleground in which God and the Devil strive for each individual soul. It would appear that the Devil wins most of the time, for the mill folk believe that more people are on their way to hell than to heaven. In testimonies and in prayers, in Sunday School lessons and in sermons, the Devil is depicted as tempting men and women to do the wrong thing by enticing them and tricking them. Personal struggles with the Devil are related in vivid terms, how he tried to keep someone from church, or tried to get someone not to go into the ministry, or led someone to commit adultery. While the Devil is blamed for leading people astray, the individual who succumbs to his wiles is also held responsible. While no one can avoid completely the temptations of the Evil

One, he can be helped from yielding if he calls on Jesus. At the same time the evils of the world are attributed to the Devil, "who is stronger today than ever." There is hope and assurance for the righteous, however, because Christ will return in the clouds and whisk them away to everlasting happiness. The final outcome of the battle between God and the Devil is never in doubt, for eventually God will triumph.

Sincerity in Religion

The rules of religion are taken very seriously. Those who commit sin, as defined by their congregations, admit they are not real Christians. Mill people who said that they did not belong to or attend a church frequently added that the reason was that they were not living as they should. A man in the Townsend village lives with a woman to whom he has never been married, and he goes on weekend drunks. When asked what church he attended, he replied: "I used to belong to the Baptists out in the country, but there ain't no use in me a-going to any church until I start living right." We have already seen the defense mechanism used by some nonchurchgoers to the effect that many in church are worse than they. They hold that at least they are honest, while many who go to church are "Sunday Christians," sinning all during the week and being good on Sunday. To them, the "Sunday Christians" are hypocrites in addition to being sinners. To the mill people, religion means living in accord with certain definite, easily discerned rules. Those who do not live according to the rules should either change their way of living or get out of the church. Members have been expelled from all the mill churches, far more from the Holiness churches than from the Cromwell Baptist. But rather than waiting for expulsion, a miscreant usually stops going to church when he becomes involved in wrong doing.

Members take seriously the injunction to give a tenth of

their income to their church. Tithing is expected of every true Christian, and among the Holiness people, with their frequent special offerings, more than a tenth is given. The fact that the mill people can support three full-time pastors and maintain three church buildings attests to their high per capita giving. The incentive for tithing is related to punishment and reward, both in the present life and in the life to come. Sermons on tithing try to show that people who give the Lord his due prosper, while those who "withhold" from the Lord suffer. Former tithers are quoted as saying, "We always had more money when we tithed." Examples are given of men who were punished for not tithing: a man was severely injured by a mule a short time after he said he could not tithe; another nontither lost everything in a fire. On the other hand, a young boy who raised a hog and gave a tenth of the meat to his preacher was able to raise an even fatter and bigger hog the following year.

Reward and Punishment

Mill people are convinced that God continually rewards and punishes people in much the same manner as in the biblical accounts of the wrath of God, e.g., the victory and plague sent to the Israelites. An epidemic, a death, destructive storms, ravages of the boll weevil, these and other occurrences not readily understood are "explained" as the result of the displeasure of God. On the other hand, victory in war, a narrow escape from death, a sudden stroke of good fortune, these are interpreted as evidence of God's approval.

During a recent polio epidemic in Kent, prayers were offered in the churches for a speedy end to the spread of the disease, and for God to let the people know what they were doing wrong that they should be made to suffer so. An elderly man said that the disease was a visitation from God on parents for not bringing up their children right. The Baptist preacher disagreed, saying that punishment of the children for the sins of the parents had been set aside by certain Bible verses:

In those days they shall say no more, the Fathers have eaten a sour grape, and the children's teeth are set on edge. But every one shall die for his own iniquity: every man that eateth the sour grape, his teeth shall be set on edge. (Jeremiah 31:29–31.)

The preacher went on to say that polio had never become really bad until the March of Dimes dances were held to raise money to combat polio. God did not approve of these dances, and he sent more polio than ever to show his displeasure.

Personal misfortune is often attributed to God's wrath. A woman who is an ardent member of the Wesleyan Church was greatly upset when both her son and husband were "roaring drunk" one weekend. "Whatever could I have done," she asked, "for God to bring all this on me?" At the same time she prayed continually that God would not let her son and husband rest until they gave up drinking. When they began to complain to her that they were feeling restless much of the time, the woman was convinced that this was the result of her prayers. She added, "I'm not a-gonna let up praying, no matter how hard God gives it to them, until they change their low ways of living."

Anyone who denies the power of God to touch individual lives through prayer or in other ways is taking unnecessary chances and just inviting trouble. Carl Jones, a twenty-three-year-old veteran of World War II, told of a soldier in his company who claimed that God could take no credit for his having gone through the war safely. He had never called on God for help, and he had not even prayed before and during battles. The mill hands listening to Jones agreed that the soldier "was jes' too smart for hisself." One said that God might have spared him in order to let him have another chance to repent and act right. Another said that it was the prayers of many mothers at home that saved him. All agreed that the soldier's attitude was not only despicable but dangerous as well.

A short homily in the Cromwell Baptist Sunday Bulletin illustrates and supports the mill explanation of why God does not always punish directly:

> An atheist challenged God to strike him dead in five minutes. When the five minutes had passed, he jeered to his audience, "What did I tell you!"
> A woman standing by asked, "Sir, have you any children?"
> "Yes, why?"
> "Well, if one of them handed you a knife and said, 'Daddy, kill me,' would you do it?"
> "Why, no," replied the astonished man. "I love them too much."
> "That is exactly why God did not strike you dead," said the woman. "He loves you too much."

In one of his sermons, the Church of God preacher predicted, "There's gonna be a funeral around here," implying that certain Kent people who were criticizing the Church of God would be struck down by God. "God won't just stand around and let his people be talked about like that. I'm sorry for those people, that's all. But it's their own fault."

The consensus is that prayer is answered by God if offered earnestly and continually. "It may require several years for an answer to come, or it might be after the person praying had done passed away, but God will answer prayer," was the way a widow of sixty put it. Numerous incidents were related of how specific prayers have been answered. Mrs. Emma Allen told of a time when she had not heard from her daughter for more than a month, and she had no idea where her daughter might be. One night she prayed long and earnestly that God would help her find her girl. That night, shortly after her prayer, the telephone rang, bringing a call from a distant city. It was the daughter, saying she just could not sleep for thinking of her mother and that she would soon be on her way home. Mrs. Allen said this was a certain sign that her prayer had been answered.

RELIGION AND NEED

These religious activities and beliefs indicate that certain needs of the mill people are being met through such channels, and logical deductions can be made concerning the relationships between religion and need. Although difficult to test, they are suggestive of why the customs in the religious area are maintained, and they can therefore contribute to an understanding of these customs.

Adjustment to Death

Religion in the mill-village subculture, as in all cultures, affords an adjustment to the unknown portions of the environment, including (1) the forces at work in the world that appear stronger than man and (2) the inevitability of death. Mill-village religion teaches that God is the ultimate force in the universe, and, although he might be challenged by Satan, he is really the Lord of life and of death. God rewards or punishes people, both in this life and the next, depending on whether they live according to Christian precepts. Mill people believe without question that these precepts are revealed in the Bible, especially in the teachings of Jesus, and as long as they follow them they can be assured that death will be a great victory. It is true that mill religion itself creates deep anxieties [5] by maintaining that everyone is a sinner, by birth, by "nature," and by practice; everyone, therefore, is doomed

---

5. See Gillin, *Ways of Men*, p. 230, for an elaboration on anxiety as a secondary or acquired drive. Although it is true that all known societies have anxiety about death, mill-village people hear repeatedly about the terror of death for the unsaved, and this no doubt increases such anxiety.

to an eternal hell of punishment unless he can be saved. But at the same time, everyone has open to him the path of salvation through repenting of sins and believing that Jesus is God's son, the saviour from damnation in the afterlife. It is true that one can backslide and be threatened with eternal punishment if he does, but salvation is readily available for those who wish to seek it, later if not now.

Compensation for Low Economic and Social Status

Mill-village religion emphasizes the rewards of the life to come for the faithful. The present life is not nearly so important as the one in the future, and worldly rewards are not comparable to heavenly ones. Christians are only pilgrims passing through this world of sin, and heaven is their real home. The sufferings and trials of the present are, in effect, a testing of those worthy of a future life of happiness. So the concern is not to build up wealth and status on earth, but rather to do so in heaven, "where neither moth nor rust doth corrupt, and where thieves do not break through nor steal." In heaven the faithful will have "a robe of pure white," in place of their "old tattered garments," and they will live in "a mansion on Glory Square" instead of in a small, crowded mill-owned house from which they can be evicted. We have seen, especially with the Holiness people, how they have repudiated the "world" and equated the secular order with something evil. The Holiness members speak of themselves as "the saints of Kent." In their own minds they really have a higher status than those town people who own large houses, make large salaries, and play important roles in the affairs of the town. Excluded from town social circles, they set up their own standards of exclusion, in regard to both town and mill. They exclude from their fellowship those who engage in worldly amusements, and in the place of the social and economic status denied them by the world, they substitute spiritual status.

Feeling of Individual Worth

Not only does mill-village religion help to promote the feeling of group importance, but it also gives the individual a feeling of worth. Inherent in the mill-village interpretation of Christianity is the belief that every person, no matter what his ability or accomplishment, is of infinite value and concern to God and to Jesus. The church is deeply interested in the soul of each person and in the desire that each person live "right." Every individual is considered valuable and important from the simple fact that he is a human being, a "child of God." No matter what his sense of failure or shortcoming, a person can find solace and comfort in Christianity.

The Church of God goes to the trouble of driving its bus to all parts of Kent in order to give a ride to those who do not have other transportation. Preachers visit homes and show interest in all members of the family. Sometimes there is resentment of preachers who put on too much pressure or count numbers in order to enhance their own prestige. But these preachers are abusing their position, and "true Christianity" clearly evinces interest in a person for his own sake, or, perhaps, for his soul's sake.

Opportunity for Self-Expression

Religion, through organized churches, gives an opportunity for self-expression. The mill churches offer to a people on the periphery of participation in community affairs of Kent a chance to have their own organizations and their own buildings, to call their own pastors, and to staff their own Sunday schools. Local leadership was needed in the Cromwell Chapel before the mill churches were founded, but this was always a project directed by the downtown churches and the mill superintendent. It was not a movement among the mill people themselves.

The Holiness churches, especially, give opportunity for emotional expression. Testimonies, prayers, receiving the "rapture," singing swingy hymns—all of these things allow for an emotional release along paths highly approved by a tightly knit in-group. Young people are attracted to the lively Holiness services, which do not have "draggy old preachers" and where one can get up and move around during the meeting. The numerous revivals and prayer meetings provide a form of recreation for those who cannot engage in the "worldly" pursuits of dancing, movies, and drinking. Numerous church organizations give leadership roles that are readily filled and chances for participation by women who have few outlets for expressing themselves outside of their families and mill work.

It is true that Kent mill people are rather repressed emotionally and tend to avoid responsibility of leadership. To arouse them to overt expression at a revival or other church meeting is not easy, but once they are stirred up, they appear to enjoy emotional expression. Although most of them are reluctant to take over the duties of teaching a class or filling a church office, enough of them can be persuaded to provide the necessary leadership. After they are in such positions, they seem to enjoy them.

Using Leisure Time

CHAPTER 7   THE RURAL HERITAGE OF mill people is reflected in their favorite uses of leisure time. The majority of men are enthusiastic hunters and fishermen. Relatives visit each other almost every weekend if they live within the county, and they get together for various activities during the week if they live in Kent. Gardening, raising hogs and chickens, crocheting, informal visits with neighbors, women's auxiliary meetings at the church, and a strong preference for square dancing and hillbilly music parallel the rural pattern. For its part, the town has brought in the radio, movies, television, a swimming pool, pool rooms, and school activities.

Outdoor Sports

Hunting and fishing are highly popular forms of recreation among the men of the Kent mill villages. The woods around Kent have rabbits, squirrels, and 'possums in fair abundance, and suitable hunting spots are within a few miles of the town. Restrictions have been placed on hunting by farmers who claim that their crops are damaged by careless hunters, and mill people are careful to hunt only on the property of those who do not object or to get permission before hunting elsewhere. Ardent hunters raise their own hunting dogs, mainly beagle hounds and 'possum dogs, and they prefer the type of hunting in which their dogs give chase to the quarry. They take great pride in the keenness and ability of huntings dogs and in the range and accuracy of shotguns.

Mill villagers like 'possum hunting best, which also indicates the motivation of sport for sport's sake. These hunts begin shortly after dark and sometimes last all night. Some men brag about having gone directly from the hunt to their work in the mill. The hunt is organized almost on the spur of the moment, although it is generally understood during the hunting season that a hunt will be held on weekends if the weather is good. Several men are rounded up, the dog placed in the trunk of the car or in a specially designed trailer, and the group moves off to a likely spot. A typical hunt includes five or six men and two or three teen-age boys. The dog is turned loose in the woods, and the hunters sit around on logs, waiting for a sign that the dog is on the trail of a 'possum. While waiting they munch on pecans, "nigger toes," and peanuts, and perhaps they will drink, depending upon their religious affiliation. They swap "tall" tales and "dirty" stories, related only in the presence of men. When the hound begins to bark as though it were on the trail of a 'possum, the hunters cut short their talk, jump to their feet, and run rapidly in the direction of the barking. The trail might lead across streams, over ploughed fields, and through brambles and burrs. Sometimes a chase lasts three or more miles before the baying of the hound can be heard indicating he has treed a 'possum. When the hound and tree and 'possum are located, the 'possum is shaken out or knocked out with a stick. It is picked up by the tail, thrust into a gunny sack carried by one of the teen-age boys, and the hunt continues. Sometimes the hound gets too far ahead of the hunters and becomes lost, and it might take the rest of the night to find it. Some of the villagers eat 'possum meat, but most do not like it. More often the 'possums are turned loose deep in the woods, so that they might be hunted again.

The backwater of the Iroquois River provides numerous fishing places well stocked with bass, carp, perch, and bream. Several mill families, usually three or four related families co-operating, have rented property along the banks of the backwater from the Prince Power Company for thirty dollars a year and have constructed rough log cabins for overnight stays. From wartime wages some of the mill workers were able to buy boats and motors, but the majority of those who fish do not rent property, and their boats are ones they have made themselves and are propelled by homemade paddles.

Seining is typical of the energetic type of fishing preferred by millhands. It is done either at night or in the early morning, in a season when the weather is warm enough to permit the men to remain in the water several hours. A group of seven or eight men, composed basically of relatives and near neighbors, will decide on a seining trip a short time ahead and drive out to the backwater, about fifteen miles away. The cost of the automobile ride is shared by the group, each person giving enough for the price of a gallon of gasoline. Both going to and coming from the seining places the group will stop by roadstands for coffee, cokes, candy, beer, or cigarettes. Seiners must go in and out of the water numerous times, so that they have to wear two or more shirts and old overalls, along with a pair of tennis shoes, as protection against the cold and against snags in the water. The seine, costing from forty to sixty dollars, and the boat are owned jointly by the men. They have made the boats for as little as four or five dollars. The men paddle down the river to a good seining place, usually a clump of willow trees near the river bank. They prefer muddy water because the fish are more easily surprised. The net, which is usually over a hundred feet long with floats at the top and weights at the bottom, requiring at least six men to manipulate it, is carefully placed in a semicircle around the willows. Two men remain to hold the ends of the net while the others drive the fish into the net, shaking the willow trees and sunken logs as they do so. Then the net is closed, making a complete circle, and the fishermen begin feeling up and down the inside circle of the net. They trap the fish against the sides of the net and must struggle to secure a firm grip on the fish, sometimes getting finned in the process. Turtles and snakes are also encountered while feeling against the net in the muddy water, but rarely is anyone bitten. As many as ten to twenty fish of more than half a pound each may be caught in a single "set." Bass are not legal catch for seiners, but the men find it hard to throw away two- and three-pound bass they have worked so hard to catch. They keep this "illegal" catch in a sack separate from the one with the "legal" fish, hiding the former so that if the game warden happens along, he will not see it. Those catching illegal fish bite them on the tail in order to identify and claim them later. The other fish are divided equally among the group. Seiners are not popular with fishermen who rely on rod and reel because of the noise they make and their large catches. Laws have been threatened in the state legislature to outlaw seiners, but these have never been passed. The mill men might very well let their vote be decided for a candidate sympathetic to their modes of fishing. Seining trips last from six to seven hours or they might be all-night affairs if the men are in a suitable place for making coffee. As on hunting trips, the men carry on constant banter with one another. They tease each other about being too lazy to paddle, or too fat, or too thin. All such kidding is good natured, and there is no scolding or angry outburst if one of the fishermen makes a miscue. Much of the joking is the type that men use only in male company. Typical is the reply to a question about a dilapidated cabin on the far bank of the river: "Why, that's a whore house where they give curb service." The depth of the water is "pecker high," and "it's really not so cold until it hits your balls; then, man, oh man!"

Baseball is the most frequently played organized game in the villages and the only one many of the villagers are interested in. Football and basketball are popular with the school-age group, and more and more mill people are beginning to attend Kent High School football and basketball games. But baseball predominates, and the Kent town baseball team, which plays in an amateur county league, is made up largely of mill boys. The games are played at the Cromwell field and attended mostly by mill workers and their children. Uniforms for the team are furnished by downtown firms, including the whisky stores, which advertise their names on the uniforms. The games are free, but a voluntary collection is taken by passing a hat among the audience along about the fifth inning. Some of the men spectators drink during the game, going behind a clump of bushes or behind a car to do so. Few townspeople attend these contests, perhaps because they consider them largely mill affairs. Throughout there is good-natured razzing of the opposing team, and joking comments are made to the Kent players when they make errors. The umpire is given a difficult time by both teams and by the spectators, and this is expected by all involved.

Sports such as golf and tennis are looked upon with contempt by most mill workers, for they believe that only "sissies" and townspeople play them. One mill worker expressed it thus: "I don't see no sense in trying to knock a little ball in a hole with a stick or in standing in the same little space and knocking a tennis ball back and forth." Swimming has always been popular but used to be limited to dammed-up creek water or to the backwater of the river. Recently Kent has opened a municipal swimming pool to which the younger mill villagers go several times a week during the summer months.

Gardening

At least half the mill families have vegetable gardens and raise chickens and hogs. If a mill house does not have enough land surrounding it for gardening, land can be shared with a neighbor. The number of gardens increases during a slump in textiles. Corn, green beans, lima beans, lettuce, tomatoes, onions, sweet potatoes, beets, cabbage, and turnips are among the vegetables raised. The older people plant their vegetables according to the phases of the moon, and they slaughter their hogs in the "dark" of the moon, so that the meat will not curl up when cooked. One of the men reported that he did not bother to follow the signs when slaughtering a pig for someone else, but when he himself was to use the meat he was very careful to observe the signs. The younger mill workers, thirty-five and under, however, pay no attention to the lunar phases.

Mill people are generous with their vegetables and meat, and they send friends baskets of vegetables or several pounds of sausage. Some of them smoke their meat, but the majority take their freshly slaughtered animals to the community freeze plant to be cut up and kept at low temperature. The cost of this service is four cents a pound per month.

Primary responsibility for the gardening and hog raising falls to the husband, but the wife and children help. In preparing the ground for seed, a mule and plough are often borrowed from a relative or friend in the country, or, if the garden is small, a hoe is used. A few families have cows, but there is not much pasture land available. While this small-scale vegetable and animal raising is a valuable means of increasing income, generally the mill people regard it as recreational in distinction to "work."

The front yards of many of the mill houses are bordered with flowers, and flowers are sometimes planted in the outside rows of vegetable gardens. Some of the women regret that they cannot have flowers, however, "because there are so many youngsters on the mill hill who tromp them down." About as many men as women raise flowers.

Visiting

Visiting is a universal form of recreation among the mill villagers. Most of it is informal. A housewife will drop by her neighbor's, using the back door rather than the front, chatting while her neighbor continues her housework. A family out for a walk will stop and "set a spell" on the front porch with neighbors. Mill houses are readily accessible, and neighbors are friendly and seem always to have time to talk a while. Rarely are refreshments served during visits, but if they are, the visitors are invited to the kitchen for coffee, cold drinks, cake, or pie. Inviting a guest back to the kitchen is a way of making him "home folks" and indicates intimacy. When visitors get up to leave, they invariably say, "Come on home with us," often shortened to "Well, you all come," or just "You come." "You come" is so well established a phrase that it is used as a part of the invitation on the bulletin board standing before the Cromwell Baptist Church.

On weekends relatives have all-day visits during which meals are served. On special occasions, such as birthdays, reunions of the immediate family, or a visit from the preacher, elaborate meals are prepared. All the women, both visitors and residents, help to prepare the food while the men sit in the front room talking. A typical meal loads the table with many kinds of dishes: fried chicken, sliced roast pork, sliced ham, lettuce salad, potato salad with hardboiled eggs, string beans (cooked with fatback), biscuits and butter, iced tea with lemon. Desserts are especially numerous, with as many as seven being served at the same meal. They appear to be brought on for display as well as for food, and they might include two or more three-layer cakes (pineapple, cocoanut, and chocolate are most popular), banana pudding (a favorite among mill people), fruit cocktail, jello and whipped cream, two or more pies (custard and lemon are the most common). Often the group on such occasions is so large that they must eat in shifts.

The men eat first, while the women wait on them. Then the women and children eat. Apparently these elaborate customs of eating are direct carry-overs from farm life and are a form of conspicuous consumption.

These findings on visiting are quite similar to those reported by S. W. Hutton in her study of a mill-village section of Greer, South Carolina:

Of particular interest is the pattern of behavior followed in a social visit. In some communities women drop in for tea, or they call and inform the person they are coming, or they wait to be invited.... Instead of an announced visit, Mrs. B. drops in for a chat and she more than likely comes in through the back door rather than the front, for the woman being visited is usually to be found in the kitchen or in the back of the house. These women do not consider it necessary to go into the living room and sit down to talk, and it would be rather unusual if the woman visited entertained her visitor with other than conversation. Nor is it a practice among the people to have neighbors over to eat meals. Only two women out of the sample [of 75] had neighbors who ate meals with them. On the other hand, it is very common for relatives to have meals together. One family in particular gathers at least once a week for a meal. This family is composed of sisters and their husbands. Most of the relatives who come for meals are of the immediate family—sons, daughters, or parents. There are times when relatives come to visit for several days or as much as two weeks. These longer visits are usually from relatives who live outside of the Greer area.[1]

Reunions and Holidays

Special occasions, such as the birthday of a grandfather or grandmother, Mother's Day, a funeral, Christmas, the Fourth of July, or a wedding anniversary, are marked by fam-

1. Social Participation of Married Women in a South Carolina Mill Village, pp. 51-52.

ily reunions of fifty persons or more. One such occasion was the annual gathering on July 4 of the Watson kindred group, composed basically of ten brothers, three sisters, and their wives, husbands, and children. Altogether seventy were present, including more distant relatives and friends. The reunion was held on the Iroquois River at a rough cabin built by the Watson brothers on property rented from the Prince Power Company. A small pier, also built by the brothers, was used as an embarkation point for two motor boats owned by the brothers, and swimmers used the pier for diving into the water. After several hours of swimming and boating, attention was turned to the meal being prepared. This consisted primarily of a stew, made from thirty-nine pounds of beef and several pounds of corn and onions, cooked by one of the brothers. The beef came from cattle raised and slaughtered by another of the Watson clan and stored in the community deep-freeze locker. The stew was cooked in a large, three-legged black pot, the kind commonly used by mill people for boiling clothes when laundering. White "store-bought" bread, dill pickles, iced tea, and hot coffee rounded out the menu. The Watsons carried on a bantering relationship with one another throughout the afternoon. They played with all the children and teased each other about incidents in their childhood. There was no drinking, either in the open or behind bushes. Most of the Watsons do not drink, but even if they did, it would have been considered improper to have taken a drink in the presence of women and children.

Christmas is an important occasion for family and village celebrations. In fact, Christmas is the single most important holiday among mill people. Preparations begin several weeks in advance, with encouragement from the Kent Chamber of Commerce and advertisements in the newspapers and over the radio. In 1948, Christmas lights were strung up by the town in early December, and a large fir tree in front of the courthouse was decorated. Santa Claus arrived officially in a Christmas parade on December 3. The parade consisted of four floats, two bands from Stone Valley, and several beauty sponsors from Kent and nearby towns. Almost all the mill people attended, especially those with children. Each mill home had a gaily decorated Christmas tree, placed in the corner of the front room with curtains and shades drawn back so that the tree lights could be seen from the street. It is customary to go in to see and admire the trees of one's relatives and near neighbors. Gifts are piled at the base of the tree and given out on Christmas Eve and Christmas Day. Parents buy their children the best presents they receive during the year: skates, bicycles, wagons, fountain pens, clothing, electric trains. One father spent nearly a hundred dollars on his two-year-old son, and another saved two unemployment compensation checks to spend entirely on his children. Young children anticipate these gifts far ahead of time and are on their best behavior in order that Santa Claus will bring them what they want, for they are taught to believe implicitly in him. The kinship group is included in the gift list. One housewife, for example, gave thirty-three gifts to her brothers and sisters and their offspring. Husbands and wives exchange practical gifts, such as clothing, refrigerators, stoves, washing machines, and radios. Christmas dinner is an elaborate affair and follows the pattern of the special meals described earlier. Each of the mills gives recognition to Christmas by granting a week or more of holidays. In 1948, the Cromwell Company gave a bonus check, averaging fifteen dollars per worker, and the Reginold Company gave Christmas parties with gifts of fruit, candy, and clothing for each family. Special programs were held at the schools, and the mill churches had Christmas Eve programs of carols, plays, and exchanging of gifts.

Halloween is a special night for children. The younger ones dress in masks and clown suits, and walk up and down the streets, blowing horns and knocking on doors (since there are very few doorbells). When the owners come to the door, they give the children "treats" of cookies and candies, so they will not play "tricks" on them. The small children stop their activity about nine o'clock, and the older boys take over. Some of their favorite pranks are smearing soap on car windows, throwing rolls of toilet paper over telephone wires, throwing trash on porches, and breaking out street lights. In the past they turned over outhouses, especially those at the Cromwell School, but stiff fines by the mill superintendent have stopped this.

Stork and House Showers

Important social events for mill women, especially those in the Cromwell village, are stork and house showers. A stork shower is a surprise party given for an expectant mother, and is usually arranged by near relatives. A typical shower was one for Mrs. Wills, five months pregnant, given by a cousin, an aunt, and a sister-in-law, all of the Cromwell village. Notices were posted in the women's rest rooms at the mill, on days Mrs. Wills was not working and a day or two before the party. However, almost all who came were relatives and close friends who were invited personally. The honoree knew nothing about the party, for all such parties are planned as surprises, "because surprises are so much fun." By 7:30 on Friday evening (chosen because the mill was not running on Saturday) the guests had arrived in the home of the cousin, and then the honoree was lured over on the pretext of seeing a newly installed hot-water heater. When the honoree entered the house, the guests burst forth from an adjoining room, surprising her. Each person attending brought a baby gift, and each present was opened and passed around the room. Most of the gifts were baby clothes: bootees, dresses, knitted caps and sweaters, and diapers. Other items included baby powder, blankets, and small hot-water bottles. Cards or scraps of paper with names written on them served to identify the givers, although no formally printed cards were used. About thirty-five attended, and this was considered an excellent turnout. Prizes were given for unscrambling the letters in such words as "bottle," "cradle," and "diaper," and for the best drawing of a baby. The winners of these prizes, which were inexpensive toys, promptly presented them to the mother-to-be. During the party the women talked about their hard work in the mill and in the home. Some of them spoke of how nervous they had become as a result of so many duties, and the older women described at length the details and effects of their operations. In a lighter vein, the women teased each other, hinting that the stout ones present would be the next for whom a stork shower would be held. They kidded one another about their husbands' showing attention to other women or about the boy friends they had. There was very little gossip of a malicious nature. The party was ended with refreshments of pimiento-cheese sandwiches, chicken salad, toll-house cookies, and coffee.

House showers follow much the same pattern as stork showers. Relatives give a surprise party for the wife of a couple that have secured a mill house of their own. Newly married couples go to live with the parents of the groom or bride. There they have one room and share the kitchen. They are not recognized as a family until they are granted a house by the mill superintendent. A short time after this happens the shower is planned in the home of a close relative and, as in the stork shower, all the women in the mill are invited, those in close association groups receiving a special verbal invitation. Gifts include aluminum pots and pans, electric toasters and coffee pots, sets of drinking glasses, and mixing and serving bowls. Since wives have their own source of income, they usually do not consult their husbands when buying these gifts. As part of the program, humorous recipes are given the honoree by the guests. One might be on how to cook: "Take a can opener and remove the top from any #2 can; pour the contents into a pan, place on the stove, and just hope and pray you don't burn the stuff." Prizes are given for the best recipe and for unscrambling letters to spell various kitchen items. The winners of the prizes turn them over to the honoree.

Organizations

The Kent chapters of the Oddfellows and Woodmen of the World are composed mostly of mill workers. The Oddfellows meet above the Cromwell mill office, and their membership is composed of men who come almost entirely from the Cromwell village. The Woodmen meet downtown above one of the department stores and admit rural men and women, as well as men and women from the mills. Meeting weekly, these groups follow a secret ritual. One of the main attractions of both is their insurance benefits. Only the "better" type of mill worker is invited to join these organizations, and membership brings a certain amount of prestige.

The religious meetings themselves might be thought of as recreation, particularly the revival and prayer services. Young people's groups have occasional outings, and mill women have such church organizations as the women's missionary societies. The latter organization at the Cromwell Baptist Church meets once a month on Friday night for a discussion of missions and stewardship presented from standardized materials. These societies are also responsible for preparing church suppers and refreshments for special occasions and provide the women opportunity for approved social participation.

Radio, Music, Movies

In the more than one hundred mill and country homes where I visited, I found only one which did not have a radio.[2]

2. Television first came to Kent and to the mill-village sections early in 1949. When I left in the summer of that year, two mill homes had TV sets, subject to approval, which were treated as curiosities. Since then, most of the mill homes have acquired them, and the importance of the radio has decreased.

As their favorite programs, mill people listed "string," or hillbilly, music, preaching services, soap operas, and murder and
mystery stories. Housewives often turn on the radio as soon
as they come in from the mill and clean their houses as they
listen to whatever happens to be on the air. Listening to the
radio is an established part of the mill subculture and has never
come under the condemnation heaped upon movies by the religious organizations.

Mill workers' preference for hillbilly music was obvious
in their relative attendance at a concert of classical music and
at a performance of the Thistle-jumpers, a hillbilly radio team
from Metro City. Only two or three mill villagers (high school
students taking piano lessons) attended the concert while
almost the entire audience was made up of mill people when
the Thistle-jumpers appeared. The mill people were unusually
responsive to the hillbilly musicmakers, and they apparently
felt right at home. They cheered and laughed vigorously when
their favorite songs were sung and when a clowning fiddler,
"Hank Thistle-jumper," did tricks and told jokes. Most of the
songs were announced as being from the Hillbilly Hit Parade,
and of the eight songs sung in this group, seven had as their
theme spurned or unrequited love: "I traded a heartful of love
for a handful of kisses," "One has my name, the other has my
heart," "I let my heart fall into careless hands," "Candy kisses,
wrapped in paper, mean more to you than any of mine,"
"Waiting in Old Oklahoma" (for his "darling" who never
showed up), "Lovesick Blues," "Tennessee Border" (where
she broke my heart). Three songs with religious themes were
sung at the close of the program: "Atomic power—it came
from the mighty hand of God," "Let's have a little talk with
Jesus," and "I'm on the Road to Glory." All were sung in the
swingy style of the Church of God hymns. This program is
representative of the type of music mill people prefer and
listen to over the radio.

Movies are a popular form of entertainment, although they

are shunned by Holiness church members and older members of the Cromwell Baptist as sinful. There is one movie house in Kent and a drive-in theater three miles beyond the city limits. Double features shown on Wednesday and Saturday draw the largest number from the mill villages, especially children. Pictures shown then are the kind preferred by mill people—westerns. Serious movies or those with little action are not especially well liked.

Loafing, Gambling, Dancing, Drinking

Loafing at the mill grocery stores or on the downtown street corners or around the pool rooms is an important pastime for the men. Women do not have the time, or do not take the time, to loaf. Loafing groups are highly informal, although the same individuals are usually seen together, swapping stories, listening to baseball games over the radio, or just sitting.

Favorite loafing spots for many of the mill workers are Monk's Billiard Parlor and Bradford's Grill. These places are the hangouts for those who like to play pool, drink, and gamble. Both Monk's and Bradford's sell beer and chasers for liquor bought at adjoining liquor stores. Beer is drunk at the counter or while playing pool, but whisky is taken less openly, usually in one corner of Bradford's or in the rear of the pool room. Monk's and Bradford's, along with Nadine's Dance Hall, are considered the most disreputable spots in Kent, by most of the mill people as well as by the town people.[3]

Monk's place opens directly on Main Street in downtown Kent. It is one of the few buildings having a roof extending over the sidewalk, and men congregate on the sidewalk under this roof. Townspeople consider Monk's a disgrace and would

---

3. Even the mill children do not approve of these places. When they were asked on their compositions what they would do to improve Kent, their most frequent answer (22 out of 92, or almost 24 percent) was that they would do away with the pool room, beer joints, and dance hall.

like to have it removed. Some townspeople will avoid going down the side of the street where Monk's is in order not to have to pass by the group of "roughnecks" usually standing in front of it. At the same time townspeople are quite curious about what goes on in the dimly lighted, smoke-filled, liquor-smelling billiard parlor. The proprietor of Monk's also operates the ABC liquor store next door. He is considered one of the biggest gamblers in town and is said to be "shacked up" with a woman to whom he is not married. His friends say that he takes care of half a dozen bums who hang around the pool room.

Just to the right of the entrance to Monk's, there is a counter over which beer and soft drinks are sold. Five pool tables, each with a fluorescent light above, two pin-ball machines, a "piccolo" or juke box, a coal stove, and benches along the walls make up the rest of the equipment in the room. The walls of the building are dirty, and the floor is covered with cigarette and cigar butts, candy and chewing-gum wrappers, and mud tracked in from the rear lot. A toilet in a small alcove in the back of the room gives forth a strong odor of urine. A door in the rear leads to the back lot adjoining Bradford's Grill. Two large barrels on either side of the rear door collect empty liquor bottles and have to be emptied twice a week.

A game of pool costs five cents a person, and in a nongambling game it is customary for the loser to pay. But among the better players, pool is strictly a gambling affair, and as much as five dollars might be bet on a single point. The most common version is French pool, in which the balls are knocked into any pocket in sequence. But the favorite gambling game is called "points." Six points are possible: the 1, 5, 10, and 15 balls count one point each, and the highest total score and most balls knocked in make up the other two points. "Eight-ball" is another gambling game, and in it the 8-ball is scored last after the other balls have been sunk. In "Kelly" the players draw two numbers, representing the balls they must score, and "Crazy Kelly" is a game in which no sequence is followed and any ball may be knocked in at any time.

Each Wednesday afternoon, which is payday, mill workers gather in Monk's in preparation for poker and dice games. Cars take the men out to secluded spots in the woods, or to a room rented in a nearby town or perhaps in Kent itself. A few mill men are well known for gambling, and tales are told of the large sums they have won and lost. Foremen from the mills sometimes join in these games, although the superintendents discourage them from doing so.

Bradford's is the only "beer joint" in Kent patronized by both whites and Negroes. But the races do not mingle, for the Negroes keep to the rear of the room, and the whites to the front. A long counter with stools, two juke boxes, and two pin-ball machines make up the furnishings of the Grill. On Friday and Saturday, especially, Bradford's is crowded with mill workers and with the "rougher" groups from farms. The men drink beer and whisky, crack jokes, pass around trick pictures of nude women, and occasionally center attention on the Negroes at the far end of the room when a quarrel or "hot" jitterbugging is under way there. Negro women go regularly to Bradford's, and occasionally a white woman will be seen, although she would not be considered respectable. No respectable town person of either sex would appear at Monk's or at Bradford's. Occasionally there are fist fights between those who have had a great deal to drink, and once during my twelve-months' stay there was a serious knifing at Bradford's. But most of the time is consumed in joking among men who have shed their reserve with a few drinks. They do such things as wager who has the longest penis or who can "jerk off" in the shortest time, or who can drink the most liquor without getting drunk. These wagers are talked and laughed about but are not carried out in the Grill.

Friday and Saturday nights at Nadine's Dance Hall and, more recently, at the newly constructed Armory find many of the pool-room-drinking group and their dates dancing. Nadine's is considered "pretty rough," even by those who go there. Others call it the "bloody bucket" of Kent, where it is necessary to take along a pair of brass knucks "if you don't want to get your face smashed in." Such a reputation is exaggerated, although there are continuous drinking and occasional fist fights among those who have become "high." The Armory is considered more respectable and is frequented by high school mill children as well as by older people.

Music at both places is provided by a three- or four-piece band, including a fiddle, bass violin, guitar, and perhaps a piano. Almost all the numbers are square dances done to hillbilly music. Between the strenuous square dances, a juke box plays popular tunes, and some of the younger people jitterbug and fox trot during these intervals. Most of the dancers rest or take time out for a drink then.

At both the Armory and Nadine's drinking is an important part of the evening's entertainment. There is a beer joint adjoining Nadine's where much of the drinking goes on. At the Armory all of the drinking is done outside the dance hall. Sometimes the women join the men, one of the few occasions when men and women drink together, but more often the men go out alone. Outside in the shadows someone passes a pint or half-pint bottle around, and those present drink directly from the bottle, often not bothering to use chasers. In case anyone runs out of liquor, there is always a bootlegger on hand. He is looked up, and those who want a pint or so go with him out to his car. There, usually in the glove compartment, are several pint and half-pint bottles which sell for almost twice the amount charged in the ABC store. Almost all the bootlegging in Kent is done with ABC liquor, which is sold after dark and on Sundays, when the ABC stores must be closed. Mill people say that the police know who these bootleggers are—that in fact almost everyone in Kent knows who they are. Church people complain about them, but no one does anything about them. They must be caught in the actual sale of liquor, and this is difficult, for money transactions are made in the shadows or charge accounts are allowed. Officers are said to make no serious efforts to catch the bootleggers, and, for their part, the bootleggers do not flaunt the law openly. Apparently, the bootleggers serve a felt need, for men do run out of liquor after dark and on Sundays, and bootleggers are their only source. And as a rule mill men cannot keep liquor at home for fear their wives will throw it out. Several men reported that one reason some become drunk before going home is that they feel they have to "kill" the bottle, since they cannot take it home with them.

Several of the women interviewed during the study openly despaired of their husbands' drinking, frequently in their presence. When asked what organizations she and her husband belonged to, a Townsend wife replied that she was a member of the Church of God, "but my husband don't belong nowhere but the liquor store, at least that's where he spends all his time." And from a wife in the Cromwell village when asked about how she and her husband spent their leisure, "All he does is drink, but don't put that in your book." And from her husband sitting across the porch, "You better. If you write about Kent, you got to."

Few women drink openly. One long-time resident reported that "a great many" drank secretly in the pantry with neighboring housewives, but no direct evidence of this could be found. There is no social drinking in homes. One of the women from outside the South who had married a mill worker while he was in the service tried to serve beer in her home but was so severely criticized by neighbors that she gave it up.

A number of mill people complained that there was not very much a person could do in his spare time in Kent, and they blamed much of the heavy drinking and gambling on this fact. The teen-age mill group showed particular dissatisfaction with Kent's recreational facilities. In their compositions they frequently mentioned as a way of improving Kent the need for a teen-age club where parties, dances, and plays could be given.[4] More than one older mill person said that a former recreational leader was greatly missed because she kept the children entertained and off the streets at night, and they thought the mill superintendent should be petitioned to employ another such leader.

Recreation and Need

Recreation is not only a reflection of a rural heritage in many of its aspects but it also meets needs in the semi-urban, mill-village environment. One of the main functions of recreation is that it offers variety and relief from the monotony of mill work. Most mill workers seem to perform their jobs only as a means of securing their weekly pay check without enjoying what they do. Fishing, hunting, gardening, drinking, movies, and revivals offer emotional and physical expression that does not come from the routine of mill work. The machines, the orders of the bossmen, the blowing of whistles, company control of houses and of wages—all of these things are restricting. The forms of recreation affording self-expression and freedom might be considered expressions of what Gillin has termed a primary psychic drive for new experience.[5]

Family reunions, visits and exchange of meals among members of kindred groups, and the kinship basis of a great deal of the recreational activities contribute to the reinforcement of family ties. We have seen that the kindred group forms one of the foundations of security and that almost every phase of mill-village recreation reaffirms family unity. At the same time, neighborhood associations maintain the tightly knit, in-group

4. Out of 92 mill children, 15, or 16.3 percent, mentioned this. It was the second most often mentioned improvement.
5. *Ways of Men*, p. 228. He elaborates, "... we might also call it 'restlessness,' 'desire to escape boredom,' 'the exploratory drive,' 'the activity drive,' and so forth."

feeling that prevails among Kent mill people. Excluded from intimate association with townspeople, they have their own social groups which exclude those outside the mill village. Stork and house showers provide an expression of mutual aid through the presentation of gifts to newly established mill families. Also, groups within the villages exclude other groups, which in turn form their own associations: the Holiness church members, drinking-gambling cliques, the bossmen (who are almost social islands between town and mill).

Success in recreational pursuits affords a basis for prestige that mill work does not give. Men are known as expert 'possum hunters, excellent fishermen, good pool players, or industrious gardeners. These are strong compliments: "He's the best fisherman on the hill." "He can knock the cover off a baseball." "He just can't be beat at 8-ball." "He can down a pint and never feel it." "He knows a thousand jokes." "She's awfully nice and friendly at her parties." There is no overt striving to excel in fields of recreation, however, and it is appropriate for an air of modesty to be assumed. A person who brags or shows much self-confidence in any of these areas comes under censure.

Town, Country, and Mill

CHAPTER **8** KENT MILL PEOPLE ARE American and southern, and as such they share some culture traits with all southern Americans. They have the same national and regional historical heritage, the same national government, the same language, the same religion, and many of the same attitudes of the vast majority of those who live in the South. A Kent mill worker has far more in common with those in downtown Kent than he has with those who live outside America, or even outside the South. The similarities are highlighted when a Kent millhand is compared on the one hand with a prominent Kent citizen and on the other with someone of an entirely different cultural background, for example a textile worker in China. These likenesses must not be lost sight of as we regard the differences between mill people and their town and country cousins.

The customs which make up the way of life in the Kent mill villages differ to such an extent from those of the town and surrounding rural areas that we might consider the village dwellers as forming a subcultural group. Concomitant with the development of this subculture has been the emergence of the mill people as a social class, and the two phenomena appear to be interdependent. What happened in Gaston County, North Carolina, apparently has also happened in Kent County. Liston Pope, in his *Millhands and Preachers*, points out that before the coming of industry there were no clearly distinguishable social classes among the white independent farmers of Gaston County.[1] While this appears to be an oversimplification of the early Kent County social structure, there is little doubt that industrialization brought sharper class divisions, so that three distinct social classes emerged, "clearly separated in geographic, economic, and cultural terms."[2] Pope designates these classes as the town group, the farmers, and the mill workers. Each of these three groups in Kent and its environs may be broken down into several subdivisions,[3] and Negroes compose a separate, castelike subgroup.[4] However, for the purposes of this chapter, it is sufficient in the delineation of class lines to recognize the broad divisions of town, country, and mill, with only a brief reference to the Negro group.

RECOGNITION OF CLASS LINES BY THE GROUPS THEMSELVES

A primary indication of the existence of class distinctions is that those involved think of themselves as different.[5] In general the town and country look down on the mill, and in turn the mill looks down upon the Negro. Our main concern here is what the town and country think of the mill and how the mill feels about the town, the country, and the Negro.

Attitude of Town toward Mill

The keynote in the town's attitude toward the mill is found in this statement by a young person from the upper classes in

1. Liston Pope, *Millhands and Preachers*, pp. 49–69.
2. *Ibid.*, pp. 49–50.
3. Ralph Patrick, in his study of Kent reported in A Cultural Approach to the Stratification System of a Southern Town, designates three subdivisions among the "Blue Bloods," or "Old Kent," and three subdivisions among the "Red Bloods," all of whom are ranked above the mill people.
4. Hylan Lewis in *Blackways of Kent*, a study of Negro life, speaks of two categories of Negroes, the "respectables" and the "nonrespectables."
5. Ronald Freedman, *et al., Principles of Sociology*, p. 461, speaks of this as "class consciousness" or "the degree to which those whose class status is the same are aware of their common status."

Kent: "It makes all the difference in the world whether you are from the mill or from the town." When pressed for what this "difference" might mean, this townsperson said that the two groups comprised different social worlds that seldom overlapped. Boys and girls from the town did not date those from the mill, and Kent adults had very little in common with those in the mill sections.

Town people make a distinction between the mill people who live in the Cromwell village and those who live in the Reginold mill sections, although Cromwell workers are not accepted socially by the town any more than are the other mill workers. Town people agree that the ones who live in the Cromwell village are on a "higher" level—more stable, better educated, and more reliable than those in the Reginold villages.[6] Reflecting the Kent emphasis on the importance of ancestry, one town informant said that the Cromwell people are "old-time Kent County people, from some of the best families in the county." Kent doctors reported that Cromwell people are much more sanitary than the Reginold "crowd," and those who had business dealings with the mill workers agreed that they could talk intelligently with the Cromwell people but that they wanted to hurry away from the Reginold workers, "because they are so dull and uninteresting."

Most of the town people regard mill people, in general, as inferior.[7] The reason mill people are where they are, according to the town, is that they either did not work hard enough on the farm, or have less ability than those who "succeeded," or do not have "get-up-and-go." The stereotype of the mill worker is someone improvident, unambitious, poorly educated, unclean, and on a lower moral level than those who live

6. Patrick, op. cit., p. 8, states that town people tend to think of such workers as "mill people, but not mill type."

7. According to Patrick, op. cit., p. 6, "The Mill People are defined from the point of view of Uptown Kent as innately low in competence, as lazy, unambitious people." But, he adds, "He [a Mill Person] is expected to be moral and dependable, and not to 'live like a Negro.'"

in town. Townspeople agree that mill people get into an unimaginative routine. As one informant put it, "The men do so many hours of work in the mill, walk down to favorite hangout spots to sit around and talk, get 'high' on weekends, and then go home to beat their wives or do whatever else they are accustomed to doing." [8] Mill people, according to those in town, vote as they are told by whoever takes them to the polls, and they are perfect "suckers" for whatever salesman happens along in the villages.

Occasionally a vigorous disparagement of mill people will break forth from town people, although they are usually guarded in their criticism. A Kent doctor dismissed several Reginold patients from his office and with great disgust told the next person who entered (a townsperson), "God damn it, I hate these mill people. They're the dirtiest, nastiest people in the world." Thereupon he raised the window for a few minutes "to let the air clear" before talking to his next patient. On another occasion a man at the top of the town social scale was talking to me in his office when three or four Nielson mill villagers came in. While these workers were sitting where they could clearly hear, he continued his conversation in which he said that those in the Cromwell village were superior to the dirty, unsanitary, and ignorant Reginold workers. There was apparently no respect for the feelings of these people. After the mill visitors had gone, he expressed great relief that he was at last rid of "that horde."

The cleavage between town and mill bothers the consciences of some of Kent's upper-class citizens. One Old Kent lady said that she hated the word "class" because there just should not be any in a true democracy. But she agreed that

8. Like many of the stereotypes town people hold of mill people, this accusation of wife beating was not found to have factual basis. When mill husbands and wives disagree, the most likely reaction of the husband is one of withdrawal, either through drink or merely leaving the house until feelings cool off. What little wife beating I heard of was done by husbands who were drunk at the time.

social distinctions were made between the two groups. Sometimes a sympathetic note will be expressed for the mill workers, blaming the mill owners, especially the Reginolds, for paying low wages and providing poor houses. One person who took the side of the workers said that the entire town would be better off if the standard of living of the mill people could be raised and that the main responsibility for this was in the hands of the mill owners. But this attitude toward mill owners is rare, and most of the town people accept the line between town and mill in much the same way that they accept the line between white and Negro. This was expressed by a lawyer who observed that his daughter, now in the seventh grade, would soon be growing apart from her mill playmates at the town school. As the age for dating approaches, the line between town and mill children becomes more clearly defined. The killing of a rural textile worker employed from time to time in the Townsend mill demonstrates this attitude toward the "lower class" of mill worker in rather extreme fashion. His estranged wife reportedly confessed to the shooting, but a jury composed primarily of town men quickly acquitted her and attributed the killing to "persons unknown" because, according to a county official, with "such people" it was worth neither the time nor the money to try the case.

Attitude of Country toward Mill

The country-mill distinction is practically nonexistent at the tenant-millhand level, for the tenants and millhands share a similar status. We have seen that most of the mill workers were formerly tenants or from the families of tenants and that they still have relatives doing tenant farming. Children of mill workers and tenants intermarry, but marriage does not take place between the offspring of mill workers and those of well-to-do farmers, nor do millhands visit the homes of these farmers. The country attitudes given here are those of the independent farmer and more often of the large-scale farmer rather than those of renters, tenants, and sharecroppers at the bottom of the rural social scale.

These independent farmers in such towns as Phillippi, Lebanon, Gilead, and Shalem look upon cotton-mill workers as tenants and sharecroppers who had failed at farming. The consensus is that they were lazy: they would sit around the stores during the winter, chewing tobacco and spinning yarns rather than repairing their barns and houses and fences and doing other things to keep their farms in shape. "If they had worked as hard the year round on the farm as they do in the mill, they would have been successful in farming." The implication is that these "failures" at the farm had the same chance to succeed as the farmers who are now successful and it is their own fault that they could not make a go of farming, for "anybody who works hard enough and has a little foresight can be a success in farming." Note the attitude of country toward mill in the case of one woman who for financial reasons had to leave the farm and go to the mill, and also how those who left their farms shared the general attitude of farmers toward themselves: This woman, whose husband had died, said, "I knew what I was gittin' into"—that is, that she was lowering herself in the eyes of her neighbors—but she said she could make more by herself working in the mill than she and her children could make on the farm. So she moved the family to Kent, "realizing what everybody would think about me."

When asked directly, successful farmers admit that technological improvements in machines and harvesting methods have probably had a part in forcing some of the tenants and small farmers off their farms. They agree that the day of the one-mule farmer is over, and that to be profitable, farming must be done with machinery on a comparatively large-scale basis. At the same time they say there is still plenty of room for good tenant farmers and that there is, in fact, a shortage of tenants in Kent County. During the wartime boom, beginning in 1940, almost all the white tenants around Kent were attracted into the mills by the high wages and shorter hours of work, so that most of the present tenant farmers are Negroes. With the postwar curtailment in textiles, some mill workers have moved back to farms, usually to help friends or relatives already set up as tenants or as renters. Some of them supplement their two- and three-day mill week with cotton and peach harvesting whenever farmers provide them with transportation to their fields.

Informants say that these mill workers who return rarely stick to the farm. Having once received the weekly pay check, they become dissatisfied waiting until the end of the year before clearing something from the farm. A prominent farmer of Phillippi knows of only one former mill worker who has made a success in his return to farming. Living in the mill village "does something to them." They return with an attitude of suspicion and arrogance, and when trading at the rural stores they act as though they were going to be cheated on each transaction.

These farmers agree that textile workers living in the country are on a low moral level, even allowing their children to steal. One farmer told of a rural mill family that protected their son who had been caught "red handed" stealing from a store. Instead of punishing the boy and teaching him not to steal, they blamed the store owner. Such action contributed to the delinquency of the boy and was typical of the lack of cooperation of this family with the community, the farmer maintained. He continued by saying that dishonest practices had appeared among the tenant-mill group in the thirties when the federal government tried to help these people make a new start of farming by providing them with mules, seeds, cows, and other materials. "Ninety-nine out of a hundred beat the government out of the loan and even slipped their cotton off and sold it." Rural community leaders generally feel that this tenant-mill group is difficult to help because they are not particularly interested in improvement and show no real appreciation when something is done for them. A county welfare worker who has visited numerous tenant-mill families agreed with the farmers, telling about the attitude of many who receive welfare checks: "Oh, I get a small check from the Welfare, but it isn't enough to do much good." The observation of a farmer concerning the shooting of the rural mill worker mentioned above is significant. He remarked that such people were always making trouble and were "just like niggers on Saturday night," and "[killing each other] is a good way to get rid of a few of them."

Those who combine farming with work in such plants as the Stone Valley Printing and Finishing Company are in a somewhat different category from those who work in the regular cotton mill. According to such informants as the county agricultural agent, the former supplement their farm income with semiskilled factory jobs and at the same time carry on their farming with the aid of machinery and helpers, either tenants or children or both. Often their factory work enables them to purchase tractors and other equipment with which they modernize their farming. These part-time industrial workers usually take an active interest in rural community life, in contrast to regular cotton-mill workers who live in rural areas.[9]

Attitude of Mill toward Town and Country

Mill people are aware of and resent the superiority feeling that the town people and successful farmers have toward them. They react by withdrawing into themselves, by ignoring the upper-class groups, and by living an almost completely separate existence. Consequently, they have built up strong in-group feelings, and they are suspicious of all "outsiders" who

9. This concurs essentially with the findings of Dorothy Dickens, "Some Contrasts in Levels of Living in Industrial, Farm, and Part-Time Farm Families in Rural Mississippi," *Social Forces*, 18 (1939–40), 247–55.

enter the villages.[10] I have already told of the difficulties I encountered when first entering the village sections and of the continued suspicion and hostility that faced me during my entire stay. Lack of formal education and insight into the nature of a social study helped to arouse and perpetuate this suspicion, but also the strong in-group feeling contributed to the intensity of it. A nonmill worker from outside the village is considered an "enemy" until he proves himself a friend. Once his friendship is established, however, he is given a warm reception by most of the mill families.

Mill people believe that with wealth come privilege and power not available to the poorer man. When newspaper accounts are given of rich people who have been accused of committing a crime, mill people agree that those accused will not be convicted, "because they'll buy their way out." Judges, police, and others in places of official power can be bribed if a person has sufficient money and influence, but mill people without pull and with only enough money for a bare living cannot secure the same "justice" for themselves.[11] Therefore, they must suffer for things that the wealthier townspeople can get out of. Closely akin to this belief in the power and corruption of the rich is the conviction that a mill person has to be very careful lest he be cheated by someone from the town, an attitude illustrated in this seemingly trivial example: A worker from the Neilson village found a fountain pen guaranteed for lifetime use. The pen needed repairing, and some-

10. This is in substantial agreement with S. W. Hutton, Social Participation of Married Women in a South Carolina Mill Village, p. 69: "... there is an element of repellence in the social interaction of village folk and town folk. There is a feeling of class difference between the two, which has developed from the early days of the cotton mill industry in the area.... Since then, the village folk seem to have retained the feeling, which may be partly imaginary, that outsiders think themselves better and are generally unfriendly."

11. For example, when the governor of Piedmont State pardoned two prisoners who had served only a part of their time, mill workers at the boardinghouse were sure that the prisoners had paid for their freedom by bribing some official.

one suggested that he take it to one of the downtown stores to have it sent off. But the worker refused to do this, saying that he would probably be cheated out of the pen if he did. In this same connection, there is fear of town people once a villager leaves the familiar grounds of his own village. A mill girl walking to town was caught in a sudden rain, and the only way to avoid getting wet was to take cover on a townsperson's front porch. But the girl dared not go up on the porch, because she feared "the woman there would have knocked me clean off the porch if I had." A Neilson woman, looking for my apartment after I had moved from the mill village into the town, was in great fear that she would enter the wrong house "and get into a peck of trouble." This fear is largely imagined, for few townspeople would be openly belligerent to mill workers entering their premises under such circumstances. But the fact that such fear does exist in the minds of mill workers is significant, and it is with attitudes that we are concerned at this point. It is likewise indicative of separation of town and mill that the Neilson woman, although living only four blocks away, did not know who lived in any of the "big" houses. Mill people generally do not know which houses town people live in, and in turn town people do not know who lives in the mill houses. On the other hand, mill people know the names of those who live in each house in their village section, and town people know the names of the residents in each of the town homes.

There is an occasional outburst of resentment by mill people against town people for their supposed and actual superiority attitude. In one of the few overt acts of aggression that came to my attention, a mill worker and a townsman fought with each other because of a derogatory statement the mill worker said the other had made about mill people. The townsperson claimed that he had not intended to be critical and that the mill boy had imagined an insult. Both had been drinking, according to bystanders; otherwise the outburst would not have occurred. When my wife and I moved out of the mill-village section into the town section, one of the more outspoken mill women said that we would probably not return to visit them any more, since "town people don't associate with those on the mill hill." As a rule, however, this resentment is not expressed openly, and mill people react by withdrawing. This was done by three of the young Cromwell women who were attending the women's association in the downtown Methodist church. A bazaar was being planned, and the three women joined in wholeheartedly, soliciting their mill village for donations. They secured a large percentage of the refreshments to be served at the bazaar and raised two hundred dollars. Then they attended the last meeting before the bazaar opened to find out about the hours and to offer to help with the booths. But according to the woman telling the story, they could find out nothing—everyone was vague and evasive and seemed to know nothing definite to tell them. They were never once thanked for their efforts, and two town women took credit for all the work they had done. It was clear to them that they were "not good enough to have a booth" and that they were not wanted at the bazaar, although their donations were acceptable enough. They dropped out of the women's association as a result.

Mill people have an ambivalent attitude toward town people. On the one hand there is resentment, mixed with fear and suspicion, and on the other there is tacit acceptance of the town's verdict that town people are superior in certain respects. Most mill workers apologize for their lack of education when in the presence of someone who has had more education than they. They speak of themselves as "poor" and "ignorant," thereby accepting to some extent the town's evaluation of them. But they would become bitterly resentful if someone from outside their group spoke of them in those terms. And they never really accept the accusation that they are "inferior." They say that as long as a man is honest, sincere, and a hard worker, "he's just as good as anybody else." Their stereotype of the town person is someone, who, despite his power, wealth, and education, is corrupt, haughty, and hypocritical. Therefore, in certain respects, mill people feel themselves to be "superior." Kent mill villagers feel closer to rural people than they do to those who live in town. We have seen that most of them have lived on the farm at one time or another and claim to prefer farm work to mill work. Some of them maintain their rural church connections, and many go back for visits to relatives and former neighbors. Their association, however, is restricted to those in the lower rural social classes.

Some of the older mill people think that the sharp line drawn between town and mill in Kent has become less distinct over the past fifteen to twenty years. The open resentment and hostility of town people, so evident when mill people first came to Kent, have subsided. Mill boys used to "rock" any town boy who came through their village, and they would pick on the sons of bossmen, because they classified them with the town. Overt aggression has ceased in this area, but although the lines are not so clear as they once were, they are still very much present and are recognized consciously and subconsciously by both groups.[12]

Attitude of Mill toward Negro

There is little contact between mill people and Negroes, except for the few Negroes used in menial jobs in mills and for Negro nursemaids employed by mill families during prosperous times. These nurses are engaged by a few families in the

12. It would prove highly valuable to follow up this study of mill attitudes by more direct measurement of the type employed by J. G. Manis and B. N. Meltzer in "Attitudes of Textile Workers to Class Structure," *American Journal of Sociology*, LX (1954), 30–35. They employed open-end questions in interviews with ninety-five male textile workers in Patterson, New Jersey, and found that while saliency of class was generally limited, class awareness was clearly evident and that a majority viewed class as being both inevitable and desirable.

Cromwell in which both parents are working and in which there is no one with whom to leave very young children. They are paid from eight to eleven dollars a week, primarily for "baby sitting." The mill-village sections touch the Negro sections at points, and it is necessary for those living in the villages to walk through the Negro sections when they go downtown. Except for these brief and sporadic contacts, these groups have little to do with each other.

In general, mill people appear to have the same attitude toward Negroes as do the town and country. They regard Negroes as inferior because of their race. Some of the religious-minded mill people quote the Bible to substantiate the claim of Negro inferiority, asserting that the black man was created to be a servant to the white.[13] This is used as an indication that God did not mean for Negro and white to mix socially. Intermingling is taken by villagers to be wrong, even on Northern professional baseball teams, and some mill men say they will not root for teams that have Negro players. Mill people believe that as long as Negroes keep their place, white folks should treat them civilly, but once Negroes begin to think they are as good as whites, then trouble starts. Many objected to President Truman, because "he's for the niggers and wants us to eat with them." The general feeling is that the South has arrived at the best possible solution for "handling" the race problem, and that someone like Mrs. Roosevelt who wanted Negroes to stay at a white hotel in Metro City should be run back up North where she belongs.

Mill people are afraid of Negroes after dark and do not like to walk through the Negro sections at night. Children, especially, fear going through these sections when returning home from a movie or the town school after dark. Mill people say that Negroes carry knives and razor blades and will not hesi-

13. The passage quoted to support this was Genesis 9:25-27 in which the son of Noah cursed and doomed to servitude is assumed to be the progenitor of the Negro race.

tate to "carve someone up." There is fear of Negro burglary and rape of white mill women by Negroes, although I could find no evidence that either of these had happened in Kent. Mill people seem more influenced by the stereotype of the Negro and by newspaper stories than by personal experience. Actually, the relationship between mill people and Negro workers in the mills and in mill homes appears to be a friendly and pleasant one.

There are conflicts in the thought patterns among mill people regarding Negroes. For example, the head carpenter of the Cromwell mill, who has five Negroes working under him, exclaimed one day that all Negroes are lazy and shift-less and require close watching. "Even if they're ten percent or just one percent nigger, it comes out in them." A few days later he had nothing but praise for a Negro helper named Rudy: "I hate to have to admit it, but Rudy is a better worker than most of the white boys who help." Rudy could foresee the next step better than the others, and he could do "three times as much real hard work as any one of them." In one or two cases, workers have gone so far as to say that if Negroes were given the same opportunities as whites, they could do as well as white people. But in each case, the informant hastened to add, "You can't say that to anybody around here without getting your head knocked off." Although this liberal attitude is unusual, it is present nevertheless.

Students of Negro-white relations have frequently pointed out that the deepest prejudice against the Negro is held by the Southern white at the bottom of the social and economic scale.[14] They maintain that the Negro remains the only group which the "poor whites" can look down on and that they do so to enhance their own ego.[15] However, no evidence was

14. Gunnar Myrdal makes this point in *An American Dilemma* (New York: Harper and Brothers, 1944), pp. 597–98.
15. Pope, *op. cit.*, p. 69, states: "The mill worker, with nobody else to 'look down on,' regards himself as eminently superior to the Negro. The colored man represents his last outpost against social oblivion."

found in the textile villages of Kent that there is considerable difference between the attitude of millhands and that of town and country toward the Negro. In some ways town and country appear more determined than mill to keep the Negro in his place. They are more aware of the possible consequences if Negroes, making up about 40 percent of the population of the county and a majority of some counties of the state, are allowed to vote—perhaps to elect representatives of their own color and thereby threaten white supremacy. Mill people are still somewhat skeptical about politics and have only recently begun to take an interest, as we shall see later. Of course we cannot predict how the Kent mill workers would react if ever the Negro became a serious competitor for his mill job. With more than enough whites to fill the jobs in the mills and with Negroes excluded from all but the most menial or outside tasks, there is no competition at present. When a Neilson worker was asked what would happen if Negroes began working in the mills, he replied that all the white people would walk out. The C.I.O., on the other hand, claims that from a survey made in a Stone Valley mill, men would not object to working with Negroes on any job in the mill but that they would not like their women to work alongside a Negro man. During the C.I.O. effort to organize the Reginold mills, the owners posted pictures showing white and Negro working together in mills with the caption "This is what the union wants." The fact that the attempt by the Reginolds to play up the race problem as a tool against unionization did not have the desired effect of discouraging organization is significant. One of the mill workers joining the union was a Negro, and he was readily welcomed by the whites who also joined.

Mill people are prejudiced not only against Negroes but also against Jews, Catholics, and "foreigners," although there is almost no contact with any of these. Here they deal clearly in stereotypes and not from actual experience. They say: "Too many Jews own cotton mills"; "Catholics worship idols";

"It's the foreigners who are ruining this country." They identify as "Americans" those who are Caucasoid and Protestant, and Jews, Catholics, and foreigners fall into the category of "non-American," along with the Negro. At the funeral of a mill boy killed overseas during World War II, there was much speculation over the possible contents of the sealed casket. One relative remarked, "Why, there might be a German or a Jap or a nigger in that box, and we'd never know it."

SPECIFIC CLASS DISTINCTIONS

In addition to these attitudes which lead town, country, and mill people to regard each other as different and separate, there are several overt distinctions among these three classes. Mill people carry with them certain status symbols—dress, language, and rules of etiquette—which set them apart from town people and, to a lesser extent, from country people. Most of these distinctions seem to stem directly or indirectly from their lower standard of living.

Appearance

Kent mill people vary in manner of dress, but in general, as compared with town dress, their clothes are ill fitting, made of cheap materials, and not in accord with the latest styles. Expensive clothing and careful grooming are not sought-for values among mill people. As a worker in the Neilson expressed it, the reason he liked Kent was because "a body can dress most like he wants to, jes' like in the country."

Most of the week the millhands wear working clothes. For men these consist of overalls or blue jeans with blue cotton work shirts, or khaki shirt and trousers, and low-cut shoes which are no longer good enough for Sunday wear. Women wear cotton print dresses and aprons, and oxfords with low, sturdy heels, or inexpensive barefoot sandals in the summer. Women, in the Reginold villages especially, go barefooted around their immediate neighborhood when weather permits. As a rule few men or women wear hats.

When they go downtown, men put on clean overalls or slacks and a white shirt without a tie. In cold weather they wear wool jackets and wool suit pants, but rarely overcoats. Women wear to town their newest and cleanest cotton dresses, which cost on the average from three to five dollars, and in winter they wear a plain woolen coat over their dresses. The style of these dresses is much the same from year to year. Clothes are purchased most frequently from the "country" store in Kent, where goods are least expensive, or are ordered from Sears, Roebuck. On Sundays, at funerals, and for family reunions, mill people wear their best clothes. Men wear suits with matching pants and white shirts with ties, and women have their hair curled and put on their newest dresses.[16] The Cromwell women dress more expensively and more stylishly than do those in the other villages. A few of the older women wear hats decorated with flowers. Younger people dress more "in style" than do the older, the young women appearing in high heels and the young men in bright suits and ties. However, wearing suits and ties is strictly a once-a-week affair for regular mill workers. One of the few millhands who attends the downtown Presbyterian Church was very embarrassed to find himself there one Sunday morning without a tie. He was so in the habit of not putting one on that he had completely forgotten it. The majority of mill villagers feel that those in town churches dress "too fancy" to suit them, and they feel uncomfortable in their presence.[17]

16. Easter is a special time at which to buy clothing. A Neilson woman considered her eight-dollar dress bought for Easter "a real expensive dress."

17. A man from Cromwell Old Hill went to the Presbyterian Church and sat toward the rear in order to be by himself. "Before I knew it, all those high society folks had done sat down around me, and I felt real bad, dressed as poor as I was."

Cromwell New Hill children can hardly be distinguished from their town schoolmates in dress. But other mill children dress in overalls, go barefoot earlier and longer, and in general are more unkempt than town children. With several children in a family, it is customary for clothing to be handed down to younger children until completely worn out. In a family where there is but one child, clothes are bought a size or so too large so that he can "grow into 'em." Shoes are also bought too large, often two sizes larger than the child wears, and are of the most inexpensive makes.[18]

Permanent waves are considered important for younger mill women and even for eight- and nine-year-old children, particularly in the Cromwell village. Five or six dollars is the average amount spent on a permanent, and usually one a year is felt necessary. Instead of having home permanents, most women prefer to go to the Kent Beauty Parlor. The effect of repeated cheap permanent waves and the infrequent washing of hair often below shoulder length probably contribute to the dull, burnt, coarse, and unkempt appearance of many mill women's hair. Older women allow their hair to grow and roll it into knots on the backs of their heads.

While mill and farm people dress in a somewhat similar fashion, they have a different appearance in other ways. Mill men like to slick their hair down, and they rarely wear hats. Farmers, on the other hand, pay less attention to their hair and usually wear a straw or felt hat. Cotton-mill workers, spending a lot of their time in a closed building, are as a rule pale and sallow, in contrast to the ruddy, sunburned farmers. Nor does the skin of mill people possess the healthy transparency seen among townspeople, but tends, particularly among women, to look thick and coarse-textured. No doubt the lack of care and well-balanced diet is responsible. The

---

18. One Cromwell wife said that she spent as much as three dollars per pair on shoes for her three-year-old son and that this was above the average amount spent by other mill mothers.

crumbling and decayed teeth of many small mill children indicate improper nutrition and inadequate dental care. Poor posture is prevalent among old and young, and few of the women have "good figures." This may be a result of both the nature of their work and the prevailing attitude toward life.

Cleanliness

Teachers in the town school say that one sure way of identifying mill children, especially those from the Reginold mills, is their lack of personal cleanliness. Hands, faces, underclothing, fingernails, as well as outer garments, are not kept clean. Mill people, without bathrooms, find taking a bath a difficult, time-consuming procedure, and neither adults nor children feel compelled to bathe frequently. Workers perspire a great deal in the hot, humid mills, and it is very troublesome to bathe and change clothes completely each time they come from work. Most of the men sleep in the underwear they have been wearing during the day, although more are beginning to use pajamas as town standards become stronger. During months when children go barefoot, they are made to wash their feet before going to bed, and they splash water on their faces when they get up. Brushing of teeth seems to be a haphazard matter. Apparently there is very little prescribed cleaning. Many of the men and women, and also children, use tobacco in some form. Cigarettes, chewing tobacco, and snuff are the favorite forms, and children begin these habits quite early.[19] Mill women do their own laundry, sometimes paying Negro women to help. Three-legged black iron pots are a familiar sight in the backyards of the mill homes, although they are gradually giving

19. A seventeen-year-old boy on Cromwell Old Hill said that he began chewing tobacco at the age of three and has enjoyed it ever since. During my stay in Kent, some eight- and nine-year-old girls in the Neilson began their first snuff-dipping. Mill schoolboys begin smoking long before those from the town do. Parents do not like their children to begin these habits, but they can do little to stop them.

way to electric washing machines where the family has also been able to buy an electric water heater.

Language

Mill people use poor English, according to town standards, and random snatches from their conversation reveal that they pay scant attention to the rules of formal English grammar. Typical mistakes are the use of the double negative, use of the past participle for the complete verb form, and mispronunciation. Some of the conversation of mill people is reminiscent of Snuffy Smith in the comics: "Hit don't make no never mind." "They made me went to school." "Hit don't differ none if'n he ain't done hit yit." "I come in thar and kep' a-coughing and mite'n near a-choked." "Don't dirty yo' dress no wusser." "Whar is you a-gittin' it frum?" "Whar is it at?" Speech in the mill villages is filled with figures from farm life: "as pretty as a speckled pup"; "of no more use than a dead chicken head out in the yard"; "lazy as a old hound dawg that won't scratch her fleas." Mill people have certain common expressions not used by those in town: the mantelpiece is called the "far board" (fire board); the kitchen is sometimes referred to as "stove room"; afternoon is often "evening"; the mid-day meal is "dinner," not lunch, and the evening meal is "supper," not dinner, following the farm pattern. And there are pronunciation peculiarities: air becomes "are," tire is pronounced "tar," hungry is "hongry," and deaf is "deef." Such expressions as "yon side of the street" have the ring of Old English. "Our'n," "his'n," "you'uns," and "we'uns" are mill expressions also used by mountain and country people in parts of the South. Thus mill people are closer to country than to town in their use of language.

Houses and Furnishings

The general appearance and floor plans of mill houses have already been discussed in Chapter 2 and require no further elaboration here (see pages 18-22). Some of the mill homes have overstuffed furniture and woven rugs, but the majority still have cane-bottom chairs, wooden rockers, and linoleum floor coverings. Few of them have separate living rooms, for there is at least one bed in each room in the house except the kitchen. There are no separate dining rooms, and meals are eaten in the kitchen. Wood stoves and oil ranges are the most common types of cooking equipment, although a few of the workers have acquired electric ranges. None of the houses have central heating, but instead they have a fireplace or coal or oil stove in each room. Bedrooms are furnished with odd pieces or with inexpensive, two-toned matching sets of bed, chest of drawers, and dressing table. Pictures of a religious nature (bought at the five-and-ten-cent store), calendars, almanacs, and Biblical quotations are tacked to the walls of almost every home. Typical of such quotations are: "The Lord Is My Shepherd"; "As for Me and My House, We Will Serve the Lord"; "Christ Died to Set Men Free." Town people know about these religious quotations, and some of them jest about them and think they are in poor taste as wall decorations. The "fire board," or mantel, holds partly used bottles of medicine accumulated from illnesses over the past several years. Pictures of members of the family, individually and grouped (often at a funeral around the casket of a deceased family member), are prominent.

The houses of mill workers who rent places in the country are the poorest in the rural sections. Usually they are without electricity, and occupants rely on nearby springs for water. The few in the country who own their houses generally have much better facilities.

Food

Although a large proportion of their money goes for food, mill workers and their children are often malnourished. Kent doctors say that part of the difficulty is the preponderance of fried foods, the necessity for quick preparation, and the high starch content of the diet. Mill workers commonly eat thick biscuits, potatoes, rice, cake, and pudding at the same meal. Town people make fun of these enormous doughy biscuits. Less milk is used in the homes of mill people than in town homes, and much of it is canned. Some of the mill families are becoming aware of the table etiquette followed by town and upper-class country people and are trying to follow it, but they are in a minority. Napkins are rare, biscuits are as often "speared" with a fork as they are passed, coffee is frequently cooled by being poured into the saucer and blown. On the other hand, strict decorum is demanded of children. They must be quiet when adults are talking, they must eat what is put on their plates (that is, if they have asked for it in the first place), and they must ask to be excused when they leave the table. When guests come to supper, the wife habitually apologizes for the small amount of food served and belittles its preparation, explaining that she wants everyone to feel at home and that she "never puts on for nobody."

Association Groups

In the chapter on recreation we have seen that there is very little intermingling of town and mill in this area. The Presbyterian Church has a "mill circle," made up of women from the Cromwell mill, especially those who live on Charlesville Street. Each year, four town "sponsors" attend these circle meetings, but they appear to be more in the role of missionaries than anything else. A few mill women belong to women's circles at the town Methodist and Baptist churches but are not very active. The Rotary Club, Masonic Lodge, and White Rose Club, a monthly supper club, are strictly for men from the town and from the upper social class in the country. Town and mill people have no association with each other in their homes, especially not in the exchange of meals.[20] One of the aristocratic ladies in town was upset when her husband allowed their yard man to eat at her dining room table, even though it was not at a regular meal time. The yard man was from one of the "best" Cromwell mill families and highly respected in his village. We have seen that no cases could be found in which a mill person had married someone from the upper classes of town or country.

Newspapers

The Kentville *Transcript*, the only local newspaper, a weekly, and the Stone Valley *Bugle* reflect class divisions of town, mill, and country. The local paper almost completely ignores the existence of mill people, and as a rule does not give news about curtailment, expansion, or wage changes in the Kent mills. The subtitle of the paper is significant: "A Family Newspaper: for the Promotion of the Political, Social, Agricultural, and Commercial Interests of the People"—with no mention of "Industrial." When the National Labor Relations Board trial of the Reginold brothers was in session, the paper carried no mention of it, for, according to one of the staff members, "the issue was too controversial." But when part of the verdict favorable to the mill owners was announced, it was published in the paper, and, at the same time, the part of the

20. This is in accord with Pope, *op. cit.*, p. 68, who states: "It would be as unthinkable in most uptown homes of Gastonia to invite a 'common mill-hand' to dinner as it would be to invite a Negro." However, in at least one case, a Kent town person, one of the local doctors, said that he has attempted to get mill people that he knows well to eat in his home, but they will not come. The attitude of this doctor toward mill workers is much more liberal than that of the majority of "Old Kent" families.

decision unfavorable to the mill owners was omitted. Most of the people in town as well as those in the mill regard the local weekly as an innocuous, timid sheet that refuses to take a stand on any issue that might be at all controversial. The paper is delivered to most of the people in town, but so few mill people subscribe that it is mailed to them. Mill people say that the news in the *Transcript* is old by the time it comes to them and that there is not much in it that interests them. The contents of an issue chosen at random, the November 25, 1948, issue, show why: On the front page were news items about a rural overseas program, 4-H club winners and their pictures, an appeal from the Red Cross, institution of a dancing course at the college in Stone Valley with a picture of the instructor, Christmas parade plans, winner in a farm speaking contest, meetings of the Masons and Rotary Club, recession of court for Thanksgiving, Episcopal parish house puppet show, meeting of Alcoholics Anonymous. The rest of the paper had descriptions of town marriages and pictures of engaged town girls, personal mention of the illnesses and visits of town people, news and personal interest stories of the social doings of prominent farmers in surrounding rural towns, announcements of book-club meetings and of a play to be given over the Episcopal hour on the radio, the International Sunday School lesson, and a proclamation by the state governor on conservation. There were agricultural articles on grazing, winter vegetables, and buying farm lands. Advertisements by local merchants occupied fully half of the space. Editorials were about Thanksgiving (a reminder to be grateful to God), Christmas (an appeal to give to the Red Cross), and tuberculosis (a plea to buy and use Christmas seals).

The Stone Valley *Bugle*, published daily except Sunday, is the most popular paper among Kent mill people. Of the ninety-six mill families in the survey 54.2 percent subscribed to the *Bugle*, while only 9.4 percent subscribed to the local weekly (see Table 14). The *Bugle* can be depended upon to carry news of changes and special happenings in the cotton mills of the county, including those in Kent. When the Reginold mills shut down temporarily and when the Cromwell mill curtailed to three days a week, the *Bugle* carried articles about these events. The social page carries news of the marriages of Kent mill people and personal mention is made of visits and illnesses. The *Bugle* has two different reporters in Kent, one for the town people and another for the mill villages. Personal mention of Kent people is made in separate columns for town and mill, indicating their separation socially, although there is no mention specifically that any particular person is from the town or the mill.

TABLE 14. SUBSCRIPTIONS OF 96 KENT MILL FAMILIES TO NEWSPAPERS AND OTHER PERIODICALS, BY MILL-VILLAGE SECTION

		Number of Families Subscribing to:					
Village Section	Total Number of Families	Stone Valley *Bugle*	Metro City *Mirror*	Kent-ville *Tran-script*	Other Period-icals *	None	Two or More Peri-odicals
Total	96	52	43	9	11	11	27
Cromwell	54	30	30	8	6	3	20
Locksley	13	6	4	1	5	1	3
Neilson	16	9	6	0	0	2	1
Townsend	13	7	3	0	0	5	3
Percent of Total	100.0	54.2	44.8	9.4	11.5	11.5	28.1

* "Other periodicals" include church and farm magazines, with a scattering of a few popular magazines of national circulation.

The Metro City *Mirror* is popular with town, country, and mill. Almost as many mill people subscribe to it as to the *Bugle*, primarily for its coverage of national and international events and for its comic strips.

Education and Religion

Preceding chapters on these subjects have already indicated the "badges of distinction" that come with differences in education and religion. Although the average amount of education of town people was not measured, there is no doubt that it is considerably higher than that of mill people. While the difference is not so great between mill and country people, it is highly probable that the latter have had more formal education, especially the members of well-to-do farm families. However, as we have seen, mill children want as much schooling as farm children, although they do not want as much as town children.

We have seen that mill people, for the most part, have their own churches, which are more emotional and fundamental in their services than are the churches in town. Town people think that the fervid Holiness meetings and the shouting of the Cromwell Baptist minister are strange ways to worship. Mill people in turn generally feel that town services are dull and uninspiring. Although the rural communities around Kent are predominantly Presbyterian, there is no Presbyterian church in the mill villages and there are no Holiness churches in the surrounding countryside. Some of the workers have maintained their memberships in rural churches after moving into the mill, but they are usually criticized by the farmers for their inactivity.

PARTICIPATION OF MILL WORKERS IN COMMUNITY LIFE

Mill people do not play an active part in community affairs, either in Kent or in the rural towns near which they live.[21] In answer to the question about what interest and role mill

21. This conclusion is in substantial agreement with that of Hutton, *op. cit.*, p. 68: "Through a cumulation of many factors, the village people [a mill village in Greer, S. C.] have become content with a passive interest in civic problems. . . ."

people had in the community of Phillippi, one successful farmer's reply, probably an exaggeration, was "None whatsoever." Evidently, these mill people feel no concern or responsibility for helping to carry on community endeavors, but at the same time they are given little opportunity to do so. In Kent the mill villagers, in the Cromwell especially, are becoming more interested in civic affairs, although their participation is still quite limited.

Commercial Organizations

Mill workers are important buyers in the local stores. Since lack of transportation facilities restricts their going outside the town, most of them buy their clothing, furniture, and electrical appliances from Kent stores. Merchants say they feel the pinch when the mills curtail and wages of workers are reduced. Mill people make up an important patronage at the Kent movie and are beginning to go in larger numbers to the drive-in theater. They are good customers at liquor stores and they frequent local beer joints and Monk's Billiard Parlor. Several of the stores, especially the five-and-ten and grocery stores, employ young people from the mill villages as clerks. These are among the few alternative jobs open to those who grow up in the mill sections. In speaking of rural mill workers, a leader in the Shalem community, seven miles to the west of Kent, said that the only persons who knew or even often saw these cotton-mill people who lived near Shalem were the clerks in the Shalem stores. And prominent farmers in the other surrounding rural towns said the same.

Cooperative Community Enterprises

In 1948 the town of Kent converted a private residence into a civic center, designed to be a memorial to veterans of World War II. The building was set up as a place where any group in Kent could hold a party if it so desired. A public library occupies part of it, and a swimming pool and bath house have been built in the rear. Mill people were sure that the project would be for town people only, in spite of the fact that much of the money for establishing the center was contributed by the Reginold brothers, who stated that they hoped their workers would utilize its facilities. The main building has been used almost exclusively by town groups, but mill people have patronized the swimming pool so much that townspeople have termed it "the mill bathtub." This is partly in derision, implying that the only time mill children bathe is when they swim in the pool. At the same time it indicates that mill people use the pool whenever they wish and whenever they are able to pay the entrance fee of fifteen cents for children and thirty-five cents for adults. Some of the townspeople will not use the pool because of the large number of mill people who swim there.

Mill villagers turned out en masse for the Chamber of Commerce-sponsored Christmas parade, and they contributed generously to the Red Cross blood bank when it came to Kent. The Church of God minister took several groups in his car to and from the bank, making a special effort to have all of his members donate their blood. Parents of mill children who have parts in school plays go to see their children perform, and they attend local talent shows in which their children have parts, such as the annual baby contest. On the other hand, mill people are careful to avoid what appears to them to be strictly a town event. Only one or two of them bought tickets to the Kent concert series, which presented classical music and was well supported by town people. Few mill people attend special functions at school such as class parties, and mill parents are not active in the P.T.A.

Cooperative vesper services were arranged by the four downtown churches and the mill churches were invited to participate, but they did not—they already had their own Sunday evening services and preferred them. On the other hand, the town and mill churches readily cooperate in a joint service each Thanksgiving Day, but few from the mill attend, even when the service is held in mill churches. The town has a volunteer fire department which is made up primarily of workers from the Cromwell village.

Politics

A spirit of self-pity and defeatism is still evident in the attitude of many mill workers toward voting: "Well, it don't make no difference much who I vote for. Whoever's elected ain't gonna help us much." The consensus is that politicians are self-seeking [22] and hypocritical. "They'll be friendly with you and shake your hand and pat you on the back before election. Then after they're elected, they don't even see you walk down the sidewalk."

But this attitude that politics is all bad is changing. In the presidential election of 1948, mill people still remembered the depression of the early thirties, which they refer to as "Hoover days." They are convinced that President Roosevelt did much to help the working man, and they can see the tangible results of his actions in the unemployment-compensation check, old-age insurance payments, and shorter hours and more pay. With the coming of unions in Stone Valley and with the realization that benefits can accrue if a prolabor man is elected, mill villagers are beginning to see that they do possess power if they vote together. In the last city election they helped

22. In the 1948 Democratic primary, one candidate for the state senate said in his campaign speech in the Kent County Court House that his first interest in being elected was to get everything he could out of the office for himself. Then he would take care of his friends in Kent County. Mill people admired him for his frankness, for they felt he was stating what is true of all politicians, but on other grounds they did not vote for him.

elect a mayor who works in the Cromwell mill, although he has never lived in the village itself and has recently moved into a twenty-thousand-dollar home on the Metro City highway. A state senator who campaigned on promises to labor was elected in the county election of 1949. Kent mill people supported him because as a member of the state house of representatives he had had several of the Kent mill streets paved and had attempted to pass legislation requiring owners of mill houses to install plumbing. The county coroner, who lives in the Neilson village and who has wide family connections in the Cromwell village, was elected in the last primary with strong mill support.

It is certainly an exaggeration, however, to claim, as some of the town people do, that mill workers "control" town elections through their united voting power. Actually there is very little organization among Kent mill workers in getting them to support a particular candidate. Politicians try to line up votes through certain influential mill workers, especially those who are important in large kinship groups. Also, they arrange for automobile drivers to go by the homes of all workers to take them to the polls. Candidates are wary of seeking the support of the bossmen in the mills, for, as one worker expressed it, "You can be sure the workers will vote just the opposite of the bossmen." Little evidence could be found that this actually happens, but certainly if politicians pay too much attention to bossmen and ignore workmen in their visits to the mill, they do not fare well. One candidate appeared at the gate of the Kent mills as shifts changed, shook hands with the workers as they left the mill and asked for their support. He received a large majority at the Cromwell precinct.

Determining exactly how many mill people eligible to vote actually cast their ballots in the 1948 primary was impossible. The impression of the registrars at the city hall and county courthouse was that the mill people voted in about the same proportion as town people. From the survey of mill homes, I secured fifty-eight responses from eligible mill voters on whether they had voted in that election. Of these, thirty, or 51.7 percent, replied that they had (two-thirds of them were men), and twenty-eight, 48.3 percent, reported that they had not (two-thirds were women). No Republicans were found in the mill villages. However, in the presidential election of 1948 the entry of the States' Rights party caused great confusion, and the majority of the villagers who indicated how they voted were for the States' Rights candidate, claiming that he represented the "true" Democratic party. Men take far more interest in elections than women, and the survey indicated that those women who did cast ballots in 1948 followed the advice of their husbands. There is little doubt that an increasing amount of interest will be shown in political activities by mill people, and that those seeking office will attempt to improve the lot of the textile worker in order to gain his vote.

Mill People and "The Law"

Certain millhands have frequent dealings with "the law." On weekends, beginning Friday afternoon and lasting through Sunday, these millhands are inevitably arrested for drunkenness and disorderly conduct. They are locked up overnight in the city jail if they are too drunk to be handled easily. After paying a ten-dollar fine the next morning, they are free to go on their way. Officers say that almost all the "liquor-heads" are in the Reginold villages and that they have trouble with only three or four in the Cromwell village. Only rarely do these drinkers become destructive or use knives in their fights, as the Negroes of Kent sometimes do.[23] Instead they simply make nuisances of themselves and occasionally get into fist fights.

23. Hylan Lewis describes such aggression in *Blackways of Kent*, pp. 211–21, especially.

Town people who get drunk do so, as a rule, within the confines of their own homes or in the homes of friends, rather than in taverns and at public dances as the mill workers do. Consequently, town people are rarely arrested for being drunk. Sometimes they are fined, but this is exceptional. Mill people say that the police are instructed whom they may and may not arrest. They resent the fact that certain important men in town are not touched by the police, no matter how drunk they become, while mill workers are picked up immediately when they have had too much to drink. The workers claim that an important source of revenue for the city is from the fines paid for drunkenness, largely by the people who have the least money, the workers from the Reginold mills. At the same time, mill people do not hesitate to call "the law," or threaten to do so, to settle neighborhood squabbles or quiet an unruly neighbor who has drunk too much.

Conclusions

Thus the role of mill worker in community activities in Kent is a minor one, except in the area of elections. Kent mill people have not been fully integrated into the life of the town, although there is a movement in this direction. Certain factors are involved in this limited activity: (1) As tenant farmers and mill workers, these people have been "taken care of" rather than trained in responsibility. The paternalism of the mill, especially, makes them turn to mill officials when they want something done, for example setting up a recreational program for mill children. If the mill officials say "no," then that is usually the end of it. (2) The feeling of inferiority engendered by the fact that both town and country consider them "failures" (and those who had to leave their own farms to enter the mill also consider themselves failures as farmers) and by the fact that they are looked down on, especially by town people, has had the effect of making them withdraw more closely than ever into their tight knit villages.[24] They do not have confidence in themselves outside their village setting, where they are familiar with the prescribed patterns in relation to fellow villagers. (3) Mill people have not the formal education or the experience to enable them to take leadership roles. They know little outside of mill work and life in the mill village, and, isolated and segregated as they are from the town, they tend to perpetuate their own group and customs. (4) Those who have the most power in the community are not particularly interested in trying to increase the interest of mill people in community life. They feel that as he is now, the mill worker (like the stereotype of the Negro in the minds of town people) is satisfied with his lot and does not have the desire or the capacity for change.

24. Compare this conclusion with that of Hutton, *op. cit.*, p. 68, who states: "These factors which influence this patterning of social activity [a passive interest in civic problems and the lack of experience in initiating, and developing, programs of action] are primarily of a 'community' nature, enhanced by the 'passive' and 'in-group' characteristics and the common heritage of the people living in the villages."

Ranking within the Mill Class

CHAPTER 9   ALTHOUGH KENT MILL people constitute a class at the bottom of the social hierarchy of whites, there are internal lines of stratification recognized by the mill people themselves. Even town and rural people, when pressed on the point, readily admit that there are wide differences among the mill villages. They rate the Cromwell people above those in the Reginold villages, and they put the Townsend people at the bottom of the mill "scale."

The ranking among mill people is not highly crystallized, and mill villagers tend to be tolerant in their judgment of one another. What their "stratification system" amounts to is a rather loose grouping of people according to characteristics that are considered "better" or "worse" for mill villagers to have. The effect of the system is to help determine informal association groups in the villages.

GENERAL CRITERIA OF CLASSIFICATION

Village

The most obvious division among mill people is geographical. Each village is separate, and the members of each do not have very much contact with the members of the others, except where kinship lines cross. We have seen that the Cromwell workers have higher wages, live in better houses, and are generally more stable than the Reginold workers. These are the differences that are most obvious to town people, and they are also recognized by the villagers themselves. Within the villages there are neighborhood groupings which tend to differ. In the Cromwell village there are Old and New Hill, the latter being closer to the town in geography and in attitude. In the Townsend village there is notorious "Back Lane" where the "lowest" mill workers live, and in each of the villages there are colonies of kin people living almost next door to each other. Charlesville Street might be considered a transitional zone between the Cromwell village and the town. Several bossmen, including the local superintendent of the Cromwell mill, and a few of the regular workers who own their homes live on this street. Also living there are carpenters, policemen, grocery clerks and workers in industrial plants outside Kent.

Kinship

This study has stressed the importance of the kindred groups in mill society. Security, social life, and recreation are founded on kinship. For the most part, these kinship lines are parallel, for a mill person is not regarded as "better" or "worse" merely because of the family to which he belongs. Family connections as bases for establishing and maintaining status mean far less to mill people than to townspeople. Within each of the kindred groups there are often differences in status among unit-families and among individuals. In one sense, then, mill-village ranking is not affected by kinship lines, but in another it helps to determine who associates most intimately within kinship groupings.

Bossman-Worker

Among the bossmen only the foremen can be considered a part of the mill villages, and they do not form an integral part.

The superintendent and overseers are not a part of the mill group socially. Their wives do not work in the mill, and their children generally intermarry with the less important town people. The superintendent and overseers look upon mill people as separate from themselves, saying in a paternalistic manner, "There are some we are proud of, but there are others we can't say much for."

Although the foremen are a part of the village in which they live, they are on a somewhat different level from the regular worker. Their houses are larger and have inside toilets, and because of higher and more regular wages, they are able to furnish their homes better than the average worker. Their cars are better and of later models. Foremen dress more formally than millhands, wearing a coat and tie most of the time, even to and from work. They generally aspire to town standards, and their children often leave the mill village to enter other work. Some of the foremen provide leadership in the Cromwell Baptist Church, the Oddfellows, and other mill-village groups. Although they are also rated on their own personal characteristics by mill people, they are really a separate group at the top of the mill scale, along with the preachers and those aspiring to work outside the village.

Religious-Nonreligious

One of the most important general criteria by which mill people rank one another is whether a person attends church and takes an active interest in its affairs. They generally believe, even those who do not attend, that the "best" people belong to a church and send their children to Sunday School. There are exceptional people who live "right" and still do not attend church, but the majority of "good" people go to church. We have seen that a mill person takes the injunctions of his religion seriously and does not believe he should attend church unless he lives "right." Thus church membership and activity as a rule imply that the person does not gamble, drink, or engage in other "rough" or "sinful" activities. Anyone who leads a "worldly" life and attends church at the same time is considered a hypocrite and even worse than the sinful person who feels himself unworthy of going to church. The church group and the pool-room—beer-parlor group are in different strata, for a mill person cannot very well belong to both groups (except for a few in the Cromwell Baptist and town churches).

We have seen that the majority of mill people rate their churches in prestige in this order: Cromwell Baptist, Wesleyan Methodist, and Church of God. Of course the Church of God members would put them in exactly the reverse order, for they claim that they are true "saints of Kent." But the majority in the mill villages do not accept the verdict of the Church of God, for they look upon members in the Holiness groups as ignorant and bizarre in their services, and, although Holiness people may be strict about smoking, movies, and drinking, they are thought to be more lax in sexual matters than other churches. Although they are usually guarded in their criticism, non-Holiness members do indicate their disapproval of Holiness practices from time to time. A mill woman who attends the downtown Methodist Church reflected this disapproval when she said most people, including herself, are ignorant, but at least they know it, but "those Church of God people are ignorant and don't know it." She then cited an incident in which a woman suffering from a weak heart died during a highly emotional service at the Church of God, while all those about her, not realizing that she was dying, were rejoicing in the belief that she was receiving "power from on high." A Cromwell Baptist member, in speaking of laxity of sexual behavior in Holiness groups, said that during revivals men and women roll around on the floor together, bundled up in rugs in "temptation situations." He said that he would never let his wife go to such a meeting and "carry on" with another man. And mill workers who are not active in any church like to pass around jokes about "religious" experiences at Holiness revivals, especially at tent meetings; for example: A man took an attractive girl aside from a Church of God meeting, telling her he would try to "bring her the rapture," which amounted to nothing less than an invitation to sexual relations. The girl went out with him to a suitable spot, and at the beginning shouted somewhat in pain, "Oh, God. Help me, Jesus." Then, with a sigh of joy and relief, she murmured, "Oh, God, I've made it. Thank you, Jesus." As we have seen in the chapter on religion, the ideas of the people outside of the Holiness churches regarding Holiness practices are grossly exaggerated, but they are a part of the mental patterns which place the Holiness churches on a lower level than the more conventional ones.

Floaters or Drifters

"Floaters" have been referred to briefly in Chapter 3. They are highly unstable workers who drift from cotton mill to cotton mill, never staying in a mill village long enough to become a part of it. They are on the outer fringe of the mill sections and are not respected by the established workers.

These floaters are of two types. The most common is the unattached man who has never been married or who has been separated from his wife. He rarely stays over three or four weeks at a time at a mill, making enough money for whisky and the price of an evening with a prostitute. Floyd Osborne is one of these. He was born on a tenant farm not far from Kent and is now about thirty years old. He began working in a Stone Valley cotton mill at the age of fifteen and learned to be a mechanic and loom fixer. At nineteen he married but before he had lived a month with his wife, he discovered that she continued to keep company with men she had known before her marriage. He left her, never bothering to get a divorce.

"She was a no-good woman and done me wrong." (He claims that his ex-wife has been married five times since he parted from her, and he doubts that she got a divorce "air" time. "The cops would have plenty on her if they caught her.")

For the past ten years or so, Floyd has been traveling over the Piedmont and New England, drifting from town to town and from job to job, sometimes in industries other than textiles. He has hopped freight trains all over the eastern United States and has been jailed for vagrancy and drunkenness numberless times. Once in Bridgeport, Connecticut, his skull was "cracked" when a policeman clubbed him. Often when he traveled he would stay overnight at the jail, where his lodging and breakfast were "free."

Several times he has been robbed by girls he picked up. Once in Metro City when he worked in a mill there, he was paid sixty dollars and given a week's vacation. He began his vacation by spotting a good-looking girl ("a lot of them hang out at a place just below the bus station"), and he picked her up and they drove around having a good time. Toward nightfall he rented a hotel room. Both of them had been drinking all afternoon, and he was so "soused" that he slept soundly. When he awoke, the girl was gone and so was all that had been left from the sixty dollars. (According to Floyd, these girls know just how "to roll a guy for his dough." They drink less than he does, and after he gets sound asleep, they take his money, slip out of the room, and dress in the women's room in the hall.) He spent the entire morning and a tankful of gas looking for her, but never found her. If he had, he would have "taken care of her all right." He would have driven out on one of the back roads to the Iroquois River and "beaten hell out of her."

Floyd is soft spoken, mild and gentle in manner when sober, and easy going. According to the other workers, "He don't give a damn about nothin'." He came to Kent from New Orleans, where he had held a job as a mechanic. "I just decided

I had been there long enough, so I hopped a freight home."
He was penniless and hungry when he arrived at the Cromwell
boardinghouse and was wearing a pair of dirty overalls, a
blue denim shirt, and an old pair of shoes without socks. The
woman in charge of the boardinghouse knew him and allowed
him to charge his room and board until he began receiving
money from the mill. Skilled loom fixers like Floyd can usually
find a job in the mills, and often the drifter is highly com-
petent—otherwise he could not get a job so easily. Although
the Cromwell does not take drifters as a rule, they hired Floyd.
The first two weekends, Floyd caught rides to his parents'
home and stayed out of trouble. The third week he became
drunk but sobered up in time to go to work on Monday, but at
the end of the fourth week, he and the woman he had picked
up were arrested and jailed for disturbing the peace. He was
not sober enough to go to work on Monday and was discharged
by the mill. He said he planned to return to his home and
added that he would soon be restless after staying a while there
and would take to the road again to look for another job.

The other type of floater is the drifting family. They stay
in a village for about six to ten months, run up as many debts
as they can, and then quietly slip away from the village in the
night. They are rarely employed by the Cromwell mill but
are sometimes hired by the Reginold. Typical is the Wells
family, composed of a husband and wife and a daughter ten
years old. The Wellses moved into the Locksley village in a
trailer, saying they had been previously employed by a Piedmont State mill which had shut down. Both husband and wife
secured jobs at the Locksley mill, and they began to charge
things at the neighborhood grocery store, paying a little on
their accounts from time to time. But after six months they
suddenly left Kent with most of their bills unpaid. Many of
the floating families get rooms in a group of dilapidated houses
rented by the Reginold brothers near the business section of

town, and they often have a car or truck, enabling them to move from town to town. Because of heavy drinking and sexual laxity, these families do not hold together long.

Club Members

Membership in the Oddfellows, Woodmen of the World, Veterans of Foreign Wars, American Legion, and National Guard lends a certain amount of prestige to mill people. Each of these groups selects its members because they possess characteristics valued by mill people. Almost all of the members of these groups would be classed as "good," "decent" people. Interestingly, almost no one from the Reginold villages belongs to any of these organizations.

Leaders

Although the paternalistic system under which they grow up does not encourage the development of leadership traits, mill people provide leadership for the mill churches and the other mill-village organizations. Often these men are the same ones who hold positions of influence in the large family groups, the ones to whom many within the family look for advice on voting, and whose favor politicians curry. As a rule, these leaders are not aggressive but have to be pushed into official positions in the organization and sought out by fellow kindred members for advice. Most of them are regular workers and some are foremen. Almost all are men, but there are women who are "good" at giving stork showers, who lead in styles of furnishings, and whose advice is sought on methods of cooking, child rearing, etc. The preachers can be classified as leaders in the community because of their influence.

These leaders are well settled in the villages, and unlike those trying to leave the village and move into town, they are oriented toward the conditions in the village. They are not a clearly defined group and are sometimes hard to discover because of their lack of aggressiveness. They might be considered "natural" leaders, or "charismic" leaders, to use Max Weber's term.

Those Leaving Mill Work

Kent mill people tend to form a hereditary occupational group (see pages 51-52), with an estimated 75 to 80 percent of Kent mill children entering mill work, either in Kent or in nearby towns. Some of those who do not go into mill work become carpenters, electricians, and truck drivers, among other things. Some of them find jobs in the Stone Valley Printing and Finishing Company, considered a step beyond cotton-mill work. But a certain number of young people, in the Cromwell village particularly, deliberately attempt to move "up" the scale and out of the mill class altogether. This has to be a deliberate step, for unless a mill person makes an effort, he almost automatically drifts into mill work or its allied fields. Movies, newspapers, and public schools, presenting the American ideal of progress, stimulate this desire to move out of the mill village. We have seen how the conflict between the values of town and mill are reflected in school. The majority of mill pupils reject, to a large extent, those values taught in school which conflict with those learned in the mill village, and they leave school by the end of the ninth or tenth year. But the value of "getting ahead" is accepted by some of the mill children. These children face a strong internal and external struggle in trying to leave the mill village and enter other work.

There are several ways to avoid going into mill work. Perhaps the most important is through schooling. Unless mill children get at least a high school education, they rarely move on up the social scale. Girls need even more than high school training. Jobs as clerks in the ten-cent store and in cafés are available to Kent mill girls, but these pay considerably less than mill jobs (fifty cents an hour in contrast to a minimum of ninety-three cents in the Cromwell and eighty cents in the Reginold in 1948) and are more often part-time jobs after school hours. To be sure of getting work outside the village, they need special training as secretaries, nurses, or teachers, the main occupations open to them. If the girl remains very long beyond high school graduation in the mill village, she is almost sure to marry a mill worker, usually a boy from her village. The boys, on the other hand, can get out with a high school education or less. One of the favorite first steps in such a move is to join some branch of the United States armed forces. This period in the army or navy is considered an interim one only, for few make it their life work. Some of them return to the mill village and enter mill work, but others, having "been out and seen the world," are no longer satisfied to remain in the small, circumscribed mill village, and they take jobs outside of Kent. Some of these enter the celanese and finishing plants in Stone Valley.

To leave the mill village and at the same time remain in Kent is more difficult than entering nonmill work outside of Kent. Those who do so are likely to be considered "uppity" by mill people and they are open to discrimination by town people, prejudiced against anyone who comes from a mill background. However, there are procedures that can be followed by someone who wants to live in another section of town and forsake the occupation of his kinsfolk. Wallace Thomas is now in the process of doing this. He is twenty-two years old and continues to live with his parents on Cromwell New Hill in the same house in which he was born. Both his father and mother have worked in the Cromwell mill for more than thirty years, but none of the four Thomas children works at the Cromwell. One lives on Charlesville Street and is employed in the Stone Valley Printing and Finishing Company, another is studying pharmacy under the G. I. Bill, and a younger sister is working in a downtown Kent store. Wallace finished high school (eleven grades at the time) and began working at the Cromwell mill during the boom times of 1945–46. But he found that mill work did not "suit" him. He did not like the third shift and found the work dirty and unpleasant. A friend told him of an opening in a new men's merchandise shop in downtown Kent, and he got a job as a clerk. Now he has been in the shop for over two years and enjoys the work and the contacts so much that he has decided to make "store business" his life work. He hopes that the owner of the shop will promote him to manager or perhaps set up a store in an adjoining town that he can manage. In the meantime, Wallace is keeping one foot in the village and another outside. He has continued his membership in the Cromwell Baptist Church, where his family has always been active. In the church he has taken leadership roles as president of the young men's class and as leader of a quartet which sings occasionally in the church. When the regular leader is absent, he directs congregational singing at the church services. Wallace is a charter member of the Lions Club, which was organized in Kent in the summer of 1949. This club is the counterpart of the Rotary Club, which is composed of upper-status town people. The Lions include in their membership those on a somewhat lower scale in town and the "ambitious" young mill people, particularly those who have jobs downtown. Wallace is active in the National Guard, recently joined the Oddfellows, and hopes to get into the Masons eventually. His dress is different from the regular mill worker, for he never wears overalls or "rough" clothing. He almost always has on a suit and a tie. Of course his job as a haberdasher would require him to dress well, but at the same time this means that he follows the town rather than the mill pattern. His manners and habits are different from the majority who work in the mill. He is careful to use correct English, does not chew tobacco, dip snuff, drink, or frequent the pool room or Bradford's Grill. His friends are others who are apparently on their way out of the mill village. Two of them, sons of foremen in the Cromwell, have access to automobiles, and Wallace double-dates with them on weekends, going to square dances at the Armory (never at Nadine's), attending functions at the Kent High School, and driving to Metro City and Stone Valley for movies and for dinner. His dates are Cromwell mill girls who have finished high school or are about to finish and usually are daughters of mill foremen. Wallace is very quiet about his move in the direction of town. He is not considered "uppity" by mill people, because he has maintained his relation with the mill church and with the Oddfellows, and he has continued his association with mill young people, although it is true his friends are leaving the village also. Wallace likes Kent because he thinks it is a friendly place, but he is not sure whether he wants to live there all his life. This will depend, in part, on whether he has the chance to manage the store in which he is now employed. If he does live in Kent, he would like to own a house on Charlesville Street or farther over into town. Whether he will maintain his membership in the Cromwell church is hard to say. He might for a time, but if he does as his brother who works in Stone Valley did, he will join a town church.

One young man who left mill work and the mill-village sections within the last two years is a barber who gained his training in a barber college on the G.I. Bill of Rights. Another helps to run the downtown pool room and lives above one of the downtown stores. A third has built a small house on Charlesville Street and has a job as a carpenter with the Kent Construction Company. A fourth drives a taxi, and a fifth delivers and picks up laundry and dry cleaning for a Kent establishment. Each of these men looks upon those who work in cotton mills, particularly the ones their age just entering mill work, as lacking in ambition and as knowing nothing but the mill. Thus, in their attitudes those who have moved out reflect to some extent the town's evaluation of cotton-mill people. Since their parents are still in the village and are engaged in mill work, it is difficult for these men to resolve the inner conflict of town and mill values. They are still attached to their families, for family loyalty is strong, and they often visit their kin at the mill. Their children will grow up to be town people (of the "red-blood" type, according to Patrick), but they themselves might be termed "marginal men."

INDIVIDUAL CRITERIA OF CLASSIFICATION

In addition to the general criteria of ranking used by mill people, there are others that are more personal in nature. These personal or individual criteria are closely related to the general ones, and those ranking high in one set usually rank high in the other. Yet these personal ratings must be listed separately, for they do not always coincide with the more general ratings, and they emphasize the tendency of mill people to rank the individual as an individual rather than as a resident in a particular village or as a member of a particular family.

Cleanliness

Town people usually stereotype all mill people as "dirty" in personal appearance and in their homes. But mill people vary considerably in these aspects. The majority of families take pride in keeping their houses and yards as free of dirt and trash as possible, regardless of how crowded they are. However, certain mill families make no effort to keep themselves or their houses clean. Their children are unkempt, their houses are dirty and full of flies, and their yards are filled with debris. They usually "chew" or "dip" and the tobacco stains remain on their faces. Mill workers say that they are "people who don't care" and "people who live like cattle." [1] Some mill workers regret that there are not stricter regulations requiring the people who care nothing for cleanliness to do something about their untidiness.

Sexual Laxity

Although mill people might be termed lax in their sexual relations when compared to town people, they look down on those among them who flagrantly violate the monogamous ideal. Men and women who "shack up" are not respected, and neither are those who "go to the woods" with just anybody at any time. The Neilson women who had children while their husbands were overseas and those who "carry on" with others while their spouses are at work are considered to be too free. Many of those guilty of promiscuity are also the same as the "people who live like cattle," although not necessarily so.

"Roughness"

Those who drink heavily, frequent the pool room and Bradford's Grill and Nadine's, and sometimes get into trouble with "the law," are called the "rough" group. Such mill people are not active in religion, although a few of them belong to rural or town churches, or even to the Cromwell Baptist. We have seen that church attendance is considered hypocritical as long as a person does not live "right," so those "roughs" who are listed as church members do not attend. We have seen that

1. Ralph Patrick, in A Cultural Approach to the Stratification System of a Southern Town, p. 9, reports that town people refer to these mill workers as "trashy" and "people who live like Negroes."

Notice the similarity of the term "people who live like cattle" and the one West found used in Plainville, "people who live like animals" (Plainville, USA, p. 123). But unlike the Plainville people who fall into this category, those in Kent are held morally responsible by the mill people for what they do.

there is very little social drinking, especially involving both
men and women. Apparently when men drink they frequently do so to get drunk. There are few who "suck at the
bottle," for most of those who drink get "high" almost every
weekend, and it is during this time that they get into trouble
with "the law" and are fined. But drinking, even the heaviest
drinking, is not severely condemned as long as it does not prevent a parent from taking care of his children. The "rough"
group uses "rough" language, with much profanity.

Attitude toward Offspring

Parents are expected to be good to their children and to
provide them with the necessities of life. Those who are cruel
and "slap their kids around" are criticized. One girl who ran
away from home to live with an aunt was justified for doing
so because the mill people felt that her father whipped her too
often—the father had no right to rear the daughter and ought
to lose her.

No excuses are given for a man who deprives his children
of food and other necessities because of his drinking and
gambling habits. A man is "no good for nothing" if he drinks
and gambles away his wages. Even though a wife can make
a living for herself by working in the mill, it is wrong for her
to have to support the children alone. Harry Adams is an
example of a person regarded by the majority as "not worth a
Goddamn," because he will not support his family. He and his
wife are from well-known mill families, and one of his uncles
is a bossman. Adams has managed to hold his job in the Cromwell mill although he drinks heavily almost every weekend.
He and his wife have parted, for all practical purposes. She
has become too sick to work and has had to move with
her three children into the home of her mother and father
in the Neilson village. Adams contributes nothing to the support of his family but is said to spend all his money on liquor

and "keeping up" another man's estranged wife out in the country. His only associates are his drinking cronies and a few of those living in the neighborhood of the woman with whom he is "shacked up." The majority of men in Adams' category, and there appear to be about twenty-five, mostly in the Reginold villages, cannot hold jobs in the mill because of their drinking. They begin to seek jobs in other mills and might become floaters. Sometimes these men are sued by their wives for nonsupport, but it is difficult to enforce a verdict against them. Only in a very few cases have women forsaken their husbands and children to go to live with other men. In such cases the women usually leave the village, for it would be difficult for them to remain in the face of strong disapproval.

Sincerity

Mill people have no use for hypocrites, and they come in for much condemnation. They are usually not mentioned by name, but they include most of the town people and some of the church people in the mill villages who do not "live right" and yet attend church. One woman remarked that she could not bear to hear a certain man pray in church because she knew he did not pay his grocery bills. Hypocrites are people who "say one thing to your face and another thing behind your back." A strong compliment, implying consistency and sincerity of character, is a phrase often used, "You're just the same as the first day I knowed you." Even when a person violates certain taboos, if he does so in the open he is not severely criticized. Margaret Grant, a widow, had a child several years after her husband died. But the man who came to see her always did so in the open. "She didn't have them sneaking around after dark, so everybody knew what was going on." As long as she was aboveboard, even in promiscuity, she was not strongly disapproved by the majority.

Humility

Mill people object to those who are "snooty," who "put on airs," and who "think they are better than anybody else." The pattern is to ignore such people, including those in town who are not friendly and act as if they are superior. We have seen that some of those who leave the mill village for other work are considered "uppity"—the very fact that a person wants to leave the village is an indication that he thinks the village is not good enough for him. But we have also seen that if a person leaving the village continues to be friendly and humble in his relations with those at the mill, he is not criticized. It is a compliment to say that a town person is "just as common as the rest of us," for this implies that he puts on no airs. A mill worker who brags about past and future accomplishments is not well thought of.

Generosity

To say that a person "has got every penny he ever made" is a severe indictment. It implies that a person is tight fisted, and in their use of money mill people believe in spending what they have rather than saving. If they have the money, mill people contribute generously to their church, to the Red Cross, and to needy friends. The generous person is admired, while one who is selfish with his money, either by saving it or by spending it all on himself, is not esteemed.

Minding One's Own Business

There are apparently few "busybodies" in the Kent mill villages because of the strong feeling against anyone who "tries to tend to everybody else's business." Mill school children listed among the things they were taught at home (in the compositions on "The Story of My Life") "Not to go around asking questions about something that isn't any of my business" (perhaps this was aimed at the fieldworker), "Not to criticize other people," "Keep my mouth shut and my ears open," and similar statements indicating stress on minding one's own business.

Mrs. Mae Wilford, a widow who lives in the Cromwell village, is strongly critical of other people and talks about them constantly. In many ways she is a deviant among mill people because of her aggressive manner, her self-confidence, and her bitterly critical ways. Although she began working in the mill when she was ten, she married a man who did not work in the mill. They lived for a number of years in downtown Kent, where he ran a pool room, and Mrs. Wilford acquired town attitudes toward the mill. When her husband died and she was forced to return to mill work, she carried her anti-mill attitudes with her. She disdains attending mill churches and maintains association with one or two former town neighbors, the wives of a carpenter and a mechanic. Mill people both fear her and dislike her because of her sharp tongue. But they approve of the fact that she is a hard worker, is generous, and helps to take care of the children of her daughter, who is separated from her husband.

Mill people are sensitive to criticism of any type, and they themselves use it sparingly, even regarding town people. However, on a few occasions mill people have had to leave the village because of the disapproval of others. One young man who did not join the armed forces in World War II was considered a slacker, and "just could not work in the mill where people were talking about him." Another was the Holiness preacher who "squeezed the young girls too much." "Everybody knows what everybody else is doing" in each of the mill sections, but the circulation of such common knowledge is mainly the passing on of interesting information rather than malicious gossip.

Conclusion

Interestingly, the ranking within the mill class employs none of the chief criteria frequently used in America to designate social class itself—occupation, income, racial or ethnic group, education, and family descent. There is such a high degree of homogeneity among mill people in these characteristics that they provide no basis for ranking. Instead, ranking is much more closely related to the way a person behaves: in religion, in choice of recreation, in family relations, in use of money, in keeping clean, in talking about others.[2]

An over-all summary of ranking within the mill class is diagrammed in Figure 5 below. This is a depiction of the point of view of the majority of mill workers and foremen as determined by this study.[3] The horizontal line in the middle of the diagram divides the "religious" from the "nonreligious." Note that this division is different from "church" and "nonchurch." Table 12, page 108, shows that while 70.6 percent of the sample of 177 mill family heads are enrolled in church, only 41.2 percent attend as regularly as every third Sunday. But it is safe to say that fully half the sample might qualify as "religious," for they do not drink heavily or gamble, and in general they abide by the rules of religion. Those who are classified as "rough" and are also church members are the ones who have kept their names on the rolls of churches which they rarely, if ever, attend. This is the group in a

2. The kind of ranking used by Kent mill people is much closer to that used by Kent Negroes than by Kent town people. Hylan Lewis, in *Blackways of Kent*, pp. 3–5, 233–56, delineates two types of Negroes, "respectables" and "nonrespectables," based primarily on the kind of behavior they follow as individuals. On the other hand, Patrick, *op. cit.*, p. 5, especially, cites as basic in the evaluation of town people *who* a person is, meaning what family he comes from. His "blue blood," "red-blood" designations emphasize this. Evaluation by town people of each other in terms of *what* a person does, that is, in terms of his actual behavior, is secondary.

3. The type of diagram was suggested by the one developed in James West's *Plainville, USA*, p. 117.

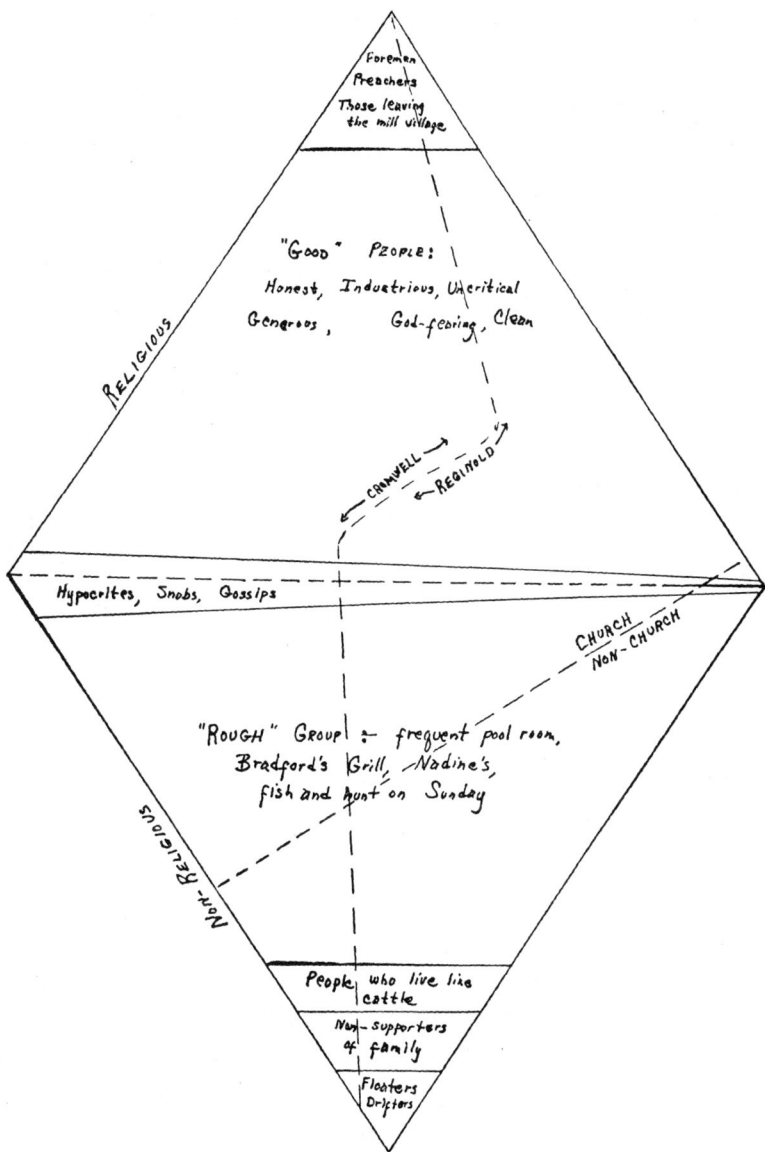

FIGURE 5. Stratification within the Kent Mill Class

"backslidden condition." Some of them have pangs of conscience about changing their ways and getting lined up with the church again, but others enjoy their "worldly" pleasures and their companions too much to consider seriously giving them up. They admit that religious people are "better" than they are, but at the same time they say "there are lots of hypocrites in the church."

Those in the lowest categories, namely "those who live like cattle," nonsupporters of families, and floaters, may move up the scale by "getting religion" and giving up their bad habits. It is the Holiness churches that take an active interest in this group at the bottom of the scale, and it would be difficult for these "down-and-outers" to enter the Cromwell Baptist or one of the town churches. Max Campbell, whose family "lived like cattle" and who was classified as a nonsupporter of his family, was "saved" at a Wesleyan Methodist revival. Subsequently, he gave up heavy drinking, is spending more money on his family, and is making an effort to keep his house and yard cleaner. He has moved just over the line among the "good" people, although many wonder how long he will remain "good." Occasionally, floaters will settle down and become a part of village life, thereby moving out of their low status. But those in the lowest categories who are saved frequently backslide again into their old ways. Sometimes they are resaved, but just as often they sink into an even lower status.

Foremen, preachers, leaders, and those leaving the mill have been placed at the top of the scale among the villagers, although some in that category, particularly those leaving the mill, might be considered snobs and hypocrites.

It will be noted from the Cromwell-Reginold division that there are many more "good" people at the Cromwell and many more in a lower stratification among the Reginold mill workers.

Personality Development in the Subculture

CHAPTER 10 ALTHOUGH KENT MILL people are individuals, differing in many ways from one another, they have much in common when considered as a group. These similarities go beyond those of housing, dress, speech, and the like to attitudes, values, and ways of perceiving and reacting to events. In other words, the similarities reach the level of personality. It is the thesis of this chapter that the manifest traits of personality which the Kent mill people evidently hold in common are directly related to the mode of life of the mill-village sections. The "press" of the mill subculture, together with the low status accorded mill workers in general, has a vital part in producing overt characteristics of personality shared by the mill villagers.

In relating selected manifest traits of personality to life in the mill sections, two additional studies of the Kent mill people supplemented the participant-observation method used by the author. These studies were carried out independently by other investigators. In one, Rorschach tests were given to a sample of seventy-five mill villagers, including a proportional representation from the four village sections, from various age groups, and from the two sexes. These tests were administered by Miss Dorothy Reynolds of Duke University, and they were analyzed by someone who knew only that the Rorschach records were drawn from a group of mill workers living in a town in Old South State. The other studied the relation between child-rearing practices and personality development. It was conducted by Miss Barbara Chartier of the University of North Carolina and consisted primarily of intensive interviews of a cross section of twenty mothers in the four village sections. In addition, Miss Chartier secured replies from fifty-seven mill children on emotional response and moral ideology tests to determine the pleasurable and painful experiences of childhood and to discover what the children considered to be right and wrong behavior for their age.[1]

The preliminary material for this chapter came entirely from the data gathered by participant observation. When the results of the Rorschach tests and the child-rearing study became available, they were incorporated as supplementary material. Therefore in the traits reported there is an emphasis on the types of reactions that could be observed by someone regarded as an outsider by the mill people. I was usually considered in the same category as a town person, and therefore reactions to me would most likely be heavily weighted toward the status-linked feelings of mill people. Thus these traits are closely akin to what might be termed "status personality."[2] No attempt has been made to treat deeper aspects of personality, such as "core personality"[3] or "basic personality type."[4]

The personality traits are drawn up for the "average" per-

1. This study is written as Weaverton: A Study of Culture and Personality in a Southern Mill Town (unpublished master's thesis, University of North Carolina, 1949).

2. Ralph Linton, Cultural Background of Personality (New York: D. Appleton-Century Company, 1945), pp. 129-30, defines "status personality" as the configuration of responses linked with certain socially delimited groups within the society.

3. Gillin, Ways of Men, p. 580, speaks of "core personality" as "the essential inner organization of the person...." It is distinguished from "public or social personality," which consists of "manifestations which other persons can predict and depend upon."

4. Linton, op. cit., p. 130, states that "status personality" differs from "basic personality type" in that it is "...heavily weighted on the side of specific overt responses."

son and, like the culture constructs of preceding chapters, should be viewed as modes within certain ranges of variation. Probably no actual mill person will show all of the characteristics discussed here, and those that are shown will be evident in varying degrees. There are deviants in mill society, as in any society, who fall outside the ranges of variation of the modal type. But this is not to minimize the fact that mill people as a group do have attitudes and values in common. It is to this "average mill worker" that the unions direct their propaganda and to whom the owners and superintendents appeal as they attempt to increase production, improve the quality of goods, or fight unionization.

The Rorschach tests were analyzed in such a manner that the results could be readily applied to the data gathered through participant observation. The chief method of analysis used was to summate the variables usually selected for consideration in Rorschach protocol. The means of these variables were computed in order to construct an "average" personality.[5] Written reactions of the Rorschach interviewer to each person tested were also used in arriving at summary characteristics.

Chartier's study not only helps to identify traits but also to show how the early training of the mill child might affect his attitudes and values and reactions. Students of personality generally accept that the way a child is trained in his earliest years is of basic importance in the formation of personality.[6] Thus the study of the effect of child care on personality development proved especially helpful in the attempt to account for the observed traits of adult mill villagers.

Before discussing the manifest personality characteristics, it

5. From the Rorschach Analysis, pp. 3–5 (on file in the Institute for Research in Social Science, University of North Carolina).
6. Ralph Linton in the Foreword to Abram Kardiner's *Psychological Frontiers of Society* (New York: Columbia University Press, 1945), pp. vii–viii, stresses the importance of child-rearing patterns in accounting for the similarities of individuals in the same society. Gillin, *op. cit.*, pp. 582–84, gives a concise summary of this position.

is essential to review in summary form the basic features of the mill subculture, since it is assumed that it plays a decisive role in the development of these traits of personality.

Foundations of Manifest Personality in the Mill Subculture

We have seen that the way of life of the Kent mill people is related to both town and country, yet it stands apart from them. Mill people have maintained many of their rural ways in a semiurban environment. The older mill workers, almost all of whom came from the farm, look nostalgically back to farm life as the ideal, but the younger workers, who have lived only in the mill-village sections, look rather toward the town for their values and ways of doing things. Because they have been a group set apart, largely separated from town and country both geographically and socially, mill people have formed a somewhat different set of values and attitudes from those of town and country.

In spite of the fact that they are industrial workers, Kent mill people possess many of the qualities ascribed to folk cultures: they are relatively homogeneous, somewhat isolated (socially, in particular), rely little upon formal education, have large families, center much of their activity and security in the kindred group, and are on much the same economic level. The farmlike houses, unpaved streets, outhouses, pigs, dogs, gardens, and farm dress are characteristic of rural conditions. But urban influences are beginning to have telling effects on this folklike subculture, for mill women want fewer children, government and factory compensation is beginning to replace a dependence upon family and neighborhood groups, and children are seeking more formal schooling and consequently acquiring town attitudes and values. Radios, newspapers, movies, and television direct mill people toward values more closely related to town than to country.

The mill operatives have been and still are under paternalistic direction. The workers are "taken care of" by the owners and superintendents, and most of their houses are owned and controlled by those who control their jobs. Mill work is essentially mechanical, requiring little initiative and few decisions on the part of regular workers. Work is directed by mill whistles, by bossmen, and by machines; and it is largely noncompetitive so far as operatives are concerned, for there is little chance to advance. The mill-village sections supply more than enough workers for the local mills, for the majority of mill children become operatives.

The culturally ascribed goals of the mill people might be termed "low" when compared with those in the town.[7] Mill operatives, as a rule, seek these things: eight to ten years of schooling, a job in the mill, early marriage, a family, a separate house (their own if possible), and a modicum of material possessions. "Salvation" is important for the majority, for mill people are deeply concerned about what will happen to them in the life after death. Recreational pursuits, particularly those in the out-of-doors, are highly valued. Like town people, mill workers are interested in making money; however, their purpose in getting money differs in some points. Money in itself does not bring prestige among mill workers, probably because they are kept on much the same economic level. Little stress is put on saving, primarily because there has been little excess money to save; instead, money is something to spend as soon as it is received, or even before it is received, for the immediate use to which it can be put.

7. It is interesting to compare the simplicity of the goals of the mill people with those of the Indians of a Guatemalan community as reported by Otto Billig, John Gillin, and William Davidson in "Aspects of Personality and Culture in a Guatemalan Community," *Journal of Personality*, XVI (1947–48), 153–87, 326–68. In contrast to the goals of the Ladinos, an upperclass group, the Indians have "low" or "simple" goals, presenting a situation somewhat similar to that existing between the mill and the town in Kent.

The subculture permits fulfillment of these goals without great effort or much frustration. Education is provided and even compulsory to the age of sixteen, and jobs in the mill are readily available for almost all who want them. Marriage is rather easily arranged at an early age, for there are few family or societal limitations, except the restriction of marriage to those within the mill class. The marriage ceremony itself is simple and quickly and quietly performed. Several different types of churches offer "salvation," which can be gained during a brief altar call, although it is difficult for some members of the society to remain saved, especially those in the Holiness groups. The surrounding countryside provides ample opportunity for out-of-door recreational pursuits.

As long as a person accepts the culturally prescribed mill goals, there are apparently few frustrations and anxieties. Only when mill life is contrasted to that of middle- and upper-class America, depicted in glowing terms by movies, radio, and television, does discontent with the mill way of life begin.

Selected Manifest Traits of Personality

I am aware that in presenting characteristics of mill people a standard has been assumed. To state, for example, that Kent mill people have relatively low anxiety if they accept the socially defined goals of the mill subculture raises the question, Relatively low in comparison to what other group or standard? Anxiety itself is difficult to measure, as are passiveness, repression, aggression, and other terms used. Ultimately this study, largely implicitly, has compared the mill people with those in town, particularly those who represent middle-class America, admittedly another vague classification. The Rorschach tests, having been standardized, and also comparisons with Hopi and Midwestern children in the emotional responses and moral ideology tests, help to balance the impressionistic tendencies of observational techniques.

Just how characteristic these traits are of mill villagers all over the South is not known. A number of company officials, union leaders, and others associated with cotton-mill operatives in various parts of the South, with whom I have come in contact, agree that the mental and actional patterns delineated here as typical of Kent mill villagers are common also to the cotton-mill people they have known. Since the patterns of cotton-mill subcultures are apparently generally the same throughout the South, it can be expected that the manifest personality characteristics of cotton-mill people are similar.

Acceptance of Life As It Is

One attitude toward environment is the attempt to control it or to change it as far as possible in accord with one's own desires. It is the "I am the master of my fate; I am the captain of my soul" approach, embodied by the American dream of "from log cabin to White House." The majority of Americans believe that any one can better himself and rise in the world if he really wants to and applies himself diligently enough. At the other extreme is the adaptation of oneself to fit in with whatever environmental situation presents itself. The Chinese, at least in the past, have used this approach, with "mei yo bon fa" ("nothing can be done") and "mei yo kwan shi" ("it doesn't really matter") philosophy, and they are renowned for their ability to adapt to varied situations and to overcome their conquerors by absorbing them slowly over a long period of time.

The attitude of mill people toward life appears to have a greater degree of acceptance and adaptation than of remolding and mastery. Examples can be multiplied to illustrate this approach. When workers were laid off from the mill, the attitude often expressed was "Oh, well, I needed the rest anyhow, and now I can spend more time with my children," or "I can draw my rocking-chair money and fix up a few things around the house." But once mill work was offered again, these same workers readily took the jobs. When wages were curtailed because of a shorter work week, many workers said that they had about as much money as during former times, because they were spending it more carefully.

Mill people seem to feel that there is little they can do to change the situations that face them. Yet this need not cause undue concern, "for everything is in the hands of the Lord." This attitude was reflected far more frequently among mill children than among town children who wrote compositions on "The Story of My Life." In reply to the question "What would you do if you could change the world to your heart's desire?" 17.1 percent of the eighty-five mill children said they would leave it alone, while only 4.0 percent of the seventy-nine town children said this. Furthermore, 62.5 percent of the mill children who said they would leave it alone added something to the effect that this is God's world and it is up to him to do something about it, but none of the town children expressed this idea.

In this same vein, mill people are cautious about expecting much of the future. When signs of an economic recession appeared in the fall of 1948, each worker thought that he would be the next one laid off, that he would end up in the county home for the poor, and that it would soon be necessary to have a federal government project comparable to the Works Progress Administration (on which many of them had worked during the depression of the 1930's). During the boom times of the war period, they were sure that the good times would not last, and when difficulties with Russia continued after the end of World War II, they were sure that America would be in war before many months. But it should be added that mill people are not unhappy because of this pessimism about the future. They apparently prepare themselves for the worst and are pleasantly surprised when it is not so bad as they thought it would be.

Summary statements throughout the Rorschach analysis bear out this characteristic of passive acceptance of things as they are:

> Most matters are dealt with in a day-to-day manner. There is little effort to anticipate events of the future. Life is lived on a day-to-day basis, with current needs determining behavior and current crises met as they arise. Attempts at long-range planning are minimal, aspirations involving subgoals not common. There is little evidence to show determinate attempts at reconstructuring the life situation, and we can expect little in the way of activity predicated to change institutions. Whatever institutions may exist will be held to with little attempt at breaking away or modifying.[8]

And, again,

> Our group, through its predominant emphasis on animal movement and only minimal utilization of human movement, would suggest a limited acceptance of roles of initiative and social responsibility, preferring instead to allow personal needs carrying less social responsibility to dominate its social perceptions.[9]

Finally,

> Thus we may recognize that our group has difficulty in associating itself with responsible social roles, and that as the associations come closer in content to the nature of the perceiver, they become more passive.
>
> We may expect that our group will not be too much concerned with assuming responsibility for change in its environment, but will be rather more concerned with accepting and maintaining the particular mores passed on to it.[10]

8. Rorschach Analysis, p. 11.
9. Ibid., p. 15.
10. Ibid., p. 16.

Several instances of hesitancy, overt at least, in accepting more responsible roles occurred during my stay. Two workers promoted to jobs as foremen did not apply for the positions or even ask for them informally. They were persuaded to take them by the overseers and superintendents. The mill worker who became the manager of the mill boardinghouse and another who took charge of a grocery store located on mill property had to be urged by the superintendent to take these jobs.

On more than one occasion, in my presence, town people criticized mill people for this passive attitude, saying that they had no ambition, no desire to get ahead, and no "hustle." They claimed that mill workers "just don't give a damn about bettering themselves."

A number of logical explanations come to mind in attempting to account for such an attitude of passive acceptance. Mill work has been highly unstable. Mills stop and curtail their working weeks almost without warning. If mill workers did seek to better themselves and if they expected much from the future economically, they would be continually frustrated. The emphasis of mill-village religion on the rewards in the afterlife might be considered both a result of this passiveness and a reinforcement of it. We have seen that one possible function of religion in the village sections was compensation for the lack of economic and social status. At the same time, it serves to promote the acceptance of existing conditions. The paternalistic system itself is very likely a contributing factor to this attitude.

The study of child-rearing practices throws light upon the reasons for this passivity and low aggression. Chartier points out that when the mother leaves the child abruptly to take up her work in the mill, the child is left to the unfamiliar and less reliable care of mother surrogates. She continues:

In addition he may at the same time be deprived of his mother's breast, receive less attention in the form of rocking and caressing, and be left to cry for longer periods.... Thus with the mother's departure the infant's world changes from one which was primarily and consistently rewarding to one in which many tensions are allowed to accumulate from unmet needs, particularly those centering about expectations of the mother's presence.[11]

This might lead to the feeling that good things do not last, and it would not promote in the child trust and confidence in a predictable world.[12] Chartier also believes that the custom of frequent teasing and frightening of children about imaginary objects might foster an attitude of skepticism about both the present and the future.[13]

Further understanding of the passiveness of mill people can be gleaned from the results of the emotional response and moral ideology tests given to 57 mill children at the Cromwell school, especially when such results are compared with those from similar tests by Laura Thompson and Alice Joseph [14] of 368 school children in a midwestern industrial town and 174 Hopi Indian children from a culture often referred to as highly nonaggressive. In response to the question "Have you ever been ashamed of something you did?" some form of aggression [15] was mentioned in 42.8 percent of the replies of the mill children, in 2.1 percent of the replies of the midwestern children, and in 10.4 percent of the replies of the Hopi. In reply to the question "Have you ever been sad?" acts of

11. Chartier, op. cit., pp. 79–80.
12. This hypothesis might be tested by comparing the attitudes of children whose mothers returned to work with the attitudes of the children whose mothers did not work in the mill, since there are a few of the latter.
13. Chartier, op. cit., p. 13.
14. The Hopi Way (Chicago: University of Chicago Press, 1944), pp. 91–92 and 145–46. Chartier included their results along with her own.
15. Chartier, op. cit., p. 135. In giving examples of answers classified as "aggression," she mentioned the following:
"When I slapped my little sister."
"When I hit a boy and he had to go to the hospital."
"When I do anything mean to anybody."
"When I would hit somebody when they fussed at me."

aggression [16] as a reason for sadness were included in 12.4 percent of the answers of the mill children, in 1.9 percent of the answers of the midwestern children, and in 13.2 percent of the answers of the Hopi. To the question "What is the worst thing that could happen to you?" 8.9 percent of the replies of the mill children included some form of aggression,[17] compared with 2.2 percent of the replies of the midwestern children and 3.9 percent of the Hopi replies. Finally, when asked "What is a bad thing for a child of your age to do?" 19.2 percent of the answers of the mill children included some form of aggression,[18] compared with 2.6 percent of the replies of the midwestern children and 9.4 percent of the replies of the Hopi tested on this question.[19] It is apparent from their answers to these questions that the mill children tested have a strong dislike for aggression, at least that of an overt, physical type. This might well carry over into adulthood in regard to the passive acceptance of life as it is.

A comment from a mill child's composition, "The Story of my Life," is highly significant in this connection. When tell-

16. *Ibid.*, p. 132. Examples of answers included under "aggression" are:
"When daddy and another man got in a fight."
"When somebody hits me and knocks me down."
"When other people get in a fight."
"When me and Joe would go out to play and he'd start a fight and I'd hit him."

17. *Ibid.*, p. 142. Examples of "aggression" are:
"For somebody to knock me down."
"For somebody to cuss me out."
"To get mad."

18. *Ibid.*, p. 147. Examples of "aggression" are:
"To sass mamma and daddy."
"To hit people."
"To kill people."
"To get in fights."
"To fuss at the baby when I have to keep her and I can't go anywhere and she won't go to sleep."

19. Thompson and Joseph, *op. cit.*, pp. 92 and 146. There were 161 Hopi children tested on this question.

ing of the things he had learned at home, a mill boy in high school wrote, "I was taught not to want more than I could expect to get."

Noncompetitiveness

Although noncompetitiveness might be considered a form of passiveness, and consequently implied above, it demands special attention because it is in striking contrast to the competitiveness associated with American life generally. The tendency toward noncompetitiveness appeared in all phases of the mill subculture. At women's parties, even when prizes were given for unscrambling words or drawing pictures, those present worked together, helping one another, rather than striving to outdo the others. On fishing trips, the men purposely helped those who had not caught anything in order to make the catch more even. Mill children did not often keep score in the games they played, nor did they seem to strive hard to win. It is true that older mill children play and succeed in highly competitive sports, particularly at Kent High School. But although involving competition, this is also a primary means of gaining acceptance by schoolmates and praise from adults, both mill and town. Teachers in the mill school reported that the children are not particularly interested in what grades they receive and that few exert themselves to make good grades. However, they do not like other students to make better grades than they do, and they complain to teachers about the lack of fairness in grading. This apparently low stress on competition might be related only to areas in which there are feelings of incompetence, but if so, these feelings cover a wide area.

Chartier was struck by this lack of competitiveness among children. When the fifty-seven mill children were asked "What is the best thing that you can think of that might happen to you?" 6.5 percent of the replies of the mill children contained some form of personal achievement,[20] in contrast to 26.0 percent of the midwestern and 18.0 percent of the Hopi replies received by Thompson and Joseph. Chartier relates this lack of competitiveness to family life. She says that sibling rivalry is low and that there is great solidarity between brothers and sisters both in and outside the home. This is attributed, in part, to the presence of many parental surrogates from whom gratification might be expected and to the fact that parents do not seem to make their love conditional upon a child's matching up to the accomplishments of his brothers and sisters.[21] She goes ahead to say that the average mill child receives little training in competitive behavior, and that this

...lack of development of a competitive drive is probably rooted in the comparatively non-competitive nature of the family situation. Competitive behavior results only under certain essential conditions. First is the presence of scarce values. Second, there must be some means by which the values may be attained by the particular individual, or he will abandon his effort to reach the goal. When viewed in this light the family situation in the mill culture would not seem particularly conducive to the development of competitive trends in the child's personality. Values, in this case, love, care, attention, and approval of the parent, are seldom exclusively available to the mill child. This may mean that they acquire either a high or low positive valence, but, what is more significant, the child is not in a position to alter appreciably the situation in which he finds himself. There are too many other conflicting demands upon the parent's time and attention over which he can exercise no control.[22]

20. Chartier, *op. cit.*, p. 129. Examples of "personal achievement" are: "Go through college"; "Pass in school"; "Be a nurse."

Most frequently mentioned as an answer to this question was some form of meeting of social expectations, for example: "Be good and help mother"; "Get saved"; "Clean up the house"; "Learn nice manners." Such an answer was given by 32.6 percent of the mill children, compared with 4.0 percent of the midwestern children and 13.9 percent of the Hopi.

21. *Ibid.*, pp. 107–8.

22. *Ibid.*, pp. 113–14.

Repression of Emotions

Kent mill people are not effusive or spontaneous. Instead they are quiet, cautious, and reserved, living by the adage (which was frequently quoted in the village sections) "a still tongue makes a wise head." Previous chapters pointed out that mill people place emphasis on minding one's own business and on not talking too much, particularly around strangers. Vicious gossip is often stifled with the remark "Well, it's their own business."[23] In trying to start conversations with mill people, I was met with a complete lack of response on several occasions. The Rorschach examiner reported numerous signs of this reserve and caution: "His attitude is cautious, though smiling continually." "He can't seem to let himself go in the testing situation." "His face held little expression and there is a stillness about him that seemed tense." "This is a rather loud, overtly hospitable and friendly woman who closes up like a clam upon testing." "He is overtly cooperative, but it is felt that his resistance never broke down during the testing."[24]

In their religious services, particularly those at the Cromwell Baptist church, the mill villagers sat almost stolidly through most of the religious exercises. Even in the Holiness churches where emotional expression is approved and encouraged, the leader of the service had to work hard to get the audience to participate. He had to start clapping his hands and tapping his feet before the congregation began to follow. The small groups composing the "amen corners" in each of the churches seemed forced rather than spontaneous in their expressions.

23. This does not imply that mill people do not talk about each other. They do, continually. And they know minute details of each other's lives. But the gossip seems to be more informational than malicious. At the same time, there is little question that this "informational" type of gossip is an important form of social control.

24. These and the quotes used later were copied from the Rorschach protocols where the examiner was asked to give her impressions of the person being tested.

The analysis of the Rorschach tests brought out this characteristic of repression more than any other trait. To begin with, the number of responses was low, on the average, and the responses made indicate that "our population tends toward careful control of its responses. . . ." [25] Furthermore, the very high percentage of form responses indicates that there is so much control that little freedom remains for the individual to respond to subtle changes in his environment. The reaction to shading and color "would indicate that our group does not permit affective values to modify their perceptions." [26] The analyzer stated that the comparatively large number of animal-movement responses would indicate the rather vigorous potential for biological need expressions, and that such biological impulses would be accepted. ". . . but the high degree of control it exercises on expression would probably result in a minimum of overt activity." [27] The general conclusion of the Rorschach analysis on control of expression states, "Thus, our group may be said to be relatively controlled in its expression of feeling, to have some potentiality for impulsive and free affective expression, but generally to resist it." [28]

Along with this tendency to allow feelings to be only carefully and cautiously brought into dealings with the demands of a real world, the Rorschach interpreter states that there is the possibility that there is a freedom in phantasy that is not found in day-to-day interpersonal relationships. "Movement responses do not seem to be directly translated into overt action, but rather to be expressions of potential action. While overt action is tied to reality, is cautious and reserved, there is a potential for expression in our group that is fairly vigorous." [29] The interpreter indicates that these phantasy productions are most likely defensive reactions to the restrictions

25. Rorschach Analysis, p. 6.
26. Ibid., p. 6.
27. Ibid., pp. 9–10.
28. Ibid., p. 10.
29. Ibid., p. 12.

of individual expression, thus reiterating the thesis of this chapter, the influence of the subculture on personality:

By living in a closely constricted community, required by local convention to inhibit individuality and to rely rather upon conformity, the potential for individuality is pushed further away from expression and becomes possible primarily in phantasy. In this case, the movement responses would reflect the degree of potential for individuality that does not find expression. They represent the unsatisfied aspirations and hopes for achievement in whatever fields have value for the group.

This large area of phantasy may well indicate the area of tension in our group. It complies and conforms, subverting its individuality to the demands of a fairly vigorous social structure. But since this pushes back individual initiative and individual expression, an area of unrest is made evident. This is the untapped source of dissatisfaction and the ever present potential that might surge into action upon sufficient frustration.[30]

My findings clearly agree with the last statement in this quotation, for I observed that many mill people tended "to go to pieces" in certain crisis situations. At deaths and funerals they frequently became "all tore up inside," and when they had not done their work well at the mill, several women reported that they went home and "had a good cry." On one occasion, when sparks from a stove almost set a house on fire, the six mill workers living there were so upset that they were unable to go to work in the mill that day. Upon further inquiry, I found this to be not unusual. There are occasional "blowups" with bossmen regarding jobs in the mill. One woman cried and refused to work when she was moved to another machine, and a man quit when he thought a bossman criticized him unjustly.[31] Several bossmen said that they had

30. *Ibid.*, p. 13.
31. Chartier, *op. cit.*, p. 65, observed that mill workers tended to walk off their jobs in the mill when faced with a difficult situation. She attributed this to emotional upset. She did not think the "blowups" with bossmen were due to the independence of mill workers, as has been attributed by some

to be very careful in scolding workers, lest smoldering resentment break out later in almost any direction.[32] These outbreaks apparently indicate the presence of an emotional dam repressing the expression of feelings.

It can be logically hypothesized that related to this evident repression of feelings under normal circumstances is the type of discipline received by mill children. Chapter 5 shows that the discipline of children tended to be inconsistent and haphazard but at the same time severe, authoritarian, and negative when enforced. Chartier reports that the general attitude of parents toward children was that they should be seen and not heard,[33] and I frequently heard parental concern over a child who was "full of hisself."

It is also reasonable to believe that such repression might be a reaction to their low status and consequent feelings of inferiority.[34] Chapter 5 points out that the town standards enforced at the schools attended by mill children imply that millways are inferior to townways. Television, movies, and contacts with Kent aristocracy might well reinforce the belief that their own way of life falls short, and that caution and reserve are the safest courses to follow, especially with strangers.

Feelings of Inferiority and Inadequacy

It was my impression that mill people lacked self-confidence and self-assurance in many situations. Many of the workers

writers, for in none of the cases was a concept of freedom or independence at stake.

32. Liston Pope, *Millhands and Preachers,* pp. 68–69, found this same characteristic among Gaston County mill workers. He quotes a pastor as saying: "Mill people are unpredictable. They take funny twists. Everything may seem all right with them, but then something comes along, and they blow up all over the place."

33. Chartier, *op. cit.,* p. 113.

34. This does not imply that the only reaction to low status is repression of feelings. The other low status group in Kent, the Negroes, does not react in this way.

spoke of themselves as "ignorant" because of their meager formal education. Foremen in the mill and other leaders in the villages were particularly sensitive about their "poor" speech. Each of the mill ministers apologized for his lack of training in English, and one spoke of "butchering the King's English," requesting that he not be quoted without having his poor English first corrected.

It is true that when with their own group and in familiar surroundings, these feelings were not so apparent, although mill people approved of those who were modest in their claims. And they expressed confidence about their mill jobs. Their conversations sometimes revolved about how much work a person had done in the mill in a day or how many different mill jobs someone was capable of doing. They were also sure of themselves when picking cotton or doing other familiar jobs on the farm. But they lost this confidence when faced with situations with which they were not thoroughly familiar. One man who wanted to move out of the village into other work, and who did become a political officeholder because of the support of the mill people, said he had felt as though "four walls and a ceiling hemmed me in." He was afraid to leave his job in the mill and run for office, despite the urgings of his friends, and he added that most mill people feared moving out of their accustomed sphere and rarely did so.

The Rorschach examiner reported that many of the mill people tested revealed feelings of inadequacy, either verbalized or shown by their manner in the testing situation: "She reacts in a puzzled sort of way as though not accustomed to approaching new problems." "He is very sensitive about his ability and covers up his lack of education by elaboration on a detective course he had." "She feels unsure of her ability and hesitates many times, often starting to give a response, then refusing to do so." "He apparently feels some inadequacy as he informed the examiner that he has lived in twenty-six states (as a soldier in World War II) in a sort of bragging manner." "She expressed some feelings of inadequacy, and it is felt that her performance could have been better if she had had more confidence." Typical of the feelings of inadequacy among the mill people tested is the following remark to the Rorschach tester by a young Cromwell male: "You can see a lot of things but don't know how to bring it out."

The Rorschach tests themselves did not reveal this characteristic of feelings of inadequacy as strongly as did observations. There is mention in the analysis of comparatively low creativity, which might reflect lack of confidence in abilities as well as lack of opportunity or motivation. The analysis states that "the mean original responses of 1.13 suggests that there is limited freedom in our group in the creative expression of new ideas." [35] The Rorschach analyzer also concluded that the cautious handling of color (stimulus potential) in the cards, coupled with freedom for spontaneous projection of activity into the cards, suggests that "phantasy, hopes, and aspirations are quite common in the group, but that activity predicated to enhance the possibility of individual achievement is quite limited." [36]

Chartier found mill people timid, fearful, and lacking in self-confidence. She points out that such traits "may have their beginnings in the unreliability and inconsistency of maternal care and in the practices of frightening, neither of which allows the child to form a picture of a predictable world in which dangers can be accurately predicted and successfully avoided by patterned and familiar means." [37]

This lack of self-confidence might also have historical roots. We saw in Chapter 2 that the successful farmers, the townspeople, and the mill people themselves considered those who became mill operatives to be taking a downward step. Mill

35. Rorschach Analysis, p. 7.
36. Ibid., p. 9.
37. Chartier, op. cit., pp. 158–59.

children, nurtured by parents who consider themselves failures in some respects, reared in a semi-isolated village, looked down on by farm and town, and brought to realize their comparative lack of ability in a competitive downtown school, could easily acquire feelings of inadequacy. The paternalistic system under which the village sections operate would appear to reinforce such lack of self-confidence. Mill owners and superintendents feel that workers cannot be trusted with responsibilities requiring much initiative. Rather, they regard the mill villagers as children who must be watched over. They prefer workers who will do as they are told, and thus it is likely that the more independent and self-confident would be eliminated.

Hostility toward Outsiders

I have repeatedly pointed out that mill villagers tend to be hostile toward and suspicious of outsiders, and the chapter on the relations between town and country and mill showed that this hostility was a reaction to the exclusion of mill people by those in town. The villagers are highly sensitive about the town's low evaluation of them and strongly resent it. They fear that those of higher status might take advantage of them and exploit them and that they are ill equipped to protect themselves. Such hostility, then, is likely a form of avoidance.

Chartier relates this hostility to child care in the following manner:

Poor maternal care, burdensome home responsibilities, severe discipline, experiences with teasing and frightening all would seem conducive to the formation of hostile impulses in the mill child's personality. Since there are strong cultural sanctions against the expression of this hostility within the family and in-group . . . and since it is not channeled into economic or status competition, the main outlet for such hostility in mill society must be through resentment of "outsiders," particularly townspeople, local, state and federal officials, Negroes, and, in fact, of almost anyone who comes from outside the village itself.[38]

Anxiety

There is conflicting evidence regarding the degree of anxiety displayed by mill people. When going through their daily rounds, Kent mill people do not show noticeable signs of anxiety. The fact that they must be at work at a certain time apparently does not bother these ex-farmers who formerly worked according to the sun and season rather than by an exact schedule. Mill workers avoid the pressure of time schedules and the need for hurrying by getting ready long in advance and by reaching the mill half an hour or so before time to enter. They exhibit some anxiety an hour or so before they must be at work if something arises which might prevent their leaving for the mill early enough. Mill children leave for school early and frequently arrive forty-five minutes before classes begin. Off the job, mill people lead a leisurely life, are rarely in a hurry and always have time to visit and chat. Thus they seem to have maintained their "folklike" attitude toward time. We have noticed that in their recreational pursuits they are relaxed and easy going. Their acceptance of things as they are and the low stress on competition evidently cushion their concern about the present and the future.

On the other hand, there are demonstrations of anxiety and tenseness when mill people deal with someone outside the mill circle. The Rorschach tester reported as evidence of tenseness chain smoking and deep concern about the results of the test on the part of many who were tested. When I sought information on a questionnaire, more than one asked,

38. *Ibid.*, pp. 164-65.

"This ain't nothin' that will git me put in jail, is it?" A worker said it was all right for me to take pictures of his hunting dogs, but that I had better not try to claim later that I owned the dogs just because I had pictures of them. Mill people reveal feelings of being handicapped through lack of education and economic equality, and those trying to leave the village show frustrations and anxieties. But for those content to remain within the culturally prescribed goals of the mill subculture and keep their contact with outsiders to a minimum, there are few indications of anxiety.

Chartier believes that the indiscriminate warnings and threatenings so prevalent in parental treatment of children cause the mill child to grow up in an environment that is constantly and namelessly threatening. She thinks that a generalized anxiety results and supports this contention with the answers of children between the ages of seven and fourteen to the question "Have you ever been afraid?" Among the answers were:

"Afraid of buggers at night," "afraid of bears," "afraid someone would grab me and kill me," "afraid of a snake," "afraid of someone tip-toeing on the porch at night," "afraid of someone trying to break into the house," "afraid of a man on a horse with his head cut off," "afraid in the house at night," "afraid in a dream that an old drunk got me and threw me in the river," "afraid of a Negro at night," "afraid when someone knocks at the door," "afraid of mad dogs," "afraid when I go to the woods alone," "afraid all night at the river when I hear motors coming," "afraid when I get into bed," "afraid when I'm home alone with my three sisters," "afraid a murderer will kill me," "afraid when my brother tells me stories," "afraid in a dream that a nigger is going to get me," "afraid that someone will come and get me at night when the dogs start barking around the house," "afraid at night when something came out of a tree at me and I thought it was a leopard," "afraid when daddy slipped through the house at night dressed up." [39]

39. *Ibid.*, pp. 92–93.

Chartier points out that most of these dangers are highly subjective. She also reports that when the children were asked whether they had ever been happy, or ever been sad, whether they had ever been angry, or ever been ashamed, the answers to these questions were rarely as full and enthusiastic as the answers to "Have you ever been afraid?"

In considering the degree of anxiety manifested by Kent mill people, it is interesting to see whether such summarizing terms as "tough" or "easy" can be applied to the mill subculture.[40] A "tough" culture makes tension-reduction difficult in filling basic needs and reaching goals, while an "easy" culture allows for ready tension-reduction in these areas. Behavioral indices of "toughness" are tenseness, nervousness, suicide, neurosis and psychosis of nonconstitutional types, crime, projection of satisfactions into afterlife, and "general malaise." The indices for "easiness" are measured by the amount of time given to nonritualistic song, dance, laughter, play, affectional activities, and nonmandatory work. "Easy" cultures have relatively frictionless interpersonal relations.

The personality type developed in the mill subculture indicates characteristics of both "toughness" and "easiness"— "tough" because of the escape resorted to in heavy drinking and the necessity for a belief in future happiness and wealth in a life to come to compensate for their lack on earth. To these should be added the tendency toward repression and, at least on the part of children, a generalized fearfulness. On the other hand, there is little friction in interpersonal relations, and friendly joking and bantering characterize many relationships. Although there is little nonritualistic singing (singing outside the church services), mill people enjoy listening to "hillbilly" music and a few play guitars in the evening while neighborhood groups sing.

The mill subculture might be termed "easy" as long as the

40. John and Jean M. Arsenian, "Tough and Easy Cultures," *Psychiatry*, XI (1948), 377-85.

culturally defined goals of the subculture are accepted. However, this becomes more and more difficult to do as the advantages of town goals are brought to the attention of mill young people. Wealth, social prestige, home ownership, college education, and the like cannot be obtained within the ways delineated by the mill subculture. A person must leave the mill and the mill-village section to have a chance at these, and the price is a heavy one to pay for a person enculturated in the Kent millways.

Summary

In drawing together the data from this and other chapters, we can form a qualified picture of the "typical" adult mill villager: (1) He accepts life as he finds it, and is not aggressive in seeking to change his condition. He is resigned to his lot. (2) He seems to be more noncompetitive than competitive, more dependent than independent, more submissive than dominant. (3) He lacks confidence in himself and feels inadequate, especially when faced with new or difficult tasks. He is humble. (4) He is reserved, quiet, and cautious, particularly when with strangers. He seems to repress his feelings more than to give them spontaneous expression. (5) He is suspicious of and even hostile toward outsiders, but he is loyal and devoted to his kindred group, and he is a warm friend to those who prove themselves friendly and uncritical. (6) He is a steady and cooperative worker, and is generous in giving his time and money to help those in need.

It is highly probable that certain of these characteristics are related to the manner in which mill people are reared and to the total situation in which they find themselves. In other words, their logical relationship to the mill subculture can be shown.

Trends and Prospects

CHAPTER **11** THE CONFIGURATION OF customs making up the subculture of Kent's mill villages is by no means static. This subculture, developed by ex-tenant farmers as an adjustment to a semiurban, industrial environment, is continually undergoing change. There have been two basic trends, almost in opposite directions. On the one hand, the mill group has grown into a distinct class, and on the other, there has been a bettering of living conditions, with higher wages and more education, which have tended to lift mill people out of their "low" social and economic status. There is a trend toward the adoption of town values, although the older and more conservative members of the villages continue to look upon the country as embodying the "good" life. Thus a complex of factors is at work making for change in mill village life. These have already been touched upon indirectly, and in this chapter the most important factors will be looked at directly, though briefly.

FACTORS FOR CHANGE

Technology and Organization of the Cotton-Mill Industry

Kent mill workers are an occupational group, and anything that affects the basis of their occupation affects their way of life. The future of the mill villages is bound up with the future of the cotton-textile industry. Exactly what is happening to the industry at the time of this writing is hard to determine. Competition between companies and between cotton fabrics and such synthetic textiles as rayon and nylon is calling for greater speed and mechanization of the industry. This in turn calls for fewer and more skilled workers, but just how much further this mechanization can proceed can hardly be ascertained. Some of the mechanical processes have changed little over the last twenty years, especially those involved in carding and weaving. On the other hand, the knot tiers, automatic spoolers, and high-speed warpers are considered wholly modern. There is little doubt that technological improvements will continue to affect the nature of the mechanical process of converting raw cotton into cloth, but it is doubtful that revolutionary changes will be made overnight. These changes are usually a matter of gradual improvements on the technological processes rather than radical innovations. Cotton goods might have an increasingly difficult time competing with synthetic products, but they are still superior in many ways to the synthetics, and experts see no serious replacement of cotton products by synthetic ones. It is highly probable, then, that the cotton mills and their workers and villages will be an important part of the economy of the Piedmont and of the nation for some time to come.

Reorganization of the industry can affect the social life of the mill villagers. A company official pointed out that there are at least three things from which the industry is suffering and which should be changed: overproduction caused by operating three shifts when two shifts would supply the demand; concentration of buying in a few hands; the method of selling through commission houses where sales agents are more interested in making a commission than in the stability of the industry.[1] If these conditions are changed, the third shift

1. From personal correspondence with John W. Clark, president of Randolph Mills, Inc., Franklinville, N. C.

would be eliminated, and employment made much more regular. The effect of eliminating the third shift was demonstrated in the Cromwell mill, which had to drop this shift temporarily early in 1949 because of the short demand for goods. Workers cut off from mill jobs were primarily the least stable workers, especially the ones who might be termed floaters, and also most of those who commuted from the country and many of the wives whose husbands worked in the mill. If the third shift were permanently eliminated, the home and child rearing would be affected, as would the husband-wife relationship. Of course, unless wages were raised considerably, the standard of living for the mill families would drop, with only one member working.

A change in the ownership of housing would have significant repercussions in mill-village life.[2] The trend in the South is to sell the mill houses to the workers living in them, and home ownership imparts greater stability, security, and feelings of importance. Certainly this is true of the workers who have bought their own homes in the Reginold villages. Thus far the Cromwell mill has determinedly maintained company ownership of houses, and according to present management will continue to do so. But the widespread sale of mill houses will affect, to some degree, the solidarity of the mill workers, for workers in other occupations of low status might eventually move into some of the houses.

Agitation for improvements in mill working conditions is going on at the present time. Bills have come up before the state legislature to require air conditioning of mills, and a few of the mills in the state have been air conditioned. Preventing cotton dust from filling the air and keeping the humidity and temperature within the human comfort zone will make cotton-mill work far less unattractive. At least a part of the low status associated with mill work has resulted from the atmos-

2. See Harriet Herring, *Passing of the Mill Village*, esp. pp. 114–17.

pheric conditions, the poor rest rooms, and the lack of places to eat. If these things can be improved, the prestige as well as the morale of mill people will be increased.

Paternalism versus Unionism

The struggle between paternalism and unionism is of great significance for the future of the Kent mill villages. The establishment of a union in Kent could seriously affect the mill subculture. The characteristics of paternalism and unionism have been discussed earlier, and we have seen that more than one outbreak between the two forces has openly occurred in Kent. With the success of the Textile Workers Union of America in nearby Stone Valley, union influence in Kent is increasing. Although paternalism is strongly entrenched in the Kent mills, as it is in 80 percent of the cotton mills in the Southeast,[3] it is being seriously challenged by the union (see pages 42-44).

The struggle is one for power and also involves standards of value. Company owners and superintendents want to maintain control over their working forces, saying when and how wages may be changed, the workload increased, or discharges made. To this end, they want a cooperative, docile, loyal worker who will do his job well. As a means of rewarding such faithful workers, the benevolent paternalists prefer not so much to raise wages as to do special things for them. They like to give them special bonuses, Christmas parties, and improved housing, and help build their churches. Their emphasis is on keeping the worker contented and dependent.

The unions, on the other hand, want the workers to have a voice in decisions affecting their wages, hours, and working conditions. This cannot be done by individuals speaking to their bosses separately, for the bosses must consult those who

3. Textile Workers Union of America, *Building a Textile Union* (New York: Congress for Industrial Organization, 1948).

are higher up the scale, and the workers have strength to demand changes only if they are united. Union literature explains:

> In union there is strength. Nobody gives you anything in this rough-and-tumble-world. It takes strength to get what you want—a decent wage, security on the job, a chance to get ahead and give the kids a better opportunity....
> If you've got strength, people have respect for you. If you can stand up for your rights, you can get results. The boss, and his behind-the-scenes bosses, can't give you the run-around now. If you've got a strong union, you get your wages raised to a decent level; you get working conditions straightened out; you get protection for your job....[4]

Through organization the unions have been able to raise wages to a generally higher level in union factories than in nonunion ones.[5] The larger nonunion mills often raise their wages shortly after union mills raise theirs, and mills like the Cromwell pay the same minimum wage as union mills do. Union contracts call for medical service, vacations and holidays with pay, overtime arrangements, minimum wage, and reporting pay. The contracts also provide procedures by which grievances may be taken up, by which disputes between workers and bossmen may be arbitrated, and by which promotions, workload adjustment, and wage adjustment may be made. The unions claim that such a contract prevents "dictatorial" control by the mill management.

Unions claim that unionization not only strengthens the position of the workers in the mill itself but also stimulates them to take part in community life and gives them the channel whereby they may do so. Through the union, which declares itself to be democratically controlled, workers are

4. C.I.O. Organizing Committee, *As Ben Franklin Said* (n.p., n.d.), pp. 2, 4.

5. U. S. Department of Labor, Bureau of Labor Statistics, *Wage Structure in the Cotton Textile and the Woolen Worsted Industries*, April, 1946 (Washington: U. S. Government Printing Office, 1947), p. 7.

represented in community projects and affairs. Union workers take an active part in local, state, and national elections because of the encouragement and insistence from union leaders, who inform them about the prolabor candidates running for office. Because of their increased power and prestige, workers can gain more respect from the communities of which they are a part. A prounion Northern journalist, returning to the South after several years' absence, reported on significant changes brought about by the union in Southern textile towns:

In the textile centers of the South I saw at first hand the new respect acquired by the industrial hands who were once the lowest paid workers and now have become buyers and voters of consequence. Acceptance of them as members in good standing of the community has come about largely through the AF of L and the CIO acting in conjunction with federal legislation. . . .

The situation in Danville, Virginia, has altered so much since then [the 1931 strike] that anyone who was there in the old violent days and saw how isolated from the community the workers were can hardly believe his eyes. The Textile Workers Union headquarters is on the main street of the town. . . . A new union hall is under construction. Almost all of the ten thousand mill workers belong to the union and Danville lives by and for its mills.[6]

The right of workers to organize has been generally recognized throughout the country and has been specifically approved by legislation:

The group basis of maintaining the individual rights of workers is reinforced by decisions of the United States Supreme Court. The Court declared in 1936, for example, that Congress is justified in protecting employees in their fundamental right to organize, choose their own representatives, and engage in collective bargaining or other activities without restriction or coercion by their employers. The basis of this right, it was stated, is the relative

6. Mary Heston Vorse, "The South Has Changed," *Harpers Magazine*, CXCIX (July 1949), 28.

weakness of the individual employee; his inability individually to resist arbitrary and unfair treatment; and his dependence on his union and equality in dealing with his employer.[7]

With such wide acceptance and success throughout the country, it appears safe to say that unionization of Southern textile plants will eventually supplant the prevailing paternalistic system. Approximately 90 percent of the New England cotton textile workers were unionized in 1946,[8] and the T.W.U.A. continually makes "drives" for greater unionization in the South. Union campaigns are aimed at overcoming the majority of workers' lack of self-confidence and passive acceptance of things as they are. These traits of personality, according to union leaders, are as great an obstacle to unionization as the direct opposition of management.

It seems logical that mill people would be more readily represented in Kent community projects if they had strong union organization. The higher wages and better living standards brought about through war earnings, and indirectly by union activities which raised wages in other textile plants, have made noticeable differences in the town's attitude toward mill workers. They have become more important to the town's economy as buyers, and their children, those on New Hill in particular, being able to dress better, are often hard to distinguish from some of those from the town. Presumably unionization would further reduce economic and prestige differences between Kent town and mill people, although it would by no means overcome them entirely. Kent is such an aristocratic place that any integration of mill workers into town life would be quite limited, even if the workers did become organized. The town people would align themselves with the mill owners, and their present attitude of passively ignoring the mill work-

7. U. S. Department of Labor, Bureau of Labor Statistics, *The Gift of Freedom* (Washington: U. S. Government Printing Office, 1949), p. 123.

8. U. S. Department of Labor, Bureau of Labor Statistics, *Wage Structure in the Cotton Textile and the Woolen Worsted Industries*, p. 7.

ers might well become one of active hostility. While this would in one sense increase their prestige, by their being recognized as worth consideration, it would at the same time make no easier their participation in town social life, for the line between town and mill would probably be drawn even tighter. Thus, in one way, unionization might paradoxically increase the isolation of mill workers as well as their participation.[9]

School

The downtown school is playing an important part in teaching mill children town standards of dress and conduct. The town school is a significant democratizing agent in Kent, for children from town, mill, and country meet on a basis of equality and are taught the same things. Of course the mill children are not well prepared nor are they strongly motivated for study, but the majority of the children from the mill villages say they want to complete high school and many of them do remain long enough to be inculcated with the patterns taught at school. They spread these modes of conduct through the villages, thereby instituting change to some degree. Through athletics, plays, and other activities in which mill children take part, the school serves as a community center. Some of the mill children and adults react against the town standards, however, ridiculing instead of imitating them, and thereby increasing the differences between town and mill ways. For example, one young mill worker delights in referring to "hors d'oeuvres" as "horse manure" and in eating with a spoon in deliberate defiance of town etiquette.

9. This is implied in a conclusion from the study of unionized textile employees in Paterson, N. J., by Manis and Meltzer, "Attitudes of Textile Workers to Class Structure," *American Journal of Sociology*, LX (1954), 34: "Union membership ... tends to be the only pattern of class-linked association in which the textile workers participate.... Hence, 'working class' cohesion tends to be implemented largely through union membership."

The mill school, on the other hand, helps to consolidate the mill group into a class. In spite of efforts to the contrary by Cromwell teachers, mill children reinforce in one another the patterns that they learn at home. But when they enter the downtown school, their mental and actional patterns are so different from the majority that they have a difficult time adjusting. Their educational foundation for high school is so poor that most of them drop out before completing the twelfth grade. There is a movement to do away with the Cromwell school and have the pupils now attending go to the town school. If this is done it would eliminate one factor of consolidation among mill people.

Church

We have seen that churches follow definite social lines and that for the most part mill people are not active in the town churches. They prefer their own churches and their own types of service. To this extent the churches contribute to the consolidation of the mill subculture. At the same time the Christian doctrine has inherent in it seeds of equality and democracy, because of its recognition of any person, regardless of his position in the social group, as important. This doctrine is undoubtedly a contributing factor in the "bad conscience" that some of the townspeople have regarding the existence of the mill class. Mill and town pastors meet in a ministerial group and exchange ideas and plans, thereby breaking down the barriers between town and mill to some extent. However, town pastors admit that there is little future for their churches among Kent mill people. The trend seems to be toward the establishment of stronger mill churches, and the very organizational setups of the mill churches place emphasis on getting more mill people into their congregations. To that extent they are competing with town churches and drawing class and culture lines even sharper.

Government

State and national legislation calling for workmen's compensation for industrial injuries, safety laws and inspection of places of work, regulation of hours and working conditions, minimum-wage laws, unemployment compensation and old-age security, compulsory school attendance, and child-labor regulations have had important repercussions on mill subculture. All of these legislative acts have, in effect, been means of giving mill workers a more nearly equal proportion of the nation's wealth and of increasing their feeling of security. Other legislation now being considered (federal aid to education, air conditioning of textile plants, and national health plans) would continue to improve the lot of mill workers and break down the barriers which separate them from other parts of their communities. Government is no longer looked upon as merely a protector of the rights of citizens and a disinterested arbiter in business. Its functions have been and are being expanded to exert a more positive control over business and industry, aimed at improving the economic and social position of the less privileged members of the state and nation. This is true not only of the federal government, but more and more state, county, and town officials of Kent are being elected on prolabor platforms.

Upward Mobility or Solidification?

No attempt has been made in this study to say whether the way of life characteristic of Kent's mill villages should continue or should be changed. That would involve value judgments outside the scope of this work. The purpose, rather, has been to describe the subculture of the mill villages in a functional framework, and in this last chapter we have glanced at some of the factors that might make for change in the configuration of customs making up this subculture. The continuation of the mill way of life is dependent upon the continuation of the social and geographical semi-isolation of the mill villagers. Those factors which contribute to this isolation, including paternalism, company ownership of houses, and mill church organizations, help perpetuate the present culture patterns followed by mill people. Factors contributing to the breaking down of isolation, including unionization and public schools where both town and mill children attend, tend to increase the upward mobility of mill workers and to change the present patterns. But barring any sudden and revolutionary invention, either within the cotton-mill industry itself or in the development of synthetic substitutes for cotton which seriously disrupt the industry, the Kent cotton mill villages will apparently continue in much the same form for a number of years to come. However, there will be gradual changes, as new adjustments must be made, and there is little doubt that these ex-tenant farmers and their offspring will eventually be urbanized.

Whatever changes do take place in the textile industry and in the mill villages will have important bearing on the Piedmont region, the South, and the nation, for the Piedmont's 320,000 cotton-mill workers, four-fifths of the nation's total, compose an important segment of the population.

APPENDIX A

SAMPLE OF SCHEDULE USED TO SURVEY
NINETY-SIX KENT MILL-VILLAGE HOMES

Address .... Name of Husband ....
                            Maiden Name of Wife ....
Place and Date of Birth: Husband .... Wife......
Occupation: Husband .... Wife......
Children: Names   Age   Sex   Occupation
                                         (or Grade in School)

Relations Living in Kent, or near Kent:
    Name   Address   Nature of Relationship

Residence:
    Years lived in Kent .... Years lived at present residence....
    Place of residence before coming to Kent ....
    Occupation before coming to Kent ....
    Original residence of parents ....
    Occupation of parents ....
    Present home owned .... Rented ...... Rental........

Education:
    Schools attended: Husband .... Last grade .....
                       Wife ....Completed .....

Social Participation:
    Participant   Organ.   Member   Attend.   Office Held
    Church Membership of children ....
    If different from parents, why? ....

Communication:

    Newspapers and other periodicals subscribed to:
    Radio . . . . Favorite Programs . . . .
    Telephone . . . .
    Automobile . . . . Make . . . . Year . . . . . .

Recreation:

    Things done when not working: Husband . . . .
                                         Wife . . . .
    How last vacation was spent:

Voting:

    Did you vote in 1948 primary? . . . . Town elections? . . . .

APPENDIX B

THE STORY OF MY LIFE

(An English assignment for students in the seventh through twelfth grades of Kent High School, April 24–29, 1949)

I. My Childhood

The earliest thing I remember
The happiest thing that happened to me when I was a child
The saddest thing that happened
The things that frightened me most when I was a child
The bad things I did and how I was punished
The good things I did and how I was rewarded
The games I played and liked best
The boys and girls I played with most
The things I liked most to do
The things I liked least to do

II. My Family

The number in my family
The occupation of my parents
The things I do to help my family
The clubs and organizations which my parents belong to
The things my parents teach me I should do
The things my parents teach me I should not do
The church to which my parents belong
The visits from my relatives
The things I do with my brothers, sisters, and cousins
The house in which my family lives

III. My Life Now

    At school: the subjects I like best and the ones I like least
                the clubs to which I belong and the offices I hold
                what I like least about school
                what I like most about school
                the games I play at school
                my best friends at school

    Outside of school:
                the work I do, at home and for extra money
                the games I play and the ones with whom I play
                what I do on Saturday
                what I do on Sunday

IV. My Life in the Future

    What I would like to be when I am grown
    How much longer I want to go to school
    Where I would like to live in the future
    What I would do if I could change Kent to my heart's desire
    What I would do to change the world to my heart's desire

The following theme was written by a seventeen-year-old Cromwell girl in the eleventh grade:

I think the happiest thing I can really remember is when one night I was at church my oldest brother was borne. When I came home I was very happy to hear about him. Then the saddest thing I can remember is when my Aunt Mary died. I was about four or five years old. It was very sad because she had helped take care of my sister, my borther and myself every since I could remember.

One of the things that frightened me most when I was little was a snake and a big black feather my mama had in her hat and she didn't get to wear it again, and she still doesn't wear a hat, nor do I like a black feather in a hat.

Some of the games I played and liked best when I was little was Hop-Scott, Black Spider, Red Rover, Giant Step, and jump rope. I think the thing I liked best to do was to play with my friends and my paper dolls. Some of the things I liked least to do was to work. I remember that when I was little and got into mischief, I would get a spanking or have to stay at home a while. Then still sometimes I would have to do work and do it good and fast I would get a piece of candy or go somewhere and play.

The number in my family is nine. I have two brothers, four sisters, and there is mama and daddy, and my self which make up the nine people. Daddy is foreman in the weave room in the cotton mill, and mama is a spinner in the same mill. I don't do so much work at home, but some I do is cook, wash dishes, sweep yards, dust, and help clean house. I live in a house made of wood. It has five rooms, a hall, and bath-room. It is a one story house on the Cromwell Hill.

My daddy belongs to the woodsman's and mama belongs to the women's circle. My daddy also belongs to something about the Jury and also the Air Raid Patrolmen. Some of the things my parents teach me I should do is to honor people, who are older than my self, good manners, to go to church, and obey them. The things they teach me I shouldn't do is talk just any way to older people, and not talk back to them. My parents belong to the Presbyterian church. They don't have any activity at church, but go to enjoy the service.

I don't have many relatives to come visit me, but when they do they usually come and stay on the week end. The ones that come most is my aunt from Lebanon come to see us about once out of every month.

I like all of my subjects at school, but I think the one I like best is Physical Ed., because we get to go out in the yard and play ball, or a rest period from hard lessons that we have. As I said I like all my subjects, but I guess I like Math least, because you have to study pretty hard on some of it.

I really don't belong to any clubs at school, or hold any office because mostly all clubs we have at school, you have to be a certain age, and I'm usually not that certain age so I'm just left out until next year. The things I like best about school is before school in the morning, lunch Physical Ed., and a few of the teachers. The thing I like least is some of the lessons, some of the teachers and the length of time we have to go to school. Some of the games I play at school is volley ball, soft ball, speed ball, socker, basket ball, and sometimes we square dance.

I don't have much time to play at home, but when I do I play baseball, innie-over, bycicle ridding, skating, swimming and sometimes walking in the woods to find wild flowers of all kinds.

I don't do much work at home for extra money, but some of them are to stay with my sisters and brothers, while they go to the show or some place, to help do extra work. Some other things I do to get extra money is to keep my neighbors children for them or help them do extra work. I don't have any hobbies, but when I have any extra time I usually go visiting or play something. On Saturday morning I usually help clean up the house, then wash my hair. After dinner I usually go to town, then go practice, then come home and get ready to go to church for Y. P. E. (at Church of God) Then on Sunday morning I go to Sunday school, then come home and help fix dinner. After dinner we go visit our relatives, or take a walk, go ridding or take some pictures, then we go to church on Sunday night (Church of God).

In the future of my life, or when I finish high school I want to go away and study to a secretary. I want to finish school, which will be through the twelfth grade, then go to a school to learn to be a secretary. Then, also some time in my future, I hope to be married. When I am married, or in the future, I want to go to Florida and stay awhile, and if I don't like it come back to Kent, or go to Georgia and live.

If I could change Kent to my heart's desire, I would want more, bigger and nicer houses, pretty streets, and stores, better schools, and the clored people to have a certain section to live in, but since I know good and well I can't change Kent, but I love it the way it is, and don't guess it was made this way for each person to have Kent like they want it.

If I could fix the world the way I want it, I would want less fighting, pretty places, more people to own their property on which they live. To have more and better churches and more people going to church. I would also want it so that we had to go to school longer than some of them do, and get a better education, and be able to take the tasks that are coming. Since I can't change the world either I guess its the same way, it's here the way God wants it to be and not for someone to change it the way they want it.

Written by a ninth-grade, sixteen-year-old boy of the Townsend Village:

My childhood was a very cheerful one. I remember when I was about six years old, I met a pretty little girl. She was older than I but then I said that she was little. This girl would come to see me and I would go to see her. I guess this was the happiest thing that happened to me in my younger childhood. I spent most of my time playing on a green hill with a lake at the foot of it. When there is a lot of happiness there come time for sadness and when as a child we had a dog. This dog had good sense. Sometimes I thought it had the sense of a man. This dog saved my life one time but in the struggle it was killed by a snake. I missed the dog very much and hope someday to find another dog that will take his place.

To my sorrow I was afraid of the dark when I was young. I believe I am right when I say that the first time I was frightened was when my father and mother was out late one night and I was alone. I was very much afraid.

When in school in the first and second grades we played dodge ball which I enjoyed very much. This game can be fun to older people. I now wish that I were playing dodge ball instead of what I am doing.

The things I like most is going swimming and boat riding that way people can forget their troubles, and of course their is some thing that I don't like to do such as go to work on Fridays when I could have been at a show or at a ball game with a pretty girl. By my childhood you can tell that I like the feminine beauty.

I did many bad things wrong when I didn't know any better, but I soon learned better by my punishments. They did me a lots of good. A whippin didn't hurt but the other punishments did the trick.

I can't remember much of the good things I did when I was little but when I was about thirteen, I saved a little girls life down at Mr. Cambell's pond and I was thanked by a very great offer which I couldn't except. The boy scouts aren't susposed to take praises from people it is a pleasure to save a persons life. That was praise enough.

My Family is one of a common class not up in society and not in a class with the people who seem to don't care. There is two boys of which one is me and one girl which makes five with my father and mother. My father works in a textile plant. My mother also works in the same plant and does her duty as a house wife. I don't do much work around home but occasionally I help add to the four room house in which we live not as good as I would like it to be But people now have to take what they can git.

My parents belong to a textile club which is not in circulation now.

My father teaches me more himsilf than I liarn at school. He is a man and I am a boy. That makes it easy for him to teach me the things I should do. He also teaches me things I shouldn't do which is very good. The things he taught me not to do will help a young boy make something of his self.

My relatives are very sociable. I thing two of my uncles come more than the rest of them but they all come occasionally.

My life now is what I have been looking forward to get to tell about. At school I study or should I say look at. The best subject is English my teacher is very good and sensible. The subject I like least is civics of which I make my worst grade. The teacher is good and sensible but I'm not interested in civics for some reason. I belong to a club in school which is called "The Green and White." This club is the best club in school in the way of inter-tainment at football games. I don't hold an office in this club but in years to come I hope to. I like most at school is the time when we have lunch boys and girls are always having fun in many ways. Girls and boys under a tree telling each other what they plan which is alright. If you don't get involved in a little court ship so young as I did in life. The things I like least about school is when the bell rings for our lunch period to be over. I guess it is because I have so much fun telling a certain little girl my secrets of life as many other boys and girls do. The games I play at school are baseball, football and basketball and occasionally Volly ball which is more of a game for girls. My best friends with which I spend most of my spare time are Herbert, Leon, Billy, and Sammy. Away from school I played with these same boys and girls. I work on friday afternoons and saturdays so that takes up saturday. I usually take my girl friend to a movie or we go out to lunch. Sometimes we go out of town to get lunch because Kent isn't a very healthy place after nine o'clock. Sundays are usually the big days in my life. I go to see my girl and we play ball or take walks.

My life in the future is yet to come but I have a good idea of what I am going to be. I want to be a coast guard on sea duty. I will get high school education and thats enough of school for what I want to be. You mostly need common sense and you don't get that in Kent High School. They teach you out of books and you can't expect a person to live on books. I want to live in Charleston that would be close to where I would be when on duty. That way I could be at home when off duty. If I had the priveledge to change Kent first of all. I would run a few of the bootleggers out of town and close a few of the liquor stores. In addition to this I would put in a recreation center for the youth of this town which these big men who have all of the money wouldn't do because they don't think boys and girls like to be together in a decent place. I would leave the world for God to take care of sense he is responsible for founding it.

This is my Autobiography up till now and my future if it is possible to do what I want.

APPENDIX C

A leaflet handed out at the door of the Wesleyan Methodist Church, summarizing certain basic religious beliefs of the majority of Kent mill people:

WHAT GOD SAYS "ABOUT YOU"
YOU "ARE" A SINNER,

"BY BIRTH"

You are BORN IN SIN. Behold, I was SHAPEN IN INIQUITY and IN SIN did my Mother conceive me. Ps. 51:5.

YOU "ARE" A SINNER,

"BY NATURE"

God says, BY NATURE YOU ARE A CHILD OF WRATH. Eph. 2:3, By one man (ADAM) SIN EN-TERED INTO the world, and DEATH BY SIN; and so DEATH passed upon ALL men, for that ALL HAVE SINNED, Rom. 3:23; 5:12; 3:19, 20. The HEART is deceitful above all things and DESPERATELY WICKED, Jer. 17:9.

YOU "ARE" A SINNER,

"BY PRACTICE"

God says, if we say that we have NO SIN we deceive OURSELF, I John 1:9. If we say: we have NOT SINNED, we make Him (GOD) a LIAR, I John 1:10. SINNER, how about those evil deeds you PRACTICE? How about that ADULTERY you commit with some one else's husband or wife? How about your LUSTFUL EYES, those FILTHY STORIES, those LIES, that HATRED, DE-

CEIT, ENVY, COVETOUSNESS, MURDER and PRIDE? LOVERS OF PLEASURE, MORE than LOVERS OF GOD. How about that DRUNKENNESS? God's curse is UPON LIQUOR, UPON the man that MANUFAC-TURES it, SELLS it, and DRINKS it. God declares that No DRUNKARD shall INHERIT the KINGDOM OF GOD, I Cor. 6:9, 10; Gal. 5:19, 21. FINALLY, how about that CURSING and SWEARING? How about TAKING GOD'S HOLY NAME IN VAIN? SINNER, God swears that for ALL THESE THINGS, HE will bring you INTO JUDGMENT, Eccl. 11:9. God will NOT hold you GUILTLESS for taking HIS HOLY NAME IN VAIN, Ex. 20:7. Let me REPEAT,

GOD'S VERDICT is, You "ARE" a SINNER, Rom. 3:2. You "ARE" CONDEMNED ALREADY, St. John 3:18.

You "ARE" LOST, Heb. 3:3.
You "ARE" on your way to an ETERNAL HELL.

BUT
YOU NEED NOT PERISH
BECAUSE

GOD LOVES YOU, and CHRIST died FOR YOU. Yea, is RISEN FROM THE DEAD. FOR YOU. It IS SIN THAT will SEPARATE the SINNER FROM GOD for all ETERNITY. God HATES SIN, but LOVES THE SINNER. By RECEIVING CHRIST as your PERSONAL SAVIOR, you will ESCAPE HELL and come out FROM UNDER the WRATH OF GOD. GOD says, "HE that HEARETH MY WORD, and BELIEV-ETH ON HIM that sent ME, HATH EVERLASTING LIFE, and SHALL NOT COME INTO JUDGMENT, but IS PASSED from DEATH UNTO LIFE, St. John 5:24; 6:37; 10:9; 20:31. WILL you ACCEPT CHRIST NOW? WILL you pass from death unto life? And doing this, come out FROM UNDER THE WRATH OF GOD? The SIN QUESTION HATH been SET-

TLED AT CALVARY'S CROSS. TODAY, it is, the SON QUESTION. What will YOU DO WITH GOD'S SON? You MUST either ACCEPT HIM or REJECT HIM. To REJECT HIM is to PERISH. It is the GREATEST DECISION you will ever make this side of HEAVEN. Upon your DECISION will depend whether you spend ETERNITY IN HEAVEN or HELL. To REFUSE, NEGLECT or REJECT GOD'S WAY OF SALVATION is to refuse HIM who SPEAKS FROM HEAVEN, Heb. 1:1, 2; 12:25. If you would not perish, DO THIS NOW:

REPENT of your SINS.
BELIEVE ON the LORD JESUS CHRIST.
RECEIVE CHRIST as your SAVIOR.
                              AND
YOU SHALL LIVE ETERNALLY.

JESUS SAID, "He that REJECTETH ME, and RECEIVETH NOT MY WORDS, hath one that JUDGETH HIM: the WORDS THAT I HAVE SPOKEN, THE SAME shall JUDGE HIM IN the LAST DAY, St. John 12:48. These are HARD STATEMENTS, nevertheless, GOD'S DECREES.

APPENDIX D

SUMMARY COMPARISON OF CERTAIN KENT CULTURE PATTERNS OF FARM, MILL, AND TOWN [1]

Type of Pattern	Farm [2]	Mill	Town [3]
Clothing: Men Everyday	Overalls, or blue denim trousers plus denim shirt. Sometimes khaki shirt and trousers. No tie. High-top work shoes. Felt or straw hat (wide brim).	Similar to farm, except shoes low-cut and hat rarely worn.	Suit and tie for majority of occupations. Felt hat, dress shoes.
Sunday and Party	Suit; dress shirt; tie; low-cut shoes; felt hat.	Suit in cold weather; tie optional; coats rare in summer; few hats.	Best suit. More stylish than farm. Tuxedos and long evening dresses exclusive to town.
Clothing: Women Everyday	Cotton dresses most of year. Bonnets. Low-heel shoes.	Cotton dresses of mail-order style. Aprons. No hats or stockings (except for Holiness people). Flat-heel shoes.	Cotton or woolen dresses or suits more stylish than farm. Semihigh heels.
Sunday and Party	Best cotton or rayon dress. Hat required, especially in church. Semihigh heels. Few fur coats.	Best cotton dress. Few hats. Stockings. No fur coats.	Best crepe, silk or wool dress or suit, of latest styles. High heels. Hats required.
Housing	Frame structures, usually two-stories, roomy with ceiled walls. Septic tanks and pumps for inside plumbing. Tendency toward more compact brick structures similar to those in town. Set apart.	Simple, country-laborer style house: one-story, frame, same design as others in neighborhood, set close together, little yard space, ceiled walls, no inside toilets, no central heating.	Best built of the houses one or two stories, brick or frame, plastered walls, one or more bathrooms, spacious lawns.

APPENDIX D (Continued)

Type of Pattern	Farm [2]	Mill	Town [3]
Industry	General uniformity of type of work. Out-of-doors, dictated only by seasons. Women in charge of household tasks. Clear division of labor.	Uniformity of jobs. In-doors, hot, humid, mechanical, under strict supervision of bosses. Women work in mill, earning as much as men.	Many alternative jobs. Majority of women in the home, although tendency for them to do part-time teaching and other jobs outside. Complex division of labor among men.
Marriage	Simple religious ceremony in church or home to which community invited. Wedding gifts prior to ceremony. Parents have important part in helping to choose mate. Announcement of engagement as a rule.	Brief, surprise civil ceremony. Marriage at earlier age than farm or town. Primarily a decision of couple. No invitations, no wedding gifts: beginning to announce wedding in paper.	Elaborate religious ceremony in church more than in home. Announcement of engagement, invitations sent to friends and relatives. Parents have strong influence in mate selection because of importance placed on "who" one is.
Husband-wife Relationship	Patriarchial. Most stable of the three.	Relatively independent, although overt allegiance to father as head of house. Least stable.	Between patriarchial and independent types. Highest degree of companionship.
Kinship	Large kinship groups important. Periodical gathering of large number of kin.	Similar to farm, with kinship even more important to individual security.	Kinship important for social classification, but few large gatherings of kin.
Children: Number per family	More than town; fewer than mill. Children still an economic asset.	Largest number of children (4.7 for all families; 5.8 for completed families). Strong tendency toward reduction	Fewest. Emphasis on "quality" rather than quantity.

of number of children per family because of economic burden and interference with recreation.

Rearing	Few baby beds, strollers, carriages, etc. Care of infants almost entirely by mother, with some aid from relatives and older siblings.	No paraphernalia of baby beds, etc. Diffused care of infant by relatives and older siblings, since mother works. Negro nurses employed when mill work steady.	Baby beds, strollers, primary care by mother, supplemented by Negro nurses.
Initiation into work	Early initiated into household and farm chores. Little encouragement of creativity in expression.	Similar to farm, but general belief that mill a much poorer place to rear children than is farm.	Few household chores. Greatest stress on self-expression and creativity.
Education	High school completed by majority, with some having gone to college.	Average of six years of schooling. Present tendency toward emphasis on completing high school. Few high school graduates. No college graduates.	Greatest emphasis on formal education. Almost all are high school graduates, with many having completed college.
Speech	Little stress on grammatical correctness. Rural figures of speech.	Almost no stress on grammatical correctness. Rural figures of speech.	Great stress on grammatical correctness. Figures of speech from literature, especially.
Magazines	Farm and church periodicals most prominent. Some popular magazines.	Same as farm, except fewer magazines, particularly popular ones, subscribed to.	Almost no farm magazines. Preponderance of popular type.

APPENDIX D (Continued)

Type of Pattern	Farm [2]	Mill	Town [3]
Newspapers	Stone Valley *Bugle* most important. Kentville *Transcript* and Metro City papers second in importance.	Same as farm, except *Transcript* unimportant.	Metro City papers and *Transcript* most important. Fewer subscribe to *Bugle*.
Meals: Nomenclature	Breakfast, dinner, supper	Same as farm.	Breakfast, lunch, dinner.
Special meals for reunions, preachers, etc.	Table overloaded in form of "conspicuous" consumption; served by women of household.	Same as farm, even to the types of dishes served.	Several courses but without conspicuous display. Served by domestic help, Negro.
Funerals	Large gathering of kin and community. Elaborate, lengthy affairs. Service held in church.	Similar to farm, but more elaborate and emotional, with more conspicuous display of flowers; stoppage of work; viewing the body, conspicuous crying; all-night watch. Service sometimes in funeral parlor.	Most dignified. Reaffirmation of unity of kin and community but not as much as in rural church service.
Recreation	Vigorous, out-of-doors: hunting, fishing, baseball, visiting, square dancing. Few movies. No mixed drinking. Little recreation by both men and women.	Similar to farm, but more movies, radio, some mixed drinking, some ballroom style dancing, pool, swimming, womens' neighborhood parties. Almost complete separation of men and women in recreation. Gardening, belief in signs of almanac.	Much mixed recreation in parties and exchange of meals. Bridge, golf, mixed drinking; ballroom form of dancing almost exclusive to town group. Movies and radio important.

Religion: Beliefs	Conservative theology, literal interpretation of Bible and total reliance on it.	Same as farm.	More liberal in theology and in interpretation of Bible.
Churches	Presbyterians slightly more prestige than Methodists or Baptists.	No Presbyterian or Episcopal groups. Consolidation of mill churches, with Holiness groups important. Most "Sect"-like.	Most formalized or "Church"-like. Church membership closely related to class stratification.
Services	Less formal than town. Fewer services because preacher must be shared with other congregations. Revivals important.	Highly evangelical. Revivals all-important. Emotional base rather than rational.	More educational than emotional. Few special services; almost no revivals or evening services. Highly active club groups.
Transportation	Trucks and some family automobiles. Bus used.	Few family automobiles. Frequent use of taxi and bus service.	Personal and family automobiles, for travel within town and for outside visits. Bus rarely used. Trains sometimes used for long trips.
General Status	Dependent largely on success of farms, community participation.	Dependent on personal achievement as mill worker, father, mother, etc. No importance attached to kinship position.	Most important emphasis on "who" you are, i.e., on family background.

[1] These summary patterns are over-all "averages." Details and varieties within each group can be found throughout the study, especially in Chapter 8. The form of the table was suggested by those in Gillin's "Parallel Cultures and the Inhibitions to Acculturation in a Guatemalan Community," *Social Forces*, 24 (October 1945), 1-14.

[2] As explained in the text, "farm" refers to the well-established farmers, not to tenants or renters.

[3] The tendency is to describe the upper classes in the town section of Kent.

Afterword

A Conversation with
Kenneth and Margaret Morland

There are three major versions or styles of living in Kent: that
of the "town" whites, that of the "poor white" mill villagers,
and that of the Negroes. These three groups form the larger
society of Kent. Each exhibits a distinctive organization of
customs, attitudes, and values. Each is a subculture—a variation of American culture, Southern Piedmont style.

Hylan Lewis, *Blackways of Kent*

John Kenneth Morland's Millways of Kent *was based on fieldwork
undertaken in the mill village of Kent, South Carolina, in 1948 and
1949. Initially Morland lived in a boardinghouse in one of the mill villages, but midway through his year in York he was joined by his new
wife, Margaret, and the young couple moved to quarters in town. Morland continued his research on the mill workers, but now with Margaret's help. In February 1992 the Morlands were interviewed about
their experiences in York. The interview took place at their home in
Lynchburg, Virginia, where Ken is retired from Randolph-Macon
Woman's College. Unless otherwise indicated, the voice is Kenneth Morland's. The photographs were taken during his stay in York.*

Portions of this interview previously appeared in John Shelton Reed, "'Millways'
Remembered: A Conversation with Kenneth and Margaret Morland," *Southern Cultures* 1 (Winter 1995): 167–214.

"How I got into it"

Well, like so many things, it was fortuitous. Howard Odum had been [a visiting professor] at Yale and he was very much interested in me, and Chapel Hill gave me a year of graduate study for the three years I had at Yale Divinity School. I had started out with Liston Pope [Yale professor and author of *Millhands and Preachers*, a study of religious life in Gastonia, North Carolina]. When I ran out of funds completely, I asked Odum about coming to North Carolina because I always just idealized Chapel Hill as the place to go.

So I did one summer, and then one full year, then another summer. And it was during that summer [1947] that Howard Odum told me that John Gillin, who had just come to the faculty, was looking for fieldworkers. John Gillin made a study, you know, these studies of the South. Morton Rubin was sent in [to the Alabama black belt, where he conducted the study reported in *Plantation County*]. Somebody went into the pine area of Georgia, never finished. Somebody went into the Kentucky mountains, and I don't think we ever heard of him again.

So John Gillin accepted me and I talked around with [Ralph] Patrick, who had been out in the field, and also with Morton Rubin. [Later] Harriet [Herring, UNC sociologist and noted authority on textile mill villages] was absolutely outdone, and so was I, because they sent me into the mill village without ever conferring with her, and that was unbelievable. I'm surprised Gillin didn't send me to her—somebody didn't send me to her. Of course, she had just written *The Passing of the Mill Village*, which hadn't happened here [in York]. I came up, and I had several conferences with her. I don't know how I got in touch with her, but I saw that book and I said, "Well, golly, I ought to go to Harriet Herring," and I did. I found her.

They needed a black to do *Blackways*, and I'm not sure how they got in touch with [Hylan Lewis]. He preceded me there, although we were able to confer ahead of time. Then we would have meetings in Chapel Hill and compare notes. Hylan would be able to give me insights about mill people that blacks had, and Patrick could give me the view of town people. And so I could talk to them about how mill people viewed blacks and how mill people viewed the town, and we could collaborate to that extent.

Then I had their written theses to follow, and they were very helpful, along with the master's thesis of Barbara Chartier, and Dorothy Reynolds, who came from Duke and did the Rorschach. I tell you, they were very curious about that, because here was this very good-looking woman would take them into a room all by themselves and show them these pictures. These dirty pictures. She wasn't dressed as she should have been, and a lot of them saw things there that people didn't. . . . Well, that was how I got into it.

"I TOLD THEM I WOULD LIKE TO TAKE NOTES"

I can always remember arriving at the bus station not knowing anybody and that sinking feeling I had when I went down. I told them outright [what we were doing in town]. When we talked to Gillin, he took me to [Charles Albert] Cannon [president of Cannon Mills] in Kannapolis. And Cannon said, "You know you will never get through to these people if they think you are studying them. You better go down there and tell them that you're a traveling salesman or something." I said, "No, I'm going to tell them exactly what I'm trying to do."

So I went down and said, "I'm helping with the study of the South." I said, "There are a lot of people who don't understand the South, particularly those from the North." And they all agreed heartily. And I told them what I was doing. I told them I would like to take notes.

But I got a marvelous recording of a snake-handling service [under somewhat false pretenses]. That's a story in itself. I went and talked to the person in charge and said, "Is it all right for me to take pictures? Is it all right for me to record the service?" He said he was always glad to have a reporter here or photographer.

So he thought I was with the newspaper, and I didn't tell him any differently.

[Ralph Patrick] was leaving York as I was arriving, and he introduced me to the major people, the chief of police, and Calhoun, who was so understanding—he was minister of the Presbyterian church. [Patrick] was great in introducing me to everybody I needed to meet in York. He paved the way. The mill people were a tight little enclave and very suspicious of outsiders, and he knew enough of the people that the mill people trusted in order to get me an entrée. And also an entrée with the Carrolls, with whom we stayed. That's where he and his wife were living, and so we moved into their apartment when he had left, after he had finished his fieldwork.

Patrick was the trailblazer for both of us. Having come from one of the families in Gastonia, which is just north of York, he had a entrée to the upper-upper part of society. He initially attempted to do the entire study himself, but found out that he really couldn't cover blacks and mill and town—they were three distinct segments almost in place in the town. So that's when Gillin called Hylan Lewis and me into the picture. So that's how I got involved. And I was delighted because here was the way to get my dissertation done. I had always wanted to do fieldwork, where you would go out and actually be with people and see them. But I wanted to do the dissertation, get the doctorate. I already had a job waiting at William and Mary.

Pat introduced me, and I used his notes. And Pat being from Gastonia, and knowing all those old families who really relish their ancestry, I think was in such a bind that he could never get that book into print. I know his wife used to put up on the mantlepiece *Blackways of Kent* and *Millways of Kent*. I think Pat did a marvelous job of getting in [to life in York]. He was going to cocktail parties while I was going to Holiness [church services]. They were two different worlds.

[Hylan Lewis] was there at the same time, but we made it a point to distance ourselves. Hylan and I, had we been seen together, it would have hurt him. "You're just feeding this stuff to the white folks." We had to meet outside of York. [But one time] Gillin came down, and Gillin and I went into the black section, followed by the chief of police, and we met with Hy and had a good session with him then. But there was such suspicion of us.

Hy said that he went into the poolroom frequented by both blacks and whites, and he came in with this hat on. One of the whites said, "Nigger, get your hat off." Hy said that the anger went over him but he said, no, I've got to do this field study, so he gradually took off his hat. But afterward the man found out that he was doing a study and apologized to him!

I sent notes to Gillin at the end of every week. He said, "In case someone breaks in and tries to steal your notes, you can destroy them and I'll have a copy of them." I think he really wanted to make sure that I was doing what I was supposed to be doing and not just taking it easy.

Sunday Mornings

I think [banker, friend, and confidant] Joe Hart and his family went to the Episcopal church, which was rather small. But the Presbyterian church was the head church. The Presbyterians had a mission in the mill village, and they met on Sunday evening and gave a service for the Presbyterians in the schoolhouse. But that was about the extent of the contact there.

The Associated Reformed Presbyterian church, in which they did not use organ music, I attended from time to time. It was attended a little more by the middle people. It was down more on the Main Street. But there was a large, enormous difference between the A.R.P. and the regular Presbyterian.

The Church of God is [a] Holiness [church], Church of God of Holiness was a Holiness church, and the Wesleyan Methodist was a Holiness church, and the snake handlers that came only in the summertime were Holiness people. These ministers sort of came and went. I got to know the minister at the Wesleyan Methodist pretty well. The difference between the Church of God and the

Church of God of Holiness is in the Church of God of Holiness they have to fly the American flag at all times.

The Church of God welcomed me and all. I didn't go as often to the Church of God as I went to the others. But my first visit there, they could spot me as one who was not one of the mill people. I remember the minister took a look at me as I tried to sit out of sight in the seat. He said, "Now, there's a lot of these people from town who think we make too much noise down here. But we make noise because we love the Lord. And let's all give the Lord a round of applause." Which they did. That's where they would have people come down, and pass out, and holy, holy, holy—and work on them and get them converted.

I was a prime target for salvation, and they would come down the aisle and ask, "Brother, are you saved?" And I never knew what to do, what to say—you know, just what do you mean by that? I was standing by my wife, and I was tempted to say, "I'm saved, but my wife is not." [*Margaret*: "So he could take notes."] But I thought, our marriage wasn't so very far along. And I couldn't do that.

I can remember learning to go to that church and the others with quarters in my pockets. Because they took collection about six or seven times, and the first time I was there I put in a dollar and that was all I had. So they expected me to put something in every time, so I put in a quarter. But they took up collection because a bus had broken down. They took up collection because they were behind on the light bill. They took up a collection because the church roof was leaking. They took up a collection for the visiting minister. So they took up a lot of collections.

Of course they were not supposed to drink if they were a member of the Holiness church, but they would backslide. Then they would have to get able through three steps. They would have to be saved, sanctified, and filled with the Holy Ghost. Then when you were filled with the Holy Ghost you would speak in unknown tongues.

I asked this guy Hank, who was not doing very well in anybody's eyes including his own—he is the one whose letter is in there and who got drunk too much and didn't support his family, got fired at the mill—I asked him, I said, "Hank, what is going to happen to you when you die?" He said, "I'm going straight to hell." I said, "Does it bother you?" and he said, "Well, I'm gonna get saved one of these days. Not yet, but . . ." He wasn't ready for it yet. But any time. As a matter of fact, they said if at the last moment Hitler walked down the aisle and confessed that he believed in Jesus Christ, he would go to heaven, and it can be done instantaneously.

It's very interesting. There was one man, and I think I use this in the book, who I asked, "Are you a member of the church?" He said, "Yeah, I belong to the Baptist," but he said, "I can't start going again until I start living right. The woman I'm shacked up with is not my wife. I plan to get straightened out."

SATURDAY NIGHTS

[Gillin] said, "You're spending too much time with the church people." Well, that was a good opening actually, because afterwards I got down to the Bloody Bucket most Saturday nights. I went to the dances and learned how to contact the bootlegger who was always present. He knew who you were and you knew who he was, and the undercover policemen didn't know. But whenever we needed to drink, he would take us outside and he had in the trunk of his car plenty of liquor, which he sold at about three times the price. So he made a very good living. He worked in the mill during the day, but he did this at night.

I had two big bills: one was photography, the other was losing at pool. All the mill people wanted to play me because I was so poor, and they always played for money. There was a place on Main Street that had reeking odors coming out of it. I remember the first time I went in there, it was so smoky I had to fight my way. That's where they played pool and drank heavily, because the liquor store is right in back of it, and they could go and get well supplied. I remember telling Joe Hart—Joe Hart said, "What goes on in there?" I said, "You come on down with me and come on in." He couldn't do that.

This was a place where all of us did a lot of drinking. They had two enormous garbage cans out in the yard full of whiskey bottles. We had to get our liquor from the liquor store, and one or two of the guys to whom they wouldn't sell liquor had me go and get it for them. I never knew if that was ethical or not ethical or what. But one of my best informants, if I didn't get to him before 11:00, was drunk. And I was told by several mill people who took me aside and said, "Ken, you're spending too much time with him." They said, "You know he's not a good one to spend time with." I thought, hot-cha, I'm coming up with a deal here, and I said, "Why shouldn't I spend time with him?" "Well, he gets drunk too much. He's not a steady worker. He doesn't support his family as he should. He never goes to church." All of those things, but a delightful guy.

Town and Mill

Well, I married Margaret, right in the middle of that, and took her on the honeymoon to the mill village, and she stayed with me despite that. The mill people trusted me a whole lot more, because a single male usually went to the mill village for other reasons than to do research, but once she was there and they loved her, then I think I got a wider reception. Of course she could go to the women's circles. She could go to whatever women did.

Margaret was getting her master's degree at Carolina [with her thesis on Samuel Taylor Coleridge's interpretation of Christianity]. When she came, we moved in with the Carrolls [in town]. After about six, seven, or eight months. In the mill village itself Margaret and I took an apartment there and we attended church service in the mill village. [*Margaret*: "They never did understand why I wouldn't go to their book clubs and bridge clubs. And that I preferred going to a Holiness meeting than to a bridge club."]

Joe Hart was the only one who ever came down to see me in my room in the mill village. He came down to see what it was like living there. Here we were about three or four blocks from each other, but they were different worlds. We had no running water and of course outdoor plumbing. But there was a swimming pool, which [town folk] called the mill bathtub. And the only time they bathed was when they went in that swimming pool, so [town people] wouldn't dare go.

I gave in, and Joe Hart would give me a bath and a martini over on the other side of the tracks. Once, [after we had moved] over on King's Mountain Road, we invited Clark and Geneva to have dinner with us. And the Carrolls took us aside and said, "We don't want you to do this any more. You have embarrassed us." [*Margaret:* "The mill people had to go to the back door."]

When Blanche [Carroll] read that book, she said, "We don't have these kind of attitudes toward the mill, do we?" And I said, "Well, I just wrote what I heard and I might have missed something, but this is the only thing I could report."

FAMILY LIFE

Margaret: He had been there about four months, I guess, when I joined him, and so it turned out that they trusted him a little more since he had a wife. And also I went to a lot of the women's events—everything from the women's Sunday school classes to the sewing circles, baby showers, and bridal showers and all that sort of thing.

Interviewer: The picture that comes out of the book is pretty thoroughly segregated, men and women, which is ironic because, I mean, this is a culture in which the women are going to work.

Margaret: That's right. They were liberated way before the rest of us were, supposedly.

Interviewer: It didn't seem to extend to much in their private lives.

Margaret: No, it did not. The man was definitely the head of the household.

Interviewer: It struck me as odd, this culture where the women all went off to work at the same time was one that was pretty segregated, even, in private life.

Ken: Very much so. As a matter of fact, sometimes in the church women would sit on one side, men on the other. Social life was quite different [for men and women]. The men had pretty rough sort of recreation and they did drink, and women wouldn't do that.

Interviewer: Well, Margaret, you know, Ken in that setting was obviously an odd phenomenon, and people were fussing about that, and I was wondering if you were even odder or if you were simply seen as a good wife who was coming along with her husband.

Margaret: No, I think that was the way I was seen because they really took me as one of their own almost immediately.

Interviewer: If you'd been like one of the other women who was doing the research, then you would have been odd, right?

Margaret: Yes, I think so, and they immediately put me to work from teaching the women's class in Sunday school to doing other things.

Interviewer: Were there single women in town?

Margaret: Yeah, the woman at the boardinghouse who had such a evil tone, she really scared me. She lived there and worked in the mill, and said she didn't even have time to get a drink of water. Said there was no time out, they just made you work, work, work. I forget what she did.

Ken: Now, there were positions higher in the mill village—there were the sweepers, and then people who worked in one part, and then finally up into the weaving room or loom fixer. Loom fixer was the most valued of the workers, because those looms would break down and you had to have somebody in there immediately. Had to go in there and repair them.

By the way, I had a gung-ho colleague, feminist, who said, "All these people that write books put women in special in the index, but they never put men there." So I gave her this, and here, lo and behold, under "men": "expectations of a husband, lenience toward conduct, sexual relations, attitudes toward perfect children, recreation of, drinking by, clothing worn by, voting of." And I said, "Look, and under women I have about the same thing: 'as mill workers, as working wives, expectations of as wives, double standard conduct applied to, concept of mother, attitude toward perfect children, prenatal care of, responsibility of for child care, visits among . . .'"

One thing the women did was to visit, the family visits. They did a lot of visiting, but it was the women who would go into the other home. The men didn't do much of—

Margaret: Well, the minute the word got around that someone needed help, the women really rallied round. They took shifts staying up with somebody or tending the children of the ill person. They really ministered unto each other.

Ken: Probably a good demonstration of that would be Geneva Warren. She had the biggest heart. She just helped everybody who was sick, everybody who needed any money. They would take up collections for people who were sick. They would visit them. They would prepare their food. They would attempt to get their job covered. It was tight. In a way, as long as they stayed in that enclave and knew one another, it was a very warm, binding relationship. That's why breaking up was so hard.

Margaret: I think the women, although they wanted everything for their child, actually what they wanted was for their child to be looked up to in their own environment. So that it would not have been a good thing for their child to want to leave, because it would mean that we weren't so satisfying and so good. So I think the influence, the parental influence, was to stay there and do what a good son or daughter does, which is to go right into the mill.

Interviewer: What about the ones that—not necessarily aspired higher, but the ones that somehow just didn't fit?

Margaret: Well, I think that if they didn't fit because they weren't stable enough or something like that, they might have been felt sorry for, but the ones who left because they wanted something better were considered uppity, and that was not admired. But still I remember when Ken asked all the little children at school what they wanted to be when they grew up, and they would all say a doctor, a lawyer, this or that or the other. And he would say, "Do you think that is what you're going to become?" "No, I'm going in at the mill."

Interviewer: What happened to a girl that didn't marry? Did she stay there and go to work at the mill, just become an aunt to her nieces and nephews, or what?

Margaret: Well, now, if she devoted herself to taking care of her ill parent or sibling's children, if they'd been killed or whatever, then that was excusable. That was all right, if she was doing that, if she had given her life to that, instead of seeking a life of her own. But I think single women were looked on as a little bit suspicious.

Ken: If any person there was straightforward, was honest, was not a hypocrite (they hated hypocrites)—

Margaret: And didn't try to steal somebody else's husband.

Ken: That's right, although you could do it out in the open. You shouldn't try to sneak around at night. If they went to church, if they were hard workers, if they loved their families, this was great. I know in one of the pictures, Kenny Jones, who did the developing of these pictures—there are two daughters there who were not married, but they lived together as a family of four.

Interviewer: You mentioned guys hanging out and drinking at the pool hall. Were there women there as well?

Ken: No, no. Absolutely unthinkable. I never saw a woman at the—now, they would go to these dances at the Bloody Bucket, that they called Nadine's, out on the highway where people would get drunk, get in fights and that sort of thing. But even going there would mean that you weren't sanctified. You had not led the kind of lifestyle you should have. So religion was a critically important variable. Now, you could backslide and get resaved pretty readily and that would be, I should think, a rather emotional catharsis, particularly if you could be genuinely sincere about it, and I think they were.

Interviewer: You mentioned some of the things that the men talked about when they were hunting, fishing, at the pool hall, the kinds of sometimes even raunchy talk that they have.

Ken: Some of it was pretty raunchy. I didn't know whether to report it or not. I reported some of it. I didn't know what to do. I didn't know whether to put in the dirty jokes. Now, only men would tell dirty jokes, not women.

Margaret: [But the women] knew what was going on in the world, and they knew men pretty well. They would say things. It wasn't like telling jokes, but more like making comments about men.

Interviewer: Where were the places you [women] would find yourselves alone to talk? Was it mostly in the kitchen around housework and things like that?

Margaret: Yeah, or in the sewing group where there were only women. They wouldn't have done it at the church, that was all good and proper. But they had a marvelous sense of humor, and they really saw people for who they were.

Ken: And they would have the *Hee Haw* kind of humor. They would love that. That's—it's a kind of rural—I guess you all don't watch *Hee Haw.*

Interviewer: Margaret, I was also curious what other kinds of work you were asked to do or you volunteered to do.

Margaret: I held babies a lot, and I guess I tended not to just step in. I waited to be invited in to do something. I would say, "Could I help in any way?" but I wouldn't presume to walk in and start doing something which the other women would do, because they knew that person and knew that person's kitchen and all that sort of thing.

Ken: And I took a good bit of her time, too. I would bounce ideas off of her because—after being in the field entirely in a boardinghouse and in this home without Margaret, I had all these things on paper, and she was an enormous help in interpreting them and helping me to draw conclusions. She was the one to say, put in "It's Kenneth come home," you know. It was a nice touch that Mrs. Moore said that when I returned after ten years. Very warm reception then. Oh, this one that was gossipy had started the rumor that we were locked up in the penitentiary.

Interviewer: Oh, that was the single woman?

Ken: Yes, she kept busy, like a busybody. She said, "Well, I never did think that you all were—anything wrong with you all, but what about that Barbara?" Barbara Chartier. They were suspicious of outsiders, and correctly so. They were vulnerable to salespeople, to total control by the mill owners. They accepted the limitations on their lives, and within those limitations they lived very rich, very full lives.

Interviewer: Most of the women were married, most of them worked, and they most often worked different shifts from their husbands. So did they socialize mostly with one another? Was there any couple kind of—was that common or uncommon, to socialize as a couple?

Margaret: I would say there was more of that than not.

Ken: Well, they didn't go out. For example, I never knew of anybody who went into town or something of that sort.

Margaret: No, they usually socialized with their families or their good friends.

Ken: And I can remember one of the women saying, "Look around and there's 75 relatives." So you had a—just a big family, and they visited one another and they supported one another.

Margaret: And sometimes somebody didn't do something really honest or ethical, and they were faced up with it.

Ken: They could get their feelings hurt, too. And if fire or something started at the mill, they could sort of go to pieces over it. But you know the one thing that I didn't look at, I should have, was how many men worked on the most desirable shift, which was from 7:00 A.M. to 3:00 P.M., and how many women worked on that shift, and how many worked from 3:00 P.M. to 11:00 P.M., and then that deadly midnight shift, 11:00 P.M. to 7:00 A.M. I don't know. The people who lived outside of the mill village and were not part of the enclave tended to take that third shift. And the husband and the wife would rarely be on the same shift, and that way one of them could be at home.

Interviewer: Who cooked supper if the woman had the 3:00 shift?

Margaret: Now, that was usually the woman. But they usually had either their mother or younger daughter who was old enough to do it. So they all were expected to do their share.

Ken: My recollection is that the women rarely complained. They didn't like complainers and—I don't know if that's right. At least publicly.

Margaret: I would say, generally speaking, yes, and those who did would be sort of teased, but still in an accepting sort of way.

Interviewer: So with one another they wouldn't often complain about their situation?

Margaret: We didn't hear that very often.

Interviewer: Or husbands?

Margaret: None of the husbands told me about—

Interviewer: I mean the women complaining about their husbands.

Margaret: Oh, they would do it in a kind of good-natured way when the women were just together, you know. Oh, he'd sleep all day if she let him, or if he doesn't stop this carousing at night he's gonna get something, and that sort of thing. And you didn't— they weren't difficult to talk to because you knew they weren't reading anything.

Interviewer: Talk was what they did?

Margaret: Talk was very much, yeah, it just about their everyday life, and what was going on among everybody.

Interviewer: No television to watch.

Margaret: Television began coming in, and when one person got a television set—

Ken: Geneva's father got the first one, and the whole village came over and we looked at it from a distance and marveled.

Margaret: Stand out in yards.

Ken: He had rented it. He didn't buy it. He had gone downtown and rented it. And that was a big event.

Interviewer: But it didn't interfere with conversation or socializing?

Margaret: I think it just added to it.

Ken: At that time it didn't interfere. Since then I don't know. You know, I should have saved those compositions that all the students in the school did. Now, this was a seventeen-year-old girl in the eleventh grade: "The number in my family is nine. I have two brothers, four sisters and there's mommy and daddy and myself which make up the nine. Daddy's in the weave room at the cotton mill, mommy's a spinner in the same mill. I don't do so much work at home, but what I do is cook, wash dishes, sweep the yard, dust, clean the house, take care of the younger children." Now, the boys would not do—they would have chores, but they would be different. You had a definite gender differentiation, and that was shown when he said, "That's a real boy for you," and the mother sort of fainted. He should say things like that. But I think secretly she was in favor of differentiation, too.

Writing the Book

Gillin did the smart thing. He said if you can finish your dissertation—and he gave us a deadline by the end of, before school would start, by the end of August—he would give us a hundred dollar bonus. So we set up two typewriters in Margaret's home in Birmingham, and we didn't have air conditioning, and it was summer and we rolled up the windows, and we typed away and we typed away. And you know, at that time you had a typewriter that would go "ding" at the end of the line—"ding." Well, the lawyer who lived next door found out finally that we were typing, and he said, "Thank God, I would wake up at night and hear these things go ding, ding, and wondered if I was losing my mind."

Millways was very well received by anthropologists. As a matter of fact it's cited several times in a book of resources on cultural anthropology. It was not particularly well received by sociologists. [One review said *Millways* and another book] are descriptive, and they really don't go anywhere. Well, that was not a very good review, but once you have the setting, once you have identified the major patterns of belief and patterns of behavior, once you understand and get an overview, then you can go into detail with your theories and test them directly, but you can't do it without the overall case study.

The White Rose Book Society in [York], they gave it a mixed review because they thought that too sharp a line had been drawn between mill and town, and that really wasn't the way they felt, wasn't as accurate a picture as it should have been. It was not, I would say, unfavorably reviewed, but not especially well received. [*Margaret*: "Now, they just wanted their reign over the rest of the town to look beneficent."]

Yeah, I guess so. I guess they were involved. And also there were newspapers that reviewed this in different ways. The Greenville textile mill paper was very critical. It said the person that came in looked at their religion and found it below par, looked at their lives, and so forth and so on. He was very critical, and he said I gave the greatest insult of all: I called it a "subculture." (They were using it to be "beneath" or "below" normal culture).

A lot of other places reviewed it favorably, particularly the union press [which] thought that it gave real insight into the workers and how they were being blocked from unionizing, which I had no intention of doing. But I know that I went to New York to talk to a T.W.U.A. organizer, and he wanted to know a whole lot about this. He said he read the book with a great deal of interest, was very, very much interested. And he said to me—I was teaching at William and Mary—"Don't you just get fed up with teaching and want to get out there and do something?" I said, "I am doing something. I'm doing something I love, and I don't want to leave what I'm doing. I'm just getting my feet on the ground." But he wanted me to go out and straighten the world out, I guess with the T.W.U.A.

[*Margaret:* "Some of them [the mill folk] were furious that they had been quoted, and Clark told them, well, they shouldn't have told them anything."]

Lewis's book—initially it was not well received by the black community [of York]. He came back to visit, and I can remember how hurt he was when somebody said, "You come back to dig up some more dirt on us?" Well, there was an entirely different picture, an entirely different attitude, when—I think it was the fortieth anniversary or something, during Black History Month, and they featured *Blackways of Kent*. And they called Lewis and I think they talked to him on the telephone. They talked to some of his major informants, contacts. So everything turned around. It was like *Middletown*. You know, when the book first went out, they were furious, but then when it was *Middletown Revisited*, they welcomed him back because it put Muncie on the map.

This Is the Story of My Life

You know, I'm delighted for anybody to read anything I've ever written. I've got an interesting set of correspondence now with somebody called Max Bloodworth, who said he was looking at a table of books and he saw *Millways of Kent*. He saw the spindles [on the cover]. He said this is probably a technical book on—he grew up in the mill village, and he picked it up and said, "This is the story of my life." He wrote and said, "How did you capture it so?" And I said, "What are you doing outside of the mill village?" He said he did not want to go into mill work, and it took an enormous effort. He was able somehow to get into radio and then to

get into other things. Well, he is working with the North Carolina state police in radio work. Now he's got a good job. He sent
me marvelous tapes of the Briarhoppers. He put them all together,
and they are great.

With the case study method, people become individuals and
you don't deal with a body of statistics. I think at times you need
to do that. The real joy of this is, is that you get to know the
people, and once they trust you, you couldn't have better friends
or more generous friends. Although they were suspicious of us
until the very end, even after we left. They just didn't know anybody who would be in this road. "Here he says he's from the University of North Carolina and he's studying us. Well, what is he
really up to?"

That's the Cannon mill, which was the major one. I started to get a job there, but they were laying off workers, and besides I didn't much care to. It would take time away from other things that were more important. I think [the building is still standing]. I think it's been air conditioned.

Now, that's the house I lived in, and those are my buddies. That is before Margaret came. I had a little room over to the right which had a little fireplace in it, holes in the floor. It was drafty.

Mr. and Mrs. Moss were my landlady and landlord. They wanted me at first to live in the parsonage, but I said I wanted to live in a mill home. They had retired and came from the farm to the mill, and they were a marvelous source of information. Of course they've died since.

Now, that's the [Baptist] minister. He said, "Ken, when you quote me be sure to correct my English, because I butcher the king's English." Well, he did pretty well. Now, he and I took long trips. He went up to other towns and we talked, and I asked him how he became a minister, and he said, well, he was there working in the mill and God called him to the ministry. And he thought, suppose it's not God calling me. Suppose it's the devil. And he said, even though I'd go to hell for it, I'd go to the ministry. Well, a lot of people said he hated mill work, so he got out of it. So I guess the call would come through, but he did have some lovely flowers.

This was the Wesleyan Methodist church. One of the Holiness churches. Marvelous young minister and wife. He had a great voice. And I used to take collection there. I used to sing in the choir. And I can remember being at a revival service sitting out there and the minister said, "Will that brother back there lead us in prayer." And I was looking all around for that brother. So I gulped a couple of times and started out with what must have been a very sort of uninspired prayer. But then everybody else prayed that way. You couldn't hear me, and gradually they would die out and then I would wind it up. And that's the way you prayed in the church. [Margaret] taught the women's Bible class.

He is with the Church of God. I forget his name, but I got into their home a number of times, and when I did the follow-up study, [I found something] interesting here. The Church of God did not permit people to go to movies. They said movies were sinful. Besides, you just don't know what goes on the dark in those movie houses. But at any rate, I wondered what had happened since television had come on. Whether they watch television or not. Well, it was all dark in there, but I could hear noise and I knocked on the door. He saw me and hadn't seen me in ten years. He said, "Come on in, the television's on." And I sat down, and it was one of these shoot 'em up westerns. And somebody would pull out his gun and shoot somebody, and I remember they would say, "It's wrong to kill people like that." And they would gamble, and they'd say, "It's wrong to gamble like that." But until that film was over, they didn't even move. He loved his garden and was real proud of it.

Oh, now this is a family we got to know very, very well. They might still be living, Earl and Wheatsie Moss. I've asked about them and they would have retired by now, but they were very, very good friends. He was the son of the Mosses with whom I boarded—with whom I lived when I first came. (I didn't board. I ate at the boardinghouse.) But both of them worked in the mill. As a matter of fact, husband and wife always worked in the mill, and as a rule grandmothers took care of children. So they were ahead of the present day. The parents, well, they usually didn't work on the same shift, so they could be at home. Most of the time—they couldn't be there all the time.

There they are—lovely girls. I don't know where they are now. I wonder. But they had a very lovely Christmas and they were nice to invite me to participate in it. And we exchanged presents.

Oh, that's the mill school. Well, they pulled them out, and they put them all into the regular school. They no longer had them separated. And I wonder what they've done about integration there. That would be real interesting. And another thing that interested me, the town people would say, "We can integrate, but you've got to watch the mill people—they'll cause the trouble." Well, the mill people said over and over again, "Doesn't matter who my children go to school with as long as they get an education." They were far less prejudiced than the town people.

These are little children who lived next door to me. I could hear them being disciplined. One way they would frighten their children and get them to [behave was to say,] "If you don't do that, the gorilla will get you." Or "If you don't do that, that anthropologist over there is going to get you."

I remember one of them was swinging in the swing, this one second from the left—went way up high, and she fell out and started crying. I wanted to rush over and help her. I said, no, my job is to see how they would react to this. So her big sister went over and gave her a kick and said, "Get up, you're not hurt," and she got up. She wasn't hurt. She was just looking for attention.

There's Eddie expressing himself. Yeah, that's typical. He's a wonderful little boy. [He's a salesman now in Arkansas.] He's gone way up into sales. He's done very, very well. When Eddie was, I think, three years old, we ate with the Warrens, and they served pinto beans. I think that's all we had, ketchup and pinto beans. Well, Eddie had one helping of pinto beans, two helpings of pinto beans, three helpings of pinto beans, and finally his mother said, "Eddie, you've had all you can have." So she put it on a table next to the dining table. And Eddie said, "I want my beans," and he stood up in his high chair and said, "God damn it, give me my beans!" His mother said, "Now, Eddie," and his father said, "That's a real boy for you."

This is ice that you have some kind of sweet stuff squirted into. That's the main street of the mill village. Those are the best houses there.

This is Halloween. Their favorite trick on Halloween was to push over the out-houses. They always found out if somebody was in there. They didn't push it over if anybody was in there. They did all sorts of tricks.

There's a coon dog. I went on some. . . . So they would be sure to have coons to hunt, they kept them boxed up, and then they put them out in the woods and gave them about an hour's lead and took the dogs out. We stayed all night. They would sit, eat peanuts, and chat, know where the dogs were, know other things. These youngsters didn't do well in school, but their knowledge about how to fish, how to hunt, and how to do other things indicated a very high level of intelligence, but they scored very, very low on [standardized tests].

Joe Hart [*right*] was in the banking business, and his father owned the main bank there. Joe knew I was doing an anthropological field study, and he would ask, "Ken, how are we aborigines doing?" I would say, "Joe, you're doing just fine now, acting naturally." [Ralph Patrick Jr. is to the left.]

[This] is the beginning of the Cannon village. That's where their houses start. These houses were assigned and there was a—you didn't get a house until, usually, a child came to the family. Otherwise you stayed—when you married, you stayed with your parents. Once that happened you could go to the house, and then there were the more desirable and less desirable houses. You sort of worked to get the more desirable houses. Also they were all pretty much the same.

This is our water supply, and I really learned what it is to prime the pump. We had running water in town.

Now, the boardinghouse would be right across from the mill, and that's where I could get any kind of gossip going if I asked the right questions. And this would house workers that would sometimes come and go. They were called floaters. Some of them were excellent mechanics. They could just repair anything. I know my bicycle went bad and in about half an hour, he had gotten all those gears out and put them together. He didn't stay there very long. It was alcohol that got most of them.

This is Earl Moss's daughter with the cat. All their cats got named after the presidents. I wonder if she went into the mill or whether she didn't, because she was—they were, I thought, an exceptionally attractive family, and really put a lot of effort into their homework. The mill people had a very mixed feeling. On the one hand they wanted their children to get ahead and get out of the mill, but on the other they always feared they would take on the town attitude toward the mill, and they could never go home again, really.

And this was a store where they always charged. The mill people were one week behind. They'd always charge their next salary. This is where the people that ran the store live. I hung out at the store for a little bit, but I never did go into the tents.

You know, my time was getting along and there wasn't any funeral, and I had sort of hoped there would be one, but I couldn't do anything to rig it up. One of the matriarchs died, and it was a marvel, the kind of ceremonial arrangement. They had artificial flowers, which they take, and of course she was in the Church of God, and everybody went by the coffin, which was open, and many of them kissed her goodbye. Then they got in their cars and went to the cemetery, but they went the long way around with their lights on. They went three times the distance they needed to to go, and people would wonder who that was.

This was at a [later] funeral we were attending. It was a serviceman who was brought back from World War II, and so they fired the salute. [The army] kept the coffin sealed. It was very interesting. The relatives said, "You know, we don't really know who's in that box. It might be a Jap in that box."

Ken: This is a Sunday dinner, family reunion, which I attended, and where I took pictures.

Margaret: Whenever we were invited to dinner, it was just more than you could eat. And we would eat several kinds of meat—fried chicken, ham, or whatever—and dessert came with everything from cakes to candy bars, like Hershey bars. They had four or five desserts, and you had to try them all.

(*left, below & overleaf*) They loved children and they passed them around, and the children were at home and they were accepted, and, um, greatly made over.

Index